EVENT PLANNING

*The Ultimate Guide to Successful Meetings,
Corporate Events, Fundraising Galas, Conferences,
Conventions, Incentives and Other Events*
(ISBN: 0-470-83188-X)

"Allen is a good teacher. Wise planners will add *Event Planning* to their personal reference library as a useful working guide."
— *Meeting Professional Magazine*

"A blueprint for executing events for 50 or 2,000, with budgets of a few thousand dollars to hundreds of thousands."
— *Success Magazine*

"*Event Planning* will save beginning event planners from plenty of heartbreak and headaches."
— *Lisa Hurley, Editor, Special Events Magazine*

"*Event Planning* gives readers a blueprint for planning and executing special events with flair. Consider the book as preventative maintenance."
— Sales Promotion Magazine

"A guide to well planned events. *Event Planning* is a must for any PR maven."
— *Marketing Magazine*

"This book will be a help to all event planners, from rank beginners to seasoned professionals. It provides excellent guidelines as well as helpful details."
— *Katherine Kossuth, Director of Operations and Special Events, Canadian Film Center*

THE BUSINESS OF EVENT PLANNING

Behind-the-Scenes Secrets
of Successful Special Events
(ISBN: 0-471-64412-9)

"*The Business of Event Planning* is a must-read for those in the event planning business. Strategic in thought and design and user-friendly in presentation, it literally tells you the paths to follow and the pitfalls to avoid. Well told, with examples to follow and stories to relate to, it's the 'how-to' that's a 'must-do' for the meetings, incentive, and event planning industry."
> — *Peggy Whitman, President, Society of Incentive & Travel*
> *Executives; and Western Regional Sales Director,*
> *Marriott Incentive Awards*

"Written for anyone who has to prepare dynamite meetings and special events, *The Business of Event Planning* is your bible and a must-have desktop reference. Thanks, Judy Allen! You saved the day!"
> — *Susan Fenner Ph.D., Manager, Education and*
> *Professional Development, International Association*
> *of Administrative Professionals (IAAP)*

"Guidance for new planners, reminders for experienced ones, and useful tips for everyone. This book has it all! It's the key that unlocks the mystery behind event planning, and should be mandatory reading for planners everywhere."
> — *Leslie McNabb, Senior Manager Event Planning,*
> *Scotia Capital*

event *planning*

ETHICS AND ETIQUETTE

A Principled Approach

to the Business of

Special Event Management

JUDY ALLEN

John Wiley & Sons Canada, Ltd.

John Wiley & Sons Canada Ltd
22 Worcester Road
Etobicoke, Ontario
M9W 1L1

National Library of Canada Cataloguing in Publication
Allen, Judy, 1952-
    Event planning : ethics and etiquette / Judy Allen.

Includes index.
ISBN 0-470-83260-6

    1. Special events--Planning. 2. Business ethics. 3. Business etiquette. I. Title.

GT3405.A45 2002   394.2'068   C2003-902156-4

Production Credits
Cover & interior text design: Interrobang Graphic Design Inc.
Printer: Tri-Graphic Printing Ltd.

Printed in Canada
10 9 8 7 6 5 4 3 2 1

This book is dedicated to

Addie
Cheryl
Dennis
Diane J.
Diane M.
Donna
Georgiann
Jennifer
Katie
Leeron
Louise
Lowell
Mat
Monique
Paris
Patricia
Shane
Sherry
Tanya
Taryn
Terese
Todd
Tracy

... and all the other readers who have contacted me with questions, comments and information they would like to see in a future book, or have taken the time to post reviews online to help others. I value your thoughts and suggestions a great deal.

This book is also dedicated to my parents—Walter (Bennie) and Ruth—who have lived their lives both personally and in business with the highest standards of ethics and integrity, and to others who have crossed my path and shown me what a difference choosing to live a life with ethics can make to you, those closest to you, the people you do business with and others you may not know but who experience the ripple effect in their lives from the choices you have made. What we do and how we conduct ourselves out in the world matters. If we get to a place in our lives where we must justify our actions or the actions of others to ourselves, take time to listen to what you are saying and what is being said. Justification is often a quiet warning sign that the road you are heading down in life may be the road best not taken. The best business advice I have received—that can be applied to life in general—is to always put your cards on the table and be prepared to walk away from anything that does not feel morally or ethically right.

CONTENTS

ACKNOWLEDGEMENTS

After writing three books in three years, I would be remiss if I did not thank Susanne Boyce, President of CTV Programming and Chair of CTV Media Group who recommended I read *The Artist's Way* (Putnam Publishing Group) by Julia Cameron. Reading Julia's book and starting the practice of writing daily "morning pages" made the prospect of composing the 300 plus pages it takes to make a book less daunting in the beginning. Today, I have difficulty staying within my word count (a companion website was set up to handle additional information) as there are so many facets to cover in this growing—and constantly evolving—industry.

I would like to thank all the newspapers, magazines and associations that have taken the time to read and review my books. My first two books have been warmly received by the media and the event planning industry and the kind comments and support has contributed greatly to the success of both books—which are now being used as teaching tools, course adoption and recommended reading by universities and colleges worldwide

The John Wiley team works hard at creating quality products and are leaders in the field of professional books. Their care, commitment to quality and attention to detail shows in the books they produce. Karen Milner, Executive Editor, opened the door for my series of books on event planning and her vision continues to move my books forward. Elizabeth McCurdy, Project Manager, and Abigail Brown, Project Coordinator, once again have been the strong links between the book's structure and copy edit process and on top of every aspect. They are dedicated to ensuring a finely crafted book is turned out. Gayathri (Guy) Baskara, Marketing Manager, and I have just begun to work together and I am looking forward to working closely with her in the upcoming year. Meghan Brousseau, Pubilicity Manager, and Lucas Wilk, Pubilicity Coordinator, do a fabulous job promoting all of my books and are always there whenever I need their help. Michelle Wright, from Accounting, is another great addition to John Wiley and has demonstrated excellent follow through and resolution on any requests I have had. I would also like to give thanks to all of the people behind the scenes that I do not know personally but who play an important part in creating all the John Wiley books which are highly regarded by business professionals around the world

Ron Edwards, Focus Strategic Communications, manages to find a way to pull an additional 20,000 words plus from me with his thought provoking comments as we move through the structural edit. Just when I feel I have shared all I can, Ron's suggestions or inquiries from a reader's perspective, pull one more tip or paragraph from me, which helps to build a better book. Michelle Bullard, who is spoken highly of by the John Wiley team, stepped in to do the copy edit on this book when timing did not permit Ron to do so. I would like to thank Michelle for her contribution in taking this book to its next step.

Daphne Hart, my literary agent, Helen Heller Agency Inc., is a pleasure to work with—always calm, centered and committed to the clients she represents. Her expert advice is always on the mark and I value working with her. I would also like to thank Helen Heller for her assistance as well this year, it was greatly appreciated.

A very special thank you goes to Fran Mrazek-Fanning, whose telephone message I received through crossed lines, but which came at a very timely point in the manuscript and jogged a long-forgotten memory to include in the book.

Personally, I would like to thank my family—Walter and Ruth, Marilyn and Hans, Natasha and Blair, Jasmine, Emme, Munchie, Indie, Abby, Aunt Eleanor and Uncle George, Linda, Mykila, Grayson, Aunt Dinah, Uncle Alfred, Aunt Lydia and Uncle Arch, Uncle Rennie and Aunt Gladys, Uncle Alfred and Aunt Rachel, Uncle Joe and Aunt Maria, my grandparents Hannah and James Blundon and Emma and Walter Foote for being a part of my life and who are very important to me. I am also thankful for my friends who make me laugh and I look forward to spending time with them and my family in the future.

PREFACE

The question of ethics in the event planning industry is coming up more frequently than ever before, seeping into all industry relationships and areas of negotiation. As the event planning industry continues to grow, more and more event planning companies and those who were deemed event planning "suppliers" in the past, such as destination management companies, hotels, florists, decor companies and entertainment management companies, are now going head-to-head with event planners for the same client business. Today, event planners and suppliers are often approaching the same potential customer, and the established ways of conducting business have become discarded. In the past, the event planner approached the client directly and then brought their selected suppliers onboard to work on the proposal. But world events began to greatly affect how event planning would be conducted in the future.

The event planning industry as a whole struggled after September 11, 2001 when many corporate events came to an immediate halt. Before the industry recovered, corporate accounting scandals made headlines, and top executives pulled back on spending and closely monitored expenses. This was followed by talk of war. Many companies put event plans on hold as they waited to see the impact on the economy. Airlines were on the brink of bankruptcy. Hotels were sitting empty. Some destinations and venues were immediately ruled out as possible event sites. The event planning world was left reeling.

These factors contributed to an event planning industry whose members worked hard to maintain their existing client base, entice new clients to do business with them, find ways to grow their company by creating multiple money streams and look for ways to secure as much business profit as possible. Event planning companies sought ways to reposition themselves and jockeyed for client business. Event planners started taking on the roles of suppliers and destination management companies, while some suppliers, destination management companies and hoteliers began to position themselves to clients as event planners.

Questionable business practices became more visible to the industry as a whole. Event planning associations began to create ethical guidelines—professional standards of right and wrong—in response to the effect that lack of business ethics was having on the industry.

What makes the issue of ethics so tough, however, is that one person's ideas of bad ethical behavior might be different from someone else's. While a kickback—be it in the form of cash, goods, dinner out or a weekend away—to a client may be perceived by the supplier as an acceptable business practice, some clients may view it as an attempt at business bribery, while still others have come not only to accept it but to expect it.

This book was written as a guide for establishing business and personal standards, policies and procedures. It has been composed specifically to open the door to discussion on the topic of event planning business (and personal) ethics and etiquette with industry peers, in the office and with yourself. It is designed to have you asking:

"What would I do if I was presented with a situation such as this?"

"What should I do or say in this case?"

"What does our company policy say about handling matters like this?"

"What procedures should I follow?"

and most importantly

"Where do I stand on these issues?"

"What are the lines I will not cross in order to do business or to secure business?"

"What are the legal implications that I could be leaving myself or my company open to?"

It is important that proper responses are established, practiced and prepared for in advance. Left to chance or a knee-jerk reaction, the wrong ethical decision could carry a high personal and/or professional cost, as well as legal liability for you and your company. Even worse, you could become the next scandalous newscast.

The examples in the book are based on real-life instances that actually happened in the event planning industry. Reading through them will allow you to prepare a response to have at hand should a similar situation present itself. Being unadvised, ill-equipped or totally unprepared to handle sticky predicaments ethically and with finesse can lead down the road of regret and remorse, filled with *If only*, *What if* and *Why didn't I*.

One noted event planning expert got caught in an ethical whirlwind when she sold some stocks she personally owned. The timing was terrible since the stock tanked in the eyes of the business world the next day. It looked like insider trading when it was merely an alleged standing order to sell when the stock went below a certain dollar figure. The planner made a profit of US$50,000, while her actions planted seeds of mistrust in clients, suppliers and the public. The initial result was that the future of a multi-million-dollar company was placed in jeopardy for a comparably small profit. Innocence or guilty did not matter. People were quick to judge and the event planning expert's own company's stocks tumbled to previously unseen lows. The long-term result to the planner was a loss of reportedly more than US$400 million in stocks, advertising and endorsements.

What you do personally can hurt you professionally. Perception is everything. People are now seeing what your personal and company actions and choices say about you as a person or a business, as opposed to merely listening to the words being spoken. What you say does matter, but it is what you do that really counts. Do you "walk your talk"? What about the companies you work and do

business with? Do they say what they mean, and most importantly do they do what they say? We are in the midst of an ethics back-
lash, and companies are being extremely cautious about who they
do business with and how they themselves do business. They do
not want to be caught in an ethical undertow and be pulled under
by association.

A lack of ethics can and has destroyed companies and careers.
When businesses or the people within them cross ethical lines, personal reputations can be ruined and company credibility irrepara-
bly shaken, and the loss of integrity may never be completely
erased. Ethics violations are on the rise. Companies such as World-
Com, Enron, Tyco, ImClone and various areas of government have
brought the topic of ethics to the forefront with daily headlines in
all forms of media. Ethics have become a defining business issue.
Business practices are being called into question and all of this will
have a lasting impact on the event planning industry. Corporate
CEOs and CFOs will be looking closely not just at the bottom line
but at how the actual bookkeeping is being done.

People will be held accountable for their actions and that does
not refer to only in-house employees but their suppliers as well.
Reviews of whether or not company procedures are being adhered
to will not be limited to corporate organizations, but will extend to
those they are doing business with.

Corporations must impart company values to their employees.
They must teach what is and is not considered to be acceptable
business practices and procedures and clearly outline what will not
be tolerated. And, they must lead by example in both their business and personal lives. What is taught must be reinforced by constant observance of the ethical principles that have been established. In some instances, it is not the employee but the employer's
standards or lack thereof that are questionable. In these cases the
employee must decide whether to stay and work under business
practices that could be deemed shady, and compromise their
integrity in the process by affiliation, or to go elsewhere.

Transparency is a term that will be heard more frequently in
business. Openness about business practices, policies, procedures
and budget preparation with clients looking for full disclosure will
be moving to the forefront in the business world. Clients will be
looking to do business and align themselves with companies that
demonstrate corporate responsibility, have no hidden agendas or
costs and whose business dealings are aboveboard at all times.

Good business practices and high ethical standards—both professional and personal—work to build customer confidence and affect profits. Companies that demonstrate these qualities on a day-to-day basis and on all business fronts will gain a competitive edge. Controversial business maneuvers by a company or its representatives was in the past often met with a wink and a nod that said "we know we really shouldn't be doing this but what the heck?" This sort of attitude will no longer be overlooked or tolerated. Those who choose to continue unethical business behavior and practices and the people who do business with them know that they are just one step away from being tomorrow's front page headline.

Professionals in the event planning industry will be attempting to position themselves as leaders in ethical business practices. They will be reviewing, adopting and putting stringent guidelines in place with regard to who they associate with, how they do business and what expected business behavior will be—for themselves, for their office, for their peers and even for their clients. Working with a preferred list of clients and suppliers who have clearly defined and demonstrated ethical behavior will become an industry standard.

How you conduct yourself in business and even over lunch matters today. But event planning etiquette goes way beyond the food choices you make and what such decisions say about you to your clients and industry peers. That is just one tiny aspect of what it entails. Event planning by its very nature crosses over from business to social. And mastering social graces, displaying poise under pressure and knowing the meaning behind certain social entertaining elements is just as important as having industry business acumen. Event planning is an industry that has a playful party side and one with more serious business overtones.

In many cases, business and pleasure components are mixed. In either event, clients, their guests, event planning staff and their suppliers intermingle and interact with one another non-stop and at all hours of the day. All involved will walk through a minefield of social situations that could blow up in everyone's face. Not being prepared to handle potentially explosive predicaments can be damaging to both company and personal reputations. Proper etiquette and protocol on your home turf and around the world needs to be discussed. Codes of conduct in the office and on site should be clearly defined and firmly established. Business behavior must be maintained at all times, whether in the boardroom or in a swimming pool at a tropical resort. Staff need to know how to diplomatically handle being asked to step into a guest's hotel room and keep their reputation intact, as do your clients' employees if the reverse request is made.

Issues of personal safety should also be addressed in advance before you find yourself being driven to an isolated spot by someone you think trustworthy. In the event planning business there is often an atmosphere of casual camaraderie; guards can easily become relaxed and trust can be too freely given. Knowing when and what to look out for and how to handle yourself in certain circumstances is extremely important. These general "rules" of common sense need to be set out—especially for young student planners. You must always approach event planning by expecting the unexpected and being on guard but not guarded. Above all, stay on your toes. Breaches of ethics and etiquette can happen in a blink of an eye. Think situations out in advance and develop a plan for being able to execute what is being asked of you without crossing any ethical boundaries. Positioning yourself to be poised and professional no matter what happens takes preparation and training in knowing what to do, how to do it, what is rightly expected of you and what you expect from yourself in any environment.

This book is about setting and raising event planning standards both personally and professionally. Part 1 of the book discusses what it means to be ethical, why it's important to have an ethical industry, whether some people in the industry are straying from this path, why they are choosing to do so (a bad economy creates a desperation to win at all costs), some of the problems in the industry right now and how all involved in the event planning field—planners, clients and suppliers—can work towards an ethical career and industry. Part 1 also focuses on planner/supplier, planner/client and supplier/supplier relationships and addresses the diverse issues that event planners, clients and suppliers encounter. Event planning is a business where those involved are wined and dined on a daily, if not hourly basis, at home and around the world. The atmosphere surrounding event planning is one of allure, often involving exotic locales, hosted events where the alcohol flows freely, people traveling without partners—dangerous combinations for clients, guests, event planners and suppliers alike. It can also be stressful. One false step and a business relationship can explode and reputations can be in tatters. The stakes can be high. Events can range from hundreds of thousands of dollars to multi-million dollar extravaganzas. Some suppliers are in the business of wooing event planning business by offering special perks that cross the lines of ethical behavior—a free getaway for the planner and their loved one with all expenses paid (it is not uncommon to have air, private limousine transfers, hotel accommodations, meals and activities included) or cases of expensive wine delivered to the event planner's home. In other cases, it is the event planner who is making the request from the supplier in exchange for their business. For example, staging companies have received requests to build backyard decks as part and parcel of being awarded the business. When is it acceptable to receive a gift, what is acceptable and when does it begin to cross company ethics is just one area that will be discussed. Preparing yourself, as well as staff, on what to expect and how to handle the unexpected with business finesse is crucial. The door to discussion will be opened using the examples provided throughout the book.

Part 2 of this book deals with event planning business (not social) etiquette and codes of conduct—what is appropriate, what is not, when it's apropos, situations to look out for and how to side-step them successfully. In Part 3, codes of conduct, both in the office and on site, are discussed using real-life examples. Other event planning-specific etiquette issues covered include business behavior in event planning crisis management situations (such as when Murphy's Law hits), as well as event planning essentials and event planning dos and don'ts. This book will be of value to both the professional event planner, event planning suppliers and clients who are hiring and working with professional planners and suppliers.

Business Ethics

The first three chapters of *Event Planning Ethics and Etiquette* explore event planner and supplier professional working relations; the ethical cost of doing business; supplier to supplier ethics; the issue of fair competition; how to maintain ethical boundaries and delves into event planner and client interactions both in the office and on site.

Questionable behavior—personal and professional—is no longer overlooked, swept under the carpet or condoned. People are choosing who they align themselves with—as individuals and in business dealings—carefully. They know selecting the wrong business partner to work with can lead to criminal charges and legal liabilities, with not only the company they work for being held responsible, but individuals as well. For example, when using special effects at an event, a supplier, venue or planner should hold themselves to high standards of ethics in providing guest safety and demonstrate they value saving dollars more than saving lives. If they choose to sidestep terms and conditions that have to be met to ensure participants are as safe as possible, such as making sure all permits and safety codes have been met (fire marshal permits, clearly marked exits, exit ways have been clear and not locked or blocked, required number of working fire extinguishers on hand, sprinkler system in place, certified and tested flameproof material, on duty fireman to oversee event, proper insurance coverage) and a death results, criminal charges and lawsuits can be laid with all involved—client, planner, suppliers—in the event production.

Neither clients, planners or suppliers can afford to do business with those who cross ethical boundaries, crave financial gain at all cost, flaunt disregard for event planning principles and openly show a lack of respect for moral values. The cost is too high—to do so puts individuals and companies at risk personally and professionally.

Business ethics is now an industry standard. Exhibiting ethical behavior—as an individual and as a company—will be the guiding compass leading the way to those we chose to do business, work and associate with.

1
THE ETHICAL COST
OF DOING BUSINESS

EVENT PLANNER AND SUPPLIER
PROFESSIONAL WORKING RELATIONSHIPS

WOULD YOU DO BUSINESS WITH YOU?

When competition is tight and budgets are on the chopping block, cutting corners in the ethics departments may seem like a quick fix. But as many in the event planning industry will attest, a burgeoning bottom line does not always mean that you are a success. Here is an ethical question for you. You are an event planner who wants to use a specific hotel for a high-level event. You contact an audiovisual supplier you trust (as opposed to the hotel's in-house audiovisual supplier) to be sure everything will go off without a hitch. You inform the supplier of your dates and requirements. Then, about a week later, the supplier calls to say they have received a letter from the hotel stating that to do business in the hotel, the AV company must meet certain strict requirements: The crew must not sport any facial hair, or wear earrings, blue jeans or T-shirts while on site. While it seems appropriate that tech crews dress in a neat and tidy manner, something does not ring true about this letter. Techies with no beards, moustaches or long hair? Keeping in mind that most tech crews work behind the scenes, out of sight of participants and other hotel guests, and are often paying guests (their hotel rooms for out-of-town events are generally not complimentary or even at a staff travel rate; the limited negotiated allotment would have been assigned to event planning staff members first), most planners would smell a rat right about now. Are the terms merely a ploy by the hotel to promote its own in-house audiovisual company by making it difficult for outside contractors to be brought in?

From the hotel's perspective, it has the right to require anything it wants from those who set foot on its property. Perhaps there have been some bad experiences with rough-and-ready AV personnel in the past. Who is to know? And accusing the hotel of this conduct will not win you any points in the business-relationship department. The option always remains to take your business elsewhere, which was the decision of the event planning company faced with this dilemma. They did not want to jeopardize the quality of the event they were producing by using an AV company they were not familiar with. Another recourse would be to speak to the hotel's general manager or, if all else fails, the hotel chain's president. A similar situation can also occur when planners are faced with a hotel or venue's preferred supplier list. It is sometimes possible for the planner to overcome this obstacle and bring in their chosen supplier by paying a surcharge to the facility.

Such situations are thrown into the abyss of what could be called "questionable ethical behavior." All planners and suppliers have experienced it, whether on the receiving end or the giving end, and it is a tough spot to be in either way.

Event planners and suppliers develop their professional working relationships in a variety of ways. Their relationship develops through interaction that takes place inside and outside the office and in both business and social settings, which can include:

- In-Office Sales Presentations
- New Product Updates
- Business Meals
- Familiarization Trips
- Industry Functions

- Holiday Celebrations
- Proposals and Quotes
- Event Operations
- On-Site Meetings
- Business Referrals
- Confidentiality
- Business Favors

In any one of these areas, ethical lines between planners and suppliers can be unintentionally—and certainly sometimes intentionally—crossed. In business, you will always find someone who would sell their soul for a sale. Seizing an opportunity that does not ask you to compromise your company and personal beliefs and values is very different from selling your honor for a sale. It is up to you to decide whether you or your company will take part in a particular behavior that is ethically discreditable. And the time to decide that is in advance, before you are mired in the quicksand of unscrupulous kickbacks or conduct that can pull your company and your personal reputation under.

A world of available supplier talent is literally at an event planner's fingertips and on their doorstep—in their e-mail in-box, on the Web, over the telephone and delivered with the morning mail to their desk. Daily, planners are bombarded by an abundance of resources all looking to develop a long-term working relationship with them. Planners are looking to align themselves with suppliers who are creative, cost conscious, do outstanding work and offer inventive solutions. At the same time they must respect the planner-supplier boundaries, conduct themselves professionally, work until the job is done and at final billing present no surprises. Planners will often take suppliers with whom they have developed good working relationships and who have proven to produce client-pleasing results halfway around the world with them to create successful events rather than take the chance of trying someone new and untested.

Each supplier who calls on an event planner is looking for ways to establish that kind of bond. If out-of-country locations are being considered, airline representatives would like your client's participants to fly to destinations that they service. Tourist boards are looking to promote their country or area and work to keep their location at the top of planners' minds. Hoteliers and venues would like planners to select their (and related) properties to hold their event in. Destination management companies would like event planners to use their assistance all around the world or the services of those they are affiliated with. Suppliers of promotional goods and materials would be open to shipping their items anywhere in the world they may be needed rather than have planners use local sources.

Suppliers know that if they cultivate and establish good working relationships with top event planners it can lead to business referrals and serve to increase their market share. Competition is high and suppliers are always on the lookout for ways to set themselves and their company apart from the rest. As well, suppliers look for means to strengthen their personal business relationships with planners. In the event that supplier representatives should ever change companies, they would want to be able to take their established business connections with them. They look to cultivate planner loyalty to themselves as opposed to the company they represent. Some companies, in an effort to block this, have their account executives sign contracts with a two-year non-compete clause. This means that the representative would be barred from contacting their existing clientele, as well as potential clients, for two years should they decide to leave.

IN-OFFICE SALES PRESENTATIONS

Generally, event planners and suppliers initially meet over the telephone. The supplier could be calling from halfway around the world or from across the street. Their intent is to set up a face-to-face meeting to present their product. They may request to meet with an individual, the sales and planning group or the entire company team (planning, operations and on-site staffing). They may come alone or as part of a company-wide blitz. One hotel chain likes to have their top destination sales staff visit en masse once a year, in addition to individual hotel representative visits, giving planners a double dose of the same information. Planners often feel as though they are caught in event planning crosshairs if they live in a destination that can be used as a stop en route to a major industry trade show such as World Travel Mart in London, the Motivation Show in Chicago, or

The Special Event Show, which changes venue every year. At a time when planners are working frantically to clear time to attend the trade show themselves it can sometimes feel as if their offices have been invaded by suppliers flying in from around the world—sometimes showing up unannounced—in the days preceding and following the show. Wise planners learn quickly to anticipate this and limit their access to essential suppliers they need to spend one-on-one time with so that their days are not eaten up in sales meetings. Suppliers arriving on a planner's doorstep, deliberately not calling ahead to see if a meeting is even feasible, often find themselves advised by the receptionist that the staff can see people only by appointment. This is a buffer planners put in place so that they don't damage their personal working relationship by turning a supplier away themselves. Some suppliers try the unannounced arrival on purpose, because they know if they call ahead in busy times to secure a meeting they will be turned down. Their intention is to put planners on the spot and maneuver them into a meeting. Their lack of respect for ethical event planning business practices, common courtesy, regard for your time and meeting deadlines does not warrant more of an explanation from the receptionist than an appointment is required—you do not owe them more.

Sales representatives arrive in planners' offices determined to share all their company's services. Supported with Web sites, promotional material and letters of reference they set out to win over new clients. Often they arrive bearing gifts. Those that are appreciated by planners are examples of quality promotional items (trinkets, not trash) that feature the destination, facility or product that they can add to their research files. Planners can then use these items in their presentation proposal to clients as suggestions to include in their teaser mailings to guests or as one of the event elements included in their program recommendations. Planners also get to see the quality of the items firsthand, which can tell planners volumes about the supplier and its ingenuity. Promotional items deemed interesting and worthy of future consideration are filed away. The ones that are not are returned because planners, respectful of the promotional dollars being spent, advise suppliers if they would not use these particular items.

One special effects company handed out samples of small, light-as-air puff balls made of extremely soft material with a customized ribbon attached. The customized labels on the puffs the supplier handed out featured the special effects company's name and phone number so that planners knew who to call should there be a need. These puffs could be used as part of a special effects finale such as a confetti burst, and done in a client's corporate colors. Holding a sample in their hands, planners and clients could clearly see that guests would not be injured in any way by a cascade of puffs raining down on them. Whether or not these puffs would serve a purpose being visually effective or easy to clean up afterwards, for example, is a decision the planner and client could easily make after seeing a sample firsthand.

Other welcome offerings are inexpensive food items that may depict a destination or theme. One retro (1940s–1970s) candy manufacturer brought with them a sampling of fun items we loved when we were kids that could be ordered for party loot bags or used to create a centerpiece at a theme party. They brought a fair size assortment—enough for the office to partake in—but rather than eat them, they were kept on hand as props to show clients. Had they brought in a quantity of just one item, some may have been eaten and the balance filed away for promotional purposes, but the supplier brought in one of each item and it was of greater benefit to the event planning company to keep them than to eat them. Specialty food items that do not have a long shelf life are generally shared with the office and consumed. Smart suppliers who choose to bring food (or other) items on their sales calls ensure that the items are inexpensive, representative of their company product and are useful. It is essential that they bring sufficient quantities to distribute around the office. For example, a company that sells unusual party favors was remembered more because they handed out beverage glasses that glow as opposed to the tired and traditional coffee mug with the company name imprinted on it. It was an item that was intriguing, of value (could be used afterwards and would serve as a reminder of their company long after the glow had faded—it lasts up to six hours) and one that showcased what the supplier had to offer. The glass was not imprinted with a logo. A company business card was merely placed in each glass. It was small, discreet and memorable.

Suppliers bearing large cumbersome promotional leave-behind items will not be welcome with open arms. Bringing tumbleweeds or steer skull candles from Arizona would not be appropriate. Prickly pear, margarita jams and jellies, or Arizona popcorn with a southwest chili pepper kick would depict the area and be a better choice.

One Caribbean hotel on a sales call brought each staff member at an event planning company a large double-size umbrella featuring their hotel's name and logo. The umbrella was a sample of the umbrellas found in each guestroom for guests to use on hotel property to protect them from the sun or "liquid sunshine" (rain) and take home with them at the end of their stay. That gift was deemed by the receiving office to cross no ethical borders, since the hotel was one that they highly recommended to their clients and the gift was one that tied into the supplier's product. The supplier had called ahead to find out how many employees the event planning company had because they did not want to leave anyone out. It was to the supplier's benefit to have more people walking around with the umbrellas featuring their hotel's name, since it was advertising for them.

That brings event planners—individuals as well as companies—to another moral issue. By using a supplier's product, staff are openly endorsing it. You must ask yourself if this is something you are comfortable with. Is the hotel one your company supports? Is it one that represents the quality of hotels your company recommends? Is it better to be standing outside in the rain with an umbrella that endorses a specific product or to be shielded from a storm of controversy by upholding your principles with a logo-free umbrella?

Supplier gifts start to cross ethical boundaries when they are expensive, personalized or inappropriate. Companies need to establish guidelines about what can and cannot be accepted. A supplier bringing a planner, who is a known wine connoisseur, an expensive, rare vintage, specialty bottle of wine that is clearly meant—no matter how subtly it is presented—for their own personal consumption, is an inappropriate offering. Ethically, the supplier's motives can be perceived very differently from a representative scheduling a wine and cheese presentation, featuring their regional wines and cheeses or something special like an ice wine, fortified wine or new wine (such as Shiraz or Pinot Grigio) to an entire office at the end of their work day. One is aboveboard and out in the open for all to enjoy—and could be tied into destination education—while the first example is questionable because it is clearly meant to present the gift giver in a favorable light. Whether or not it is appropriate to serve wine in a business office is an entirely different matter that needs to be discussed before allowing such a presentation to take place. Whose responsibility is it (who is liable) if an employee is injured on the job or on the drive home after partaking in on-the-job libations?

Think breakfast served to an office is a better idea? It is not without its perils. One hotel decided to set up a food station in an event planning office and serve arriving employees breakfast. The number of sales calls from this supplier to the planning office was escalating and was being taken to new levels. They had opted not to bring in one of their professional chefs; instead, the hotel sales team was there in full force to cook breakfast for their guests. What was often bandied about the office was the hotel sales manager's huge (and very visible) crush on one of the (happily married) sales executives. During the breakfast proceedings, the hotel sales manager's mind was focused trying to get the sales executive's attention and not on the omelet station, which caught on fire. It was quickly put out, but along with the omelet, the hotel sales manager had burned the supplier's reputation.

What had been long apparent to the event planning staff was now obvious to the hotel's sales team. The conduct of the sales executive had always been above reproach, always extremely professional and polite and never encouraging. In fact, she took pains never to be left alone with the hotel sales manager. In sales presentations where chitchat can sometimes take a general turn while waiting for a member of the group who might have stepped away for a moment to return, she always took care to mention her husband in the conversation. There was never a question of someone being led on. But it was a situation that had gotten out of hand.

Was the office at fault for not setting sales boundaries for their staff and making sure that limits were maintained? The hotel sales manager had repeatedly shown lack of professional decorum, but it had not been dealt with. The concessions the event planning company had been receiving from the hotel, which was one of their preferred ones, made it easy to overlook questionable behavior. The event planning employee was caught in the middle. Her demeanor to the hotel sales manager was always professional and respectful and had never crossed the line. But she and her colleagues both knew that if they spoke up and asked to work with another sales manager, their clients may not continue to receive special compromises from the hotel. While they had done nothing to curry special favor, they knew they were receiving it and why. The office and their clients benefited, but there was a cost to doing business that way. After the situation literally flamed out of control, the hotel stepped in and resolved the situation by having the sales manager assigned to a new territory. They had witnessed firsthand what was to them unacceptable business behavior and took immediate action.

> **T**
> **I**
> **P**
>
> Never "drop in" unexpectedly on clients or suppliers "because you are in the area." Be respectful of one another's time, commitments and deadlines. One sales representative assures clients that she will take up no more than 10 minutes of their time and makes sure she does exactly that. A timer is set to ring in her pocket when the 10 minutes have elapsed. Always remember that no one will feel kindly towards someone they feel is holding them prisoner in their own office.

By using strong-arm tactics or engaging in unethical business practices such as courting clients with expensive gifts, customers can be turned off doing business with a company. It can be a costly mistake. Wise sales executives approach each buyer as a potential lifelong client, not a one-shot contract, and look towards building a long-lasting professional working relationship. They know that if they cross ethical boundaries, corporate business relationships can be quickly terminated, client references rescinded and their chances of future business referrals nullified. They know that individuals come and go and that their true client is the company they are doing business with. They are aware that the cost of doing business unethically can be high, should they choose to cater to the demands of one unscrupulous individual or solicit business in a manner that is questionable. The onus will fall directly back on them, damaging their professional reputation, and on the company they represent if the company is perceived as condoning a lack of ethical behavior.

COMMUNICATION BETWEEN PLANNERS AND SUPPLIERS

Keep new product mailings and updates sent by e-mail professional, not personal. What is said can be circulated around the office and around the world in a matter of minutes. Do not put anything in writing you are not prepared for the world to see or hear. E-mails and voice messages can be easily forwarded or replayed for the whole office to witness.

One owner who was ethically, but not electronically, challenged, could decipher the phone message codes from the tone being played when staff were picking up their messages using speakerphone. He knew the entire staff's telephone passwords and would monitor their messages. He discovered that one of the company's married employees was having an affair with one of their suppliers, and delighted in playing several of the "private" messages to others on their executive team. Both the owner and employee were guilty of unethical behavior. Some event planning companies record all staff conversations, with the staff's knowledge, but incoming callers are not advised that calls are being caught on tape (technically illegal in some areas).

A seemingly harmless joke can have serious repercussions and even damage someone's character. For example, a mailing from a supplier included tequila suckers (complete with worm). The handwritten note made reference to discovering a new way to drink on the job and alluded to how much they knew the recipient enjoyed tequila. Luckily, everyone in the office received the same message and supply of suckers (which were promptly thrown away). But had only one message come into the office, its contents, if opened by someone else, could have easily damaged someone's reputation. Many companies have their receptionist open incoming mail and date stamp it. No one should ever assume that only the recipient will be viewing their messages, even if marked personal, private or confidential. What comes into a place of business should be related business material and may be opened, read and circulated by anyone. In the news, we read daily how e-mails and business letters with personal requests are coming back to haunt the sender by being leaked to reporters covering business transgressions in their entirety. If an inappropriate message is received in the office, it is best to address it directly with the sender and advise them to be more circumspect in the future. Letting it go is not the answer. A lack of response could lead to a further lack of business respect being shown in the future.

BUSINESS MEALS

Many sales reps like to cement business relationships over lunch or dinner and some will try to make sure that they schedule their appointments to end just before lunch or at the end of a business day when the offer to get a quick bite or grab a fast drink may be made. Others may call and formally invite planners out to lunch or dinner. Planners who prefer to keep their business relationships professional and not cross over into their personal time and space learn to schedule supplier meetings to begin at 10:00 a.m., knowing that scheduling a meeting at 11:00 a.m. could lead to an invitation to lunch. In the afternoon planners schedule meetings to begin at 2:00 p.m., knowing that by doing so they have sidestepped being invited to go to lunch before their meeting (which would generally happen if they erred and scheduled it for 1:00 p.m.) and avoided being asked to go for drinks after work since the meeting would be ending mid-afternoon. If planners decide to stop for lunch or go for an after-work drink, they cut into time usually reserved for meeting family or friends, as their personal time can be extremely limited when deadlines are looming. Many planners work through their lunch hours on days that meetings with suppliers are scheduled so that they can minimize the domino effect of work, e-mails and messages piling up while they are in meetings. Planners can tactfully tell their sales reps that by meeting in the office and not over a meal they can both fully focus on the business at hand. This way, planners can give the representative's material their full attention and talk more freely about their upcoming events needs without the concern of being overheard or indiscreet in a public setting.

Some event planning employers may feel that going to lunch with suppliers is an expected part of the job. In their minds, relaxing over food in a casual setting can open the door to a better working relationship with suppliers and benefit their clientele. Suppliers know that the more they can discern about their client, the better they can service them and determine how to better their chances of closing the sale. Those skilled in sales will make note of their client's personal preferences, birthdays, marital status, children's names and ages, and pets. Power selling and speaking courses teach sales staff how to tell if their client connects more to visual or auditory sales techniques by the language they use. They are taught to listen to client responses. For example, do they reply to a question by saying, "I see what you mean" (visual) or "I hear what you are saying" (auditory). Knowing a client's preference can help them target their sales presentations and service style.

A top salesperson's mission—as a planner's main sales contact—is to get to know their client better than their competition and to work towards building a lasting professional working relationship.

But the same thinking can be applied in reverse. By planning companies spending time getting to better know their sales representatives at lunch or dinner, or the ideal scenario for both—over a round of golf at a charity event where an extended amount of time can be spent in each other's company and where foursomes are selected with business opportunities in mind and not left to chance—the possibility of being able to secure better rates for their clients in their future dealings with a supplier could be their main objective, not merely grabbing something to eat.

Are mealtime maneuvers ethical? Are they mandatory and part of the job requirements? Can professional and personal boundaries be crossed over something as basic as lunch? Could company secrets or private business be spilled instead of the soup during the enjoyment of a glass or two of wine or beer in a casual atmosphere? The answer to all these questions is yes. How many times have you heard a colleague return from a business lunch exclaiming "You won't believe what I just heard!" and in a matter of minutes a major industry newsflash has gone through the office and out on the streets via e-mail and the telephone before the unsuspecting teller of tales has even returned to their desk. Those practicing ethical behavior need to stop the flow of conversation when it turns to airing a company's dirty laundry or dishing dirt on the competition. Sitting silent is showing that this manner of conversation is being condoned. One planner was caught in the position of being in the know between two business peers. A colleague was about to launch into a recap of a high-level meeting, not knowing that the person she was sitting across from was best friends with the senior executive she had just met with and his wife. Had she proceeded to tell her tale the end result could have been disastrous, with the information being shared sure to get back to those she had met with. The planner had a choice of whether to say nothing or step into the conversation and ask the other person (who was sitting there quietly, not saying a word but taking it all in) in all innocence if they were friends with the senior executive, putting her peer on warning that they were being indiscreet and to proceed with caution. The planner broke into the conversation and a change of subject was quickly introduced. The world gets smaller every day and you never know who knows who—they may be sitting across from you or directly behind you during your lunch meeting, taking in everything you say without anyone being aware. Be wary of what is being said, to whom it is being said and where it is being discussed.

FAMILIARIZATION TRIPS

Familiarization trips, known in the business as fam trips, can take place in the city you live, out of state and around the world. The purpose of a fam trip is to introduce an event planner to a new service, venue, facility, hotel or destination. Airlines have been known to whisk planners away on flights to nowhere, taking off and landing in the same location, to demonstrate in-flight comfort and service, or for an afternoon beach barbecue on a tropical isle in the middle of winter. Spas try to demonstrate how their location has mastered the art of pampering, and restaurants have created special delicacies to tempt planners' palates. Hotels have walked planners up and down every inch of their facility to show off every conceivable nook and cranny. Some "fam" trips are purely business, while others are purely pleasure. Many are a combination of both, and in some cases the planner is invited to bring a personal guest. Suppliers also offer fam trips to planners' clients who may be considering a specific destination for an upcoming program.

Fam trips are not meant as a reward to administrative staff, an inexpensive vacation or an opportunity to send the company head's parents away on an all-expense sightseeing venture. They are not supposed to be a chance to do unrelated business in locations that were of personal, not professional, interest, but they are sometimes used by event planning companies that way. In each case, office reports would be filled in upon return, but what an inexperienced and uneducated eye sees is entirely different than a professional eye. Some suppliers have been misled as to who is actually a full-time, part-time or freelance (contracted) employee, or a relative, partner (spousal non-business) or friend not in the industry. They have, in some cases and at great expense, been used. Some suppliers are fine about having *any* representative of the event planning company attend. They are so anxious to show off their services. To them, it may be better to have someone—anyone—rather than no one there. But they need to know exactly who is attending and why, what their in-office responsibilities or affiliations are and whether the proposed service being showcased is a viable company option. There are times where there are no in-house staff members able to take part or afford time away from the office, and a trusted and trained eye could be sent in their stead to view a particular site that is of true interest to the office for an upcoming proposal. But the supplier needs to be provided with the facts, not half-truths, in order to make a decision.

Having said that, the planner may then be putting the supplier in a position of having to bend certain rules to accommodate them, with the event planner asking them to compromise their business ethics. A freelance trip or program director that the event planning uses on a consistent basis is an example of affiliated personnel they may recommend to represent them. They are fully trained, knowledgeable and aware of the event planning company's requirements.

T
I
P

> Bad business behavior can take place that will reflect badly on both the supplier and the event planning company when non-company representatives demonstrate unprofessional attitudes. The mother of one planning president, on a fam trip representing the company, loudly berated local airport staff for not upgrading her and her husband to first class on a scheduled flight. Her behavior was so obnoxious that the head of the airline called the planning office to complain. That was only the first leg of the trip. Things then went from bad to worse. At the hotel they were equally demanding, requesting room upgrades and free amenities. They were late to functions, held up the rest of the guests time and time again and were generally unpleasant to be with. And the company's claim to professionalism was definitely questioned by all who witnessed it. The manner in how it was handled was noted by the planners—the supplier had lost total control of the situation. In another case, when faced with unacceptable conduct, there was no hesitation on the part of the supplier, who sent the offending guest home immediately at their own expense. They were not about to reward blatant bad behavior. Those on the trip respected the supplier for standing up for ethical behavior and taking appropriate action. By demonstrating company values while conducting themselves professionally, the supplier earned a reputation for masterful handling of difficult situations. Don't be afraid to do the right thing. The business the supplier may have lost by sending the unwelcome guests home was not business they wanted to handle if this was an example of how the company conducted themselves.

Fam trips have also been used by planners to entice prospective clients or as a thank you to existing ones whose decision maker had always longed to go on a safari, sail the Nile, climb the pyramids or visit down under, but had no intention of actually going there with their group and openly said so. Once again the supplier is on the hook for the costs, has been lied to, feels used and has wasted a valuable opportunity to better grow their business by bringing a true potential client with them.

Some planners and clients prefer not to be indebted to any supplier. If a fam trip is required, they pay up front for all their expenses. They consider it an ethical cost of doing business, not an industry perk or payback in exchange for business, and accept no offers of free—or reduced fee—fam trips. That way they also get to determine exactly how long their stay needs to be and what they need to see. One event planning company made a much-needed visit to see a Las Vegas theater being used to stage their event, all in one day. Two key staff members took the first flight in and returned on the last flight out, seeing exactly what they needed to complete their presentation. Being wined, dined and wooed was not what they were about—they were there not to play in the pool or hit the slots, but for purely business reasons. They were on a fact-finding mission.

Always make sure that the fam trip being offered is on the up and up. If you have been the recipient of unwanted attention from a supplier, be wary of fam trips that are offered. One industry supplier representative (a very much married lothario) was planning a fam trip of one for an unsuspecting planner. Unknowingly, the planner was to be the only invited guest on a weekend getaway, all expenses paid for by the equally unaware supplier. On another fam trip a planner was being hit on nonstop by the sales representative, whose main ambition was to familiarize themselves with their invited guest. On the final night the planner received one last call from the sales rep asking to be let up to the room so that they could make the planner's last night in the destination "memorable." It was. With the deadbolts securely fastened and a heavy bureau pushed in front of the door to keep unwanted intruders out, their last night in the destination certainly became memorable. The planner had learned from a hotel representative that hotel room keys may be given out by "a good buddy" working on reception, and the planner decided not to take any chances and barricaded the door.

INDUSTRY FUNCTIONS

Suppliers often showcase their products at industry functions that range from large conferences to individual special events.

Some supplier events are very tasteful and their focus is on educating their guests, introducing them to key personnel and spending quality time together. Starting with cocktails with dinner, this is followed by a formal presentation after which everyone heads home. Others are pure party disguised as a professional get-together. Some come in between. Planners attending supplier special events are usually going to see a new facility or learn something new. If a supplier is holding their event at a brand-new venue that the planner has not been to or has not experienced their service firsthand, that can be a major drawing card in getting them to attend. The event planner will be more impressed by being introduced to something out of the ordinary—be it a location, food, beverage, decor or entertainment—than having to sit through something run of the mill at an overused location.

Some suppliers looking to show their clients a good time will include overflowing bars and dance bands, which can lead to being placed in a compromising situation. When partners do not accompany attendees, dancing should never be included by event planners. Preferable would be a performance that guests can all watch and enjoy. A band with a dance floor forces participants, willing or not, to get up and dance with a member of the sales team or one of their associates. For the most part many of them would rather be home, relaxing and spending time with loved ones. They attend industry functions to show support for their sales representative, to learn something innovative and to come away with new business contacts—not to dance.

T I P Introducing the newest dance and song that is about to sweep the nation, and encouraging guests to participate from their seats by doing just the arm movements, can be fun and entertaining and done in a manner that no one's reputation could be publicly jeopardized and the subject of conversation the next day.

Marital conflict was the result of one wife picking up her husband before a presentation had come to an official end. When the woman arrived she saw people drinking, dancing and in some cases being overly familiar with their industry peers. "Is this what you call working while I'm home alone waiting to spend time with you?" was the comment heard as the couple left. Event planning crosses over to party planning and supplier events can mirror that, but knowing what to include and how to present it professionally is paramount. Business decorum must be maintained. Guests attending are working, not there for a good time. The festivities and entertainment elements should be reflective of this. It is how professional event planners would strategically plan their clients' corporate events if guests are expected to attend on their own.

Where ethical boundaries also are crossed at industry functions is when the following are encountered:

- No-Shows
- Bringing Along Uninvited Guests
- Unexpected Guests
- Substitute Guests

No-Shows

When guests RSVP but have no intention of attending, it is not just rude, it is expensive. Last-minute crises do happen, but at some industry functions the percentage of no-show guests who have called in to say they will be attending, don't call and cancel, or merely don't show up is very high. They should know better. Planners know when suppliers have to call in food and beverage guarantees. After all, that is part of what they do for their clients. Not showing up when you have said that you will can strain working relationships. The supplier is on the hook for the cost of the meal and planners should consider how it feels to pay for meals for guests who have not bothered to show up. This can reflect back on their sales relationships with their suppliers. The supplier may have not been able to invite other guests due to budget or room capacity and thoughtless no-shows limit their options.

Sometimes the inability to decline the invitation in advance is driven by good intentions. For example, when the sales rep is pressuring the planner by stressing how important it is that they attend, it can be difficult to continue to give excuses and may be simply easier to say yes. What no-shows may not realize is that not only does the supplier know who RSVPs and doesn't attend, often name tags of expected guests are left at registration in the hopes that the recipient is only momentarily delayed, so departing guests often get to see who was expected and was ultimately labeled an official no-show.

BRINGING ALONG UNINVITED GUESTS

Guests may call and ask if they can bring an uninvited staff member, friend or partner. Planners recognize the importance of how an invitation is worded. They know that they leave themselves open to the uninvited if the invitation is not properly worded. "And Guest" after the invitee's name means exactly that. The invited guest is free to ask anyone to accompany them to the event. The additional company is accounted for, included in the budget and openly welcomed. Invitations bearing only one name (and not clearly marked "And Guest" or "And Staff") mean only one guest is planned for and expected to attend. Calling a supplier to request additional space can stress budgets, create extra work for them as they try to juggle responses and seating plans, and place the suppliers in the awkward position of having to say no.

 A gracious out that suppliers can use—if they find themselves unable to say no—is to simply note the request and advise the caller that if space should open up, they may be able to consider their request.

UNEXPECTED GUESTS

Guests may show up unexpectedly, deciding at the last moment to attend. They've called and sent their regrets, but on the day of the event their desk has been cleared, there is nothing slated on their to-do list that can't wait, the office is buzzing and getting ready to attend a fun evening function and an evening out with their industry peers suddenly is more appealing than being left behind or sitting at home alone. The group arrives en masse at the registration desk and the supplier is then faced with a dilemma. Do they scramble to make room for someone unexpected? Turn them away at the door and offend someone they regularly do business with and who was originally a welcome addition to the evening's festivities? Planners have been on the other side and know the ripple effect an unexpected guest can cause and, in good conscience, being respectful of industry business ethics should never intentionally cause registration chaos. Suppliers generally try to handle this awkward situation with grace, but a gracious guest does not put their host on the spot or in a position of having to incur unexpected expenses on their behalf.

Substitute Guests

Guests may pass on their invitations to others. An invitation comes in. The event is a "must do" for a number of reasons—the office wants to show support, check out the venue the host is using, see how a new theme is being done or meet additional contacts—and the person who has been invited is unable to attend. Most planners would call and express their regrets, but some take matters into their own hands. An RSVP is called in, but instead of the intended guest, a substitute is sent in their place to represent them. Invitations, unbeknownst to the sender, are often circulated around the event planning office with a note scrawled across the top that says "does anyone want to go in my place?" The invitation eventually makes its way back to the recipient and a yes is called in, but there may be no mention of a change of name. What is not taken into account is that the supplier has selected the guest name with care. An event that has been designed around company presidents attending will be uncomfortable for all concerned should the office's temporary receptionist show up in their place. Money will have been spent on someone for whom it was not intended and the supplier did not have the opportunity to bring in another guest who would be more suitable for the evening's objectives.

HOLIDAY CELEBRATIONS

Holiday celebrations are never an invitation to let loose with inhibitions or indulge in sending gag jokes that cross personal and business limits. Get-togethers may be casual, but good business behavior should never be casually discarded.

Companies vying for a major account took the holiday season to inundate one company president with very expensive gifts for him and the office staff, with the hopes that their company may be looked at more favorably when it was time to decide the winning bid. Unfortunately, company policy required that all of the gifts be returned as the companies had violated the dollar amount for what was deemed an appropriate holiday gift dollar value for a person or entire office. Red faces all around. Checking with companies in advance to see what would be a suitable gift is always advisable. General gifts for the office to share, such as inexpensive but creative food baskets, may be a better choice than individual gifts.

Suppliers who send fitting holiday gifts can have their "gifting" rights violated when the offerings they send are not used as they were intended. One supplier chose a huge container of gourmet popcorn (several flavors were sectioned off in the can) as their annual holiday gift for office staff, one that could easily be shared while at work. When the beautifully decorated canister was empty, staff decided that names would be drawn to see who would take it home. In this case, the gift was used exactly as the supplier meant. All shared in the supplier's goodwill. Not so in the following example.

Every year one candy manufacturer would send their event planning clients a large and lavish display for all the staff to share as a thank you (as noted on their accompanying card). At one office, the first thing one company president would do was call her family members to tell them the package had arrived and to come in and choose their favorites from the selection. The festive package, which came wrapped in clear cellophane, would be whisked away behind closed doors the minute it arrived. The president's family would come and later depart with their arms laden with the supplier's wares. The one or two remaining boxes would be put out for the staff to partake in. The supplier was never aware that the gift they had intended to be shared by all was being used to stock one individual's family members' shelves for the holidays—especially the one most likely to be able to afford to buy their own candy supply. The supplier would then call to find out how the staff had enjoyed their holiday treats and new products, which, of course, the staff had only seen as a moving blur as they were carried from the reception area to the president's desk. This scene was played out year after year, and in the office the president's behavior quickly became a standing joke with bets on how fast her family members would arrive. But, would the supplier have been able to see the humor in it? The staff, embarrassed by their president's actions, never told the supplier that the thoughtful gift was never distributed as intended. A better option for the supplier would have been to deliver the gift in person and be on hand to distribute it to staff.

Should an individual be able to commandeer what has been earmarked as an office gift from a supplier? Or how about others appropriating personal gifts addressed to someone else who happened to be out of the office when gifts were delivered? In the case of perishable items such as a seasonal box of Clementine oranges, it is acceptable to appropriate them if they would go bad before the addressee returned back to the office. They can always be consumed and easily replaced. Items that are not so affected should always be delivered to whom the supplier intended. If the gift is something deemed unacceptable to company policy, it is the individual's responsibility to acknowledge it, advise the supplier of company procedure and return it. A staff member whose passion was golf was gifted with a top-of-the-line golf club, which far exceeded the gift value that was acceptable by his company. In keeping with his company's policy setting the gift maximum at $25, he returned the club. Logo-imprinted golf balls or a hand towel to clip onto his golf bag would have been a better gift selection.

One supplier used the holiday gift-giving season as an opportunity to be present with their product and show a touch of creativity, all with the advance approval of head office. Hot roasted chestnuts from an actual vendor's cart, steaming hot chocolate, a specialty coffee bar, warm cinnamon buns (all skillfully prepared by professional staff—not their sales reps) and strolling carolers greeted staff as they came to work. It was an inexpensive way to add festivity to the start of their day and get to spend additional quality time with them, further developing their long-term working relationship. Staff were introduced to the supplier's serving elves, the faces behind the names most knew only from telephone or e-mail communications. Their holiday gift stood out from the rest and staff looked forward to seeing what surprises next year would bring. Their gift selection was out of the ordinary and in keeping with the services they offered.

In order to sidestep any office politics and to demonstrate social responsibility, some suppliers opt to send donations to charities to support worthwhile causes in lieu of gifts. Choosing a charity can be difficult. Many who select this option make one large donation on behalf of all their clients as opposed to supporting each client's individual charity. A donation to helping children, especially in the holiday season, may be viewed in a warmer light than one saving endangered donkeys, which may be equally worthy to an animal lover but may not be the choice of the majority. Reports in the news regarding charity spending scandals will make some suppliers skittish about continuing this trend. They will be more careful in choosing charities, especially after a major charity accepting donations for a September 11, 2001 relief fund made headlines when it was revealed that the dollars coming in were not all going to help individuals, but that some of the incoming funds would be diverted and spent on new computers and administration. Ensuring that the money received will be spent as it was intended is important, since in some cases ethics are reportedly being crossed. Make sure that the charity is legitimate. Not all charities are who they claim to be. One charity calling for donations, with police and missing children in their name, was not connected in any way to the police. Be aware. It is better to go with recognized and reputable charities.

With the holiday season come company get-togethers and parties. Some event planning companies have solicited suppliers for gifts for door prizes, decor and reduced costs for entertainment. There are many ethical reasons not to cross this line and put suppliers in the position of being backed into a corner, or accept such offers if they are presented. As planners you could be walking the fine line of being perceived as beholden or aligning your company with one particular supplier. The supplier may feel, rightly or wrongly, that they are being put in the position that if they do this for your company you will look more favorably on their next bid or proposal, and if they don't pony up they won't stand as good a chance or the opportunity could go to someone else.

Clients are not impressed by the developing trend of supplier promotional material being sent to the recipient in designer store logo-printed giftboxes wrapped as a "present." Creative packaging is appreciated. It is reflective of what we do as an industry—it showcases our talents. Take, for example, the Flexplay DVDs that were used to show scenes from the newest James Bond movie to reporters before the movie was released. In true James Bond fashion, the DVDs self-destructed. As reported by CNN's Jeordan Legon, "The discs included a letter from Q warning recipients: Once you remove the DVD from its packaging, you only have 36 hours to watch it. After the time has elapsed, Q's letter advises, the disc then makes a nice martini coaster." (Flexplay is located in New York City—www.flexplay.com.) Receiving that kind of innovative mailing would delight event planners. But sending parcels that look as though the receiver's business is being solicited by receiving expensive gifts would not. Turn instead to companies like Progress Packaging (www.progresspackaging.com) whose marketing team can design creative customized packaging and promotional mailings that will stand out. Combine the packaging with creative inclusions, such as chocolate sushi (www.chocolatesushi.com) sent in bento boxes (a Japanese box used to serve lunch or dinner in) with your message attached to chopsticks, inviting the recipient to take a moment to savor the important news inside or to take-away some new ideas to share with their clients.

PROPOSALS AND QUOTES

The time, effort and expense that goes into preparing a proposal is tremendous. Collectively, from all involved on the event planning side, well over 100 person-hours can easily be spent in researching, designing, developing and preparing a proposal and cost breakdown summary. Add to this figure all the hours spent by each individual supplier, and the cost to do a well-executed presentation to the client can be staggering. This time and money can't be recouped if the bid is not won, as most proposals are done on speculation in the hopes of winning the business. Unlike lawyers, most event planners do not charge a retainer for services rendered with no outcome guarantees. The fear in the industry is that charging a retainer may limit their chances to be asked to present, because the majority of event planners do not charge consulting fees. Some event planners do charge a retainer with the stipulation that should they win the business, the consulting fee will be applied to the management fees being charged. This is done to weed out clients who are using their services only to fulfil company policy of receiving three or more cost comparisons, which can be standard business practice (and applies to office supplies, couriers, long-distance carriers, office equipment, etc.) with some corporations. They may have no intention of changing suppliers, but are merely soliciting quotes to fulfil their required quota.

When a request for proposal is sent out to a supplier, with the initial telephone call followed up by a detailed request, the supplier is looking for reassurance that the request for proposal has been properly qualified and the event planning company is not about to waste their time preparing a quote that is pure speculation and unlikely to be awarded to them.

Suppliers expect to be informed about how much competition they face. For example, they would want to know that their proposal is one of 16 being considered so that they can determine whether they can afford to invest the time and money in preparing a quote. They want to know if there is a real possibility of landing business and that the event planning company is not just taking an opportunity to display their abilities with little chance of return. Time permitting, the supplier may welcome the chance to demonstrate their talents, but they need the facts to be able to make an informed decision. One car manufacturer was notorious for having multiple bids put out for their product launch, but year after year they went with the incumbent. Their company policy required them to solicit three bids, but in actuality they opened the door to accepting bids from everyone who had approached them throughout the year. Most suppliers would be wary of spending their energy on such a long shot and their real fear would be of being used for price comparison (the client's attempt to ensure that the incumbent is being honest in their pricing) or being mined for new ideas. Ethically they need to know where they truly stand so that they can do what is best for their business and staff. Some clients have been known to take creative content from one company and fax it over to their preferred supplier, not even bothering to remove the name of the contributor. Ethical planners will not engage in stealing ideas and choose not to do business with clients who display little regard for the work involved.

Not all planners are up front with suppliers about timelines. Often, suppliers receive frantic calls requesting a two-day turnaround on an extensive quote. Not only is their creativity and talent being unfairly taxed to produce something that quickly with expected accuracy, but in many cases they are being asked to "jump the line" and handle that request before completing one that is just on the brink of being completed and due by the same deadline.

> **TIP** Jumping the line can occur when a salesperson happens upon on a client during a cold call who is right in the middle of viewing presentations for an upcoming event.

There is a difference between planners giving a supplier a due date that is different from the actual client presentation, and giving a false deadline. The client presentation date is not the supplier due date. An event planner needs time to be able to review incoming quotes, clarify any questions regarding costs, timing and logistics and compile the information from all suppliers. There is a domino effect. For example, all electrical and lighting needs cannot be determined until decor, entertainment and catering have sent in their requirements. The planner then must analyze inclusions, finalize the cost summary breakdown, prepare the proposal, make sufficient copies and have everything ready on time for their client's presentation.

Planners cannot wait until the day before a client presentation to receive supplier information and quotes. The information cannot be turned around that quickly and in the end both the supplier and event planner will have most likely wasted their time, money and creative energy. The end result will be rushed and could be filled with errors that could become apparent during the presentation. The proposal most likely would not have been of equal caliber to the competition if they had been given the time to properly prepare, review the material, double check for errors and make sure that the finished product is reflective of their company values. Business has been lost on rushed proposals. The impression a sloppy presentation can leave will be lasting. Sales reps need time to absorb the material, ask questions and be thoroughly familiar with the proposal before they have to stand before their clients. They need to appear poised and prepared to answer any questions. There can be the odd exception, but in one case, the fast turnaround resulted in a US$100,000-plus costing error because many of the costs were not researched. Planners had been told to merely "make it up" as per the company vice president, and plaster the words "estimated costs" everywhere in an attempt to protect them should the proposal go to contract. The error was discovered *after* the proposal went to contract. The clients were greatly upset, but did pay the additional amount, since there was less than six weeks before the event was to take place and no time to begin again with a new company—but they did not do business with the planning company the following year. Ethically the event planning company was at fault. They had not done proper research and what they knowingly presented was a proposal filled with costing errors. They won the bid because their pricing came in well below the competition who had done their homework and had presented an accurate estimate. The client felt they had been part of a bait-and-switch scam, but owned part of the responsibility since they should have questioned the vast pricing discrepancy between the two bids.

T
I
P

The date that planners give to suppliers as their due date— not client presentation date—is what ultimately needs to be respected if a supplier wishes to be considered. And the timeline a supplier requires to turn around a costing that is up to their professional standards needs to be closely considered.

Just as an event planner needs time to properly prepare their proposal, so does a supplier. Suppliers lament that they are continually being hit with deadlines that are completely unrealistic and false by planners who are paranoid that their quotes will not arrive on time. Planners who do that have often experienced being left waiting and not being told truthfully by suppliers that they cannot handle another quote due to their workload. Even a reliable supplier may be loathe to turn away a business opportunity from a good planner, cautious of creating a situation where their client may end up bonding with another company if they are unable to meet the deadline. And planners want to work with suppliers they have come to trust and hesitate when it comes to working with what they consider to be less than the best to meet their event needs. One planner who was not in a bid situation kept their client waiting more than eight weeks for a quote to have one of the best in the field tent and cover over an intricate pool for dining and dancing. For something as specialized as that you want to ensure the company you are working with is tops in their industry so that no guests find themselves plunging unexpectedly into the pool mid-dance. The company quoting was in their busiest time and the proposal kept getting pushed further and further back through unexpected delays and the need for three site inspections to make sure that all specs were correct. What started out as a request in August could not be finalized and submitted to the client for review until mid-November.

The next time that planner is required to do a similar quote with the same company, they are going to enter into the negotiations wary of the supplier being able to meet their actual proposal deadline because the supplier now has a history with them of not being able to turn around a quote quickly in their busy season (although on site they are wonderful and never miss a step). Ethically, planners need to be informed if a due date is going to be highly improbable. They are placing their reputation on the line and may lose business if a quote is not received on time, so choosing the right supplier is crucial. Each party needs to be respectful of the other and understand what can actually be done in the time permitted. It can serve both supplier and planner better to say no if something is not doable, rather than taking the chance of burning business bridges by giving false hope of deadlines being met. When presented with true timelines, the planner has the option to go back to the client to ask for an extension in order to present a proposal with a supplier who will do the best job. This was the case with the pool being covered with acrylic for dining and dancing. It was better for the client to move the proposal date, knowing it meant that they would then have access to the best in the field.

A supplier left waiting for an event planning client's decisions is an ethical pet peeve. If suppliers, who often move heaven and earth to meet planning requests and deadlines, are left to chase planners to see how the presentation went and when the decision would be made, they may end up feeling of lack of business respect when they are left out in the cold. When their calls to busy planners about the status of the proposal are curtly dismissed with a "we'll call you as soon as we know," and they find out weeks later, from a friend of a friend in the industry grapevine, that the business has been awarded elsewhere, respect evaporates and seeds of suspicion and mistrust are planted.

Planners can be fiercely protective of the identity of their clients, so much so that there are times when a false name is given. Trusts have been violated in the past by suppliers who have overstepped boundaries and called the end user (the event planning company's client) directly. Planners maintain that their client is *their* client and adopt a "hands off" policy with suppliers. The event planner feels that they are the supplier's client and that is where all communication starts and ends. As everyone continues to try and get a bigger piece of the event planning industry pie, some resort to unethical means. Hoteliers have called event planning companies' clients directly and offered lower rates if they book with them as opposed to the event planners. One destination management company that an event planner had always used on their programs went directly to one of the planning company's clients, soliciting business directly with them. It was a deliberate move designed to cut out the event planning company. The client showed the supplier's proposition to the event planning company. Their loyalty was to the event planner and the client thought they should know that their "trusted" supplier had no business integrity. That destination management company's services were never used again and others in the event planning industry were alerted.

Suppliers maintain that they need to know who the client is so that if they are asked to bid on the project by more than one event company, they can make sure that all event companies involved in the bidding receive the same rates and concessions so that no favoritism can be perceived by the industry. Regardless of who wins the bid, the cost is the same. Creativity and customer service is then the deciding factor. In general, hotels let event planners know when someone else is bidding on the same bit of business. Some will give out the competition's name, while others will not. Planners have been shocked to find that clients who have said they are taking only three bids have actually opened the door to many more.

In some cases, knowing the client's name can hurt supplier negotiations. One decor company knew that regardless of who won the bid, their services would be used if the program was a go. All event planning companies had chosen to go with the same supplier for a quote. Each competing event planning company was presenting a different theme event—there was no conflict there— but the decor company knew that they did not have to come in with their best possible prices because they were only competing against themselves. The event planning companies did not know that they were all going to the same decor source because the decor company determined it was not in their best interests to tell them and they also wanted to keep client confidentiality. They were not sharing creativity nor competitors' costs and did not feel that they needed to let others know that their company would be presenting more than one idea. But without violating client confidentiality by naming names of who else was requesting a bid, they could have advised the event planning companies of the potential conflict of interest and offered the second and third planning company to call in the option of looking elsewhere, which they didn't want to do as it would limit their chances of being selected. Other companies choose to turn away business rather than compromise their integrity by being caught in conflicts of interest, and let planners know upfront that someone else has contacted them first (without divulging who).

A *New York Times* article contained a photograph of a well-known event planner's home and reported that the apartment contained decorating items from events that they had previously helped take place—everything from live flowers to Moroccan dishes. Suppliers do not usually note on their quotes whether they own items outright, are renting them from a third party or are purchasing them specifically for the event. If the items are being purchased—ethically—who owns them after the event? Should clients be advised and offered the option of having them sent to their office after the event? Can planners claim rights to the items, bearing in mind that it is the client, not the planner, who actually paid for them? Unless informed otherwise, the client generally assumes the items are rented and owned by the decor company, florist, etc., involved. If the supplier is not asked and does not tell which items have been purchased exclusively for the event, is it ethical for the supplier to then retain the goods, add them to their collection and eventually re-rent them to others without compensating the event planner's client? Hopefully, the event planner who was featured in the newspaper story had told his clients that some of the items had gone home with him for personal use or to be warehoused. The event planner could have purchased these items from the client to keep as a momento—the article didn't say—but it could give future clients of all event planners pause for thought after seeing party decor being used to decorate a planner's home displayed in the newspaper.

If an item is purchased with a client's money, it ethically and financially belongs to the client's corporation, not the individual representing their company. Event planners need to be very careful about how they hand over purchased items to a company to make sure that one individual is not personally benefiting, because this could easily put the event planner in a questionable position. Event planners can suggest having purchased items presented to a charity on behalf of the corporation and have their client's company receive a tax receipt for their donation. Planners can make arrangements to sell the item back to a supplier and have a credit applied to the final billing or recommend that they be handed out as prizes. One employee appreciation day included learning how to flyfish. The cost to rent the fishing poles versus the cost to buy them was very close and the event planner recommended to their client that they consider purchasing them. At the end of the day they could be given as a memento to the staff as a take-away gift or some of them could be used as prizes and the balance sold to another supplier that had a fishing rental shop, with the money credited back on their final reconciliation. Event planners need to ask hard questions of their suppliers for their client and to protect themselves. They need to make it their business to find out if any prop items—decor, entertainment, floral, tabletops, glassware, cutlery—are being purchased, rented from a third party or taken from the supplier's warehouse. Planners also need to be aware of costs to determine if it is better to purchase the item or rent them. At one charity event the centerpieces were rented at a special rate. There was no discreet signage stating that the centerpieces had been loaned to the fundraiser for the evening and guests did not know that they were not theirs for the taking at the end of the evening. The tables seated eight and each centerpiece was made up of eight identical sections that fit into one another. Guests dismantled them and handed one out to everyone at their table as a souvenir. The charity was hit with over US$6,000 in damage charges. The cost to have purchased or replace centerpieces could have been built into the cost of the ticket had this been anticipated. Event planners are responsible for client money management as well as event management, and need to make sure that all options have been explored and that clients have been informed of possible benefits—cost, product or otherwise.

Other rental ethic questions that have been raised in the event planning industry include the quality of rental items. One rental company's office reception furniture, for instance, was rented out repeatedly for trade shows. Their clients were from out of town; they flew in, did their shows and were gone within days. They never visited the supplier's office and had no way of knowing that the exorbitant rental fees they were being charged, plus trucking costs and labor, was for furniture that was being used every day by their supplier and not being brought in especially for them. The furniture had signs of wear and tear from daily use. It would have been less expensive for the clients to have purchased new furniture and hired an independent person to oversee delivery and set up, and discard the furniture after their event. What the customers were actually paying for is convenience, one-stop shopping, and knowing the items would be there, set up on time and taken away. The clients were trusting that the supplier would provide goods that would help them attract customers to their booths. In at least one case, the display of shabby furniture was not enticing and the client was furious when they saw the quality provided for the money being spent. The sketch the supplier had sent, depicting a fresh, sleek display setting, was misleading, and what the client ended up with was shabby cheap, not chic. It is unethical to misrepresent the quality of items being used. When a client is renting an elaborate tent, for example, they are anticipating receiving one in pristine condition. That is not always the case. Smart planners know to ask about the condition of the tent and if the tent has any visible tears or patches, if there are cracks in the material or if the tent or clear window panels have yellowed. And they make sure that their specific requirements as to what is acceptable are added to the supplier contact. The same applies to table linens and other display items. Some unethical rental companies do send out goods that have visible mending, cigarette burns and stains. Planners need to know the questions to ask and how to protect their clients from disappointment. Supplier contracts often state that the client is responsible for replacement value should any items be unaccounted for or damaged at the end of an event, but the quality of the items is seldom noted. Planners need to add a contract clause stating what acceptable condition goods are to arrive in (e.g. no visable signs of mending, stains, etc.) before signing.

There are disreputable staging companies who design "custom" staging and sets by merely reusing existing props, not creating new designs or making new purchases. One such company was put to the test. The event planner, intent on saving their client money, arranged to sell the exclusive set the staging company had designed at great cost for this event to the hotel hosting the party to use for future theme parties. There was no problem in re-selling the set as the staging had been built expressly for their event and the customer owned the rights to the goods. The client was pleased with the planner's ingenuity and cost-saving considerations. And the hotel was thrilled to have purchased a theme setting that had been built expressly to fit their ballroom specifications.

Another client found out through a questionable accounting incident that the elaborate stages that they thought had been created for them were in fact being warehoused and recycled by their event planning company with no concession to cost being received by them. The client's recourse was to pull all their business from the event planning company, which had been the agency's number one account, and sue them. Losing the business caused the event planning company to lay off staff and eventually dissolve their business. The cost to their reputation was irreparable.

In an effort to secure as much business as possible, some suppliers and planners are not being upfront about their abilities, professing to be able to do more than they have experience with. One event planner was shocked to see pictures of an event they had done in another supplier's portfolio. The supplier that sales representative had worked for had supplied only one small event component and they were now alluding to have masterminded the whole event. Everyone at times has said "we do that" to get the business, but most have not told outright lies. There is a difference between exaggeration and lying. Planners may not have actually provided an event element, but they know where to go to bring in the professionals, how to subcontract their services and include their expertise under their event planning company umbrella. An example of lying is alluding to having done and being capable of doing an event for 2,000 when the largest group a company may have handled is under 50. Another is taking credit for event design and production by another company, when all your company did was provide the floral centerpieces.

Fine lines can be crossed in contract negotiation. Be careful of inappropriate offers or concessions being asked for by planners or offered by suppliers for personal, not business, use, such as using air or hotel bonus points for individual use. One event planning company invoices their client for payment by check and arranged with the supplier to then pay them with their personal credit card, which entitles them to bonus points. The president of the company then gets the benefit of using the points for personal items or towards their vacations (the event planning company boasted they could travel the world many times over) or to purchase items selected from credit card points catalogs. One company president purchased a very expensive backyard barbecue that way, but they did invite their corporate clients over for grilled steaks (obtained through the bonus plan, too), both paid for by the client. The points were not passed back to the client in this case, nor had the client been informed of the benefits their company could receive if they paid for the travel expenses by company credit card. They were not aware that it is an option open to them. Ethically, the client should have been advised of the opportunity they are missing out on that would have benefited their company, and the event planning company should not be reaping the rewards of something they have not paid for. In other instances it may be the client who is looking to pay by their personal, not business, credit card and be reimbursed by their company, but keep the bonus points accumulated in the transaction process to use at their discretion. Companies are now starting to look into bonus points and frequent flyer points to see how they can be applied towards reducing company travel expenses, as opposed to giving them to staff for personal use. It is better to present all advantages upfront to the client rather than have them discover at a later date that they have not been made aware of added value options.

When hotels and cruise lines get requests for seven-night site inspections when three nights are more than adequate, they know they are being asked to host a mini vacation and not a site inspection. On the other hand, planners have received offers for themselves and/or their clients from their suppliers for extended stays. Approaches are sometimes made, from both sides, about whether spouses can be brought along or would like to accompany the client during the site inspection. One client wanted to take their girlfriend along on the site inspection—he was very upfront about it—and wanted to have one room for a longer stay rather than two rooms for a shorter duration. His wife and his mistress—the mistress worked for the company—would both be accompanying him on the actual trip, but no one was to know that the girlfriend had been to the resort before with the client. Hotel staff were instructed not to say anything about a previous visit.

Another client requested that creative costing be a part of their business deal. They wanted their planner to approach their prospective hotel about having the total expenses from their personal two-week family vacation (including the nanny) that would take place pre-event costed into the program and listed on the hotel bill as meeting room rental charges which they, as company owner and president, would approve and sign off on. In order to secure the business, the hotel complied and over US$30,000 worth of charges were listed under meeting room rental fees.

When one planner requested a detailed breakdown based on the quote received, the entertainment supplier was extremely evasive about what 18 accompanying crew members were actually going to do on site. This large crew was in addition to the costs for the creative director, producer, riggers and technicians. They turned out to be family members. What was questionable was not that the costs for family members were included in the talent rider—look at top celebrities and the entourages they travel with (often including family and friends)—but how the costs were being buried in the supplier proposal. The manner in which their expenses had been given and the explanations as to their purpose did not ring true. Suspicions were raised when some accompanying staff members had job descriptions and titles listed beside their name and the 18 additional members' purposes were not defined. When questioned, the planner was advised they were seamstresses responsible for the costumes and prop management, which was feasible. When names were required for air tickets, it was discovered that some of them were children. And it set the planner on guard. What else was being hidden? Could this be just the tip of the iceberg? In this case it was.

Suppliers have the right to set their prices, with mandatory inclusions, terms and conditions. Planners have the right to choose not to work with a supplier if they feel that what is being proposed is out of line or not of value to their client. What could matter most to the client is having a certain entertainer perform at their event and the cost to bring others along may not be a concern if it was that important to them. Had the 18 accompanying members been presented upfront and honestly, the planner would have held the supplier in a different light. Mistrust, however, is not something that can be easily reversed.

EVENT OPERATIONS

Event operations is often the time where there is a changing of the guards. Once the event has been contracted, the sales reps and planning staff move onto the next piece of business and the file is transferred over to the various operation departments. Supplier sales reps and the planning staff may come back together again on-site to make sure that what has been planned takes place, or it may be left to the event planning account executive and operational staff to run the program. If there are any questionable practices by either side, this is the time when they will become known and other people are drawn into the goings-on. Staff have been known to be asked to lie to cover up mistakes that have been made in planning. For example, if space has not been cancelled in time and penalties are now applicable, staff members might be advised to tell their suppliers that records show that it had been done on time when it was not, to avoid being billed for penalties. The venue may challenge the lie, that but then the matter becomes one of he said/she said. Documents can and have been forged to show fake notice was sent. The decision to continue to pursue the matter then becomes based on future working relationships and if they are being jeopardized. Or, if operations staff discover that a planner or supplier has made a major costing error that their company might have to cover, they may be asked to look for ways to disguise the cost difference during operations or at final reconciliation (e.g., increasing actual food and beverage costs, for example, as clients are not always presented with back-up billing and take the presented reconciliation as is).

Great cover-up capers have been acted out to event planning companies, suppliers and clients. Everyone involved becomes a co-conspirator. Personal ethics standards are put in peril, with people and companies becoming linked to others by association and sitting back and saying nothing. Some take a stand and refuse to take part or quit when they discover something underhanded. Their reputation, which could have been easily tarnished, is all they take with them. In some cases, departing staff have even gone so far as to present the supplier with the truth, absolving themselves of duplicity. One company executive was offered an opportunity to buy into the company they worked for. They declined the offer, stating that they couldn't because the company standards were not their own. The question that the individual needed to ask himself or herself then was if the company's standards were not theirs, why were they continuing to work there? That awakening set them on the path to aligning themselves with a company they could truly stand behind.

ON-SITE MEETINGS

The event moves forward from planning and operations to on-site orchestration. Those involved in planning at the very beginning may step back into the program at this stage, operations may go on-site and run the event with their program directors and travel staff, or freelance staff may be assigned to handle the on-site requirements. First on the scene for move-in and setup are event planning staff, followed by suppliers, the client and then the guests. Planners and suppliers will come together and interact at pre-event meetings (pre-cons), during on-site event orchestration and at post-event celebrations. The ethical boundaries for each will be covered in depth in Chapter 7: Codes of Conduct on Site. For first-time planners, all the suppliers and the client come together at on-site meetings.

BUSINESS REFERRALS

"Business is business" is the credo of a planner I know. If they refer business to caterers, florists, decor companies or other planners who have specialized skills more suited to the proposed event, they are candid about expecting a 15 percent finder's fee. You know exactly where you stand if you choose to act on their referral. With some people and organizations, referral fees are an openly acknowledged part of doing business with them, but with others it may be expected but never asked for outright, expecting others to do the right thing as a thank you for business (and shocked when they receive nothing). Many event planning companies pay commissions to sales reps and finder's fees to employees and others who provide business leads. Other companies exchange sales leads on an ongoing basis with no compensation expected beyond building goodwill and the hope of future consideration.

It can be debated that there is a difference between a lead and handing over found business. A lead is passing on the name of a company and contact that does events or may be thinking about planning one in the future (e.g., corporate anniversary coming up). Found business, on the other hand, is someone calling with a referral of a firm event that they are not going to bid on and that they are personally recommending that another company handle. It has been presented to the event planning company on a silver tray. The event planning company has had to do nothing to secure the business. One planner, unable to handle any more business during a specific time period, referred a client to a colleague who was well equipped to handle the group and one who the planner knew would do an outstanding job. This was not a bid situation but business handed over on a platter, but no mention was made of a referral fee and none was received. In fact, they did not even receive a thank you card. The next time the same situation presents itself the planner could think twice about who to refer the business to. The company that got the job in question does pay finder's fees to their staff and commissioned sales reps, but did not make the same offer to an outside source.

Adding insult to injury, the planner who passed over the business received a card from the company that handled the event requesting a donation to one of its favorite charities (to acknowledge the company president's milestone birthday in lieu of gifts). Needless to say, that raised a few eyebrows in the office of the company who had handed over the business without receiving compensation or a thank you. In their eyes they had already made a large donation to that company's well-being. Ethically, the first company did the right thing by passing the business over to a competent competitor rather than leave the client stranded when they couldn't take on their project. The matter of compensation, on the other hand, is a matter each individual office must decide on—whether it is ethical or not to give or receive money for referred business. If staff and sales reps are being paid commissions for bringing business in, event planning companies may want to consider paying referral fees to those who direct business to their company. And if someone is referring business to another company, be clear about expectations if compensation is expected. Don't assume that others will do what is right in your mind. To do so is being naive and most people are not mind readers.

Remember, business is business. Simply stating that "if a contract results from the referral, a 15 percent finder's fee would be appreciated" is not offensive. In return, the recipient of the referral has arrived at an enviable position without doing an immense amount of work. They have incurred no advertising, marketing or selling costs. In addition to saving money, they have also saved time, which in turn saved them more money. In fact, many companies feel that time is priceless, and found business a gift, and are happy to compensate those who help to build their business.

For others, compensation is not a factor and not expected. In another case, an event planner used a third-party supplier for group airline tickets for one of their incentive clients. They received no commission from the agency. They felt that the agency deserved all the money earned on the airline ticket, because the markup was not large and the clients were demanding and time consuming. Ethically they felt this was the right thing to do. What mattered most to them was that their client's guests received excellent service. They knew that the agency would earn every penny and they wanted to be fair with them. Had they received a commission, this company would have passed it back on to their customer as they worked on a flat management fee. The planning company's costs to their client were all laid out. Nothing was hidden and no additional revenue was being received from any other source. Hotel rates were net, not commissionable. The only money they earned as a company was from management fees.

This client was eventually passed onto another planning company (the original company had a change in direction), but the same supplier was still being used to purchase air tickets for the group. This planner asked for and received a commission from the agency that amounted to thousands of dollars in undisclosed income to the planner. The planner had contracted with the clients for a flat management fee and was not supposed to be making money from additional sources. The client was signing the contracts with suppliers in this case, and no mention of the commission being paid to the planner was listed. The client was unaware that this event planner was making money over and above their management fee, assuming that they were following the same standards of ethics as their predecessor. This event planner was actually making money from a number of different sources. The agency involved in handling the air tickets was operating under two different systems. If people asked for a finder's fee, they received it, and if they didn't ask, it was not offered.

The second agency boasted to the first event planning company about how much money they had received from the air bookings, knowing that the first agency did not do business that way and knowing how costs and management fees had been presented to the client. The original planning company was caught in a moral dilemma. Someone they had referred business to was operating in an underhanded way by contracting at a flat management rate and not crediting back to the client any additional revenue. Their company reputation was at risk because they had referred business to someone they thought they could trust to do business honorably under the terms that had been agreed upon with the client. They also had to decide on their ethical course of action—whether to tell the client what they knew to be true or to walk away from the situation. They chose to inform the client what was taking place. The client now has their own planner in-house where they can keep a careful eye on money going out to suppliers and money being paid out in commission from airlines and hotels. With business referrals, ethically, more is at stake than whether or not a finder's fee will or will not be paid. Who you refer and how they conduct themselves in business reflects directly back on you personally and professionally.

CONFIDENTIALITY

Confidentiality is key between planners and suppliers. Planners do not expect trusted suppliers to be visiting their competition and discussing what they are doing and who they are doing it for. If that trust is violated, so is the relationship. Suppliers need to exercise extreme caution in this area. Planners may not say anything, but they will take note if their suppliers are talking about their competition. They know it could be their company that is the subject of gossip at the sales reps' next meeting. Planners take care to remove any revealing client material that may be in a boardroom or office before meeting with suppliers and other customers. Unexpected drop-ins are not welcome, because sensitive information must be removed from inquisitive eyes. The same applies to planners with respect to supplier confidentially. There is nothing quite so shocking as to hear exactly what is going on inside your office from someone else. Ethics have been violated either by someone on staff or people who are working in partnership with your company. There is an expression that loose lips sink ships, and it is true for working business relation "ships" as well.

BUSINESS FAVORS

Be careful what you ask for and how you ask for it—not because you might receive it, but because of how what you ask for could be perceived by others. Your personal and professional credibility, as well as your company's, could be on the line and hung out for all to see if you are requesting favors that ask others to cross ethical lines. For example, asking a supplier if it is possible to receive back-stage passes to a performance for a VIP client is quite different than asking the supplier to bump people holding confirmed tickets to a sold-out performance in order that your client may attend. The first request is an easy yes or no and does not compromise anyone, but pushing a supplier to cancel someone else so that your client can go is asking them to do something unethical.

2 FAIR COMPETITION

SUPPLIER-TO-SUPPLIER ETHICS

Except for the ultimate client, everyone is a supplier. The event planner is a supplier to the client, and the venues, decor companies, caterers, entertainment companies and the like are suppliers to the event planning company. Within that mix, it gets broken down even further. Florists, for instance, may be suppliers working directly with the client, event planning company, decor company, caterer or venue. And the role they play can change from event to event. An event planner may not know if the decor company they are working with actually does their floral arrangements or sub-contracts them out. There are layers and layers of suppliers operating behind the scenes. In the dog-eat-dog world of big business, some suppliers are doing all they can to make sure that they capture as much business and profit for themselves by using any means possible—both ethical and unethical.

Some say it is a lack of respect between industry partners that is causing ethical dilemmas. Others say that the financial impact of cutbacks in the event planning industry, triggered by the events of September 11, 2001 and compounded by the corporate accounting scandals, and war being waged in Iraq, has put ethical behavior to the test, forcing those in the industry to do anything to beat the competition or squeeze as much as they can from clients, suppliers and planners alike. The question is being asked, have some forgotten what fair business practices are? Have ethics been pushed to the side just to make an extra dollar?

Planners have witnessed blatant displays of breaches in business ethics between competing suppliers for years but, as one planner remarked, when *hasn't* this happened?

Lack of respect is the first sign. It comes in many forms—done with subtlety—with "eyespeak," the flicker of an eyelid, the slightest rolling of the eyes, the lift of a singular eyebrow, to more blatant displays—from snide remarks or whispered innuendoes to complete fabrications being bandied about. For example, one hotel told a planner that another hotel didn't have air-conditioning when it did. It can be voiced as concern—real or fake. For example, "I'm glad we don't have to deal with the problem of the homeless camping outside our hotel like hotel 'ABC' does." It may be an expression of concern about all that noise from construction or outside television broadcasting starting every day at 4:30 a.m. in the case of one hotel. "I don't know how they manage to keep their guests from being disturbed." The concerns are expressed in a deliberate and well practiced manner in a way to raise concern, plants seeds of doubt and set planners' hearts beating wildly. Did they miss something that they should have seen, known or been told about that is going to impact their client or event? Ethics—the accepted principles of right and wrong that dictate the conduct of a profession—are violated when the focus of the meeting is not imparting product information and the best servicing of their client but instead taken as an opportunity to try and position themselves and their services in a better light by tearing down the competition.

Suppliers are better served by focusing on what they bring to the table and using their time with planners to tell:

- Who they are.
- What their corporate culture is about.
- How they conduct business.
- What they can do for your company.
- What systems they have in place.

- How they can meet your expectations.
- How their company can help your company do a better job.
- How they respect client confidentiality.

It is up to the planners to do their homework on supplier competition, to research their business practices and reputation. Suppliers who belittle their competition come away as the ones who are seen to "be little" in business. What you say about others reflects directly back to you.

A decade ago business seemed to be much more about the experience and relationships. Now it appears to be all about the bottom line. Clients are no longer as loyal as they once were. They are under pressure to create profits, and your company can win business by best helping them achieve their objectives. Budgets are tighter, but expectations are higher than ever. Planners are looking to suppliers to help them develop creative solutions that they can pass on to their clients. For example, clients considering an out-of-country stay are not opposed to committing to have breakfast at the hotel every day and perhaps a minimum of three food and beverage events on property in order to secure better room rates. Thus, the hotel is guaranteed revenue from another source beside room rental. Hotels whose rates include all meals and offer no flexibility, however, are sometimes ruled out because of cost considerations. For an extended stay, planners are going to want to take guests off property and offer them a change of environment. Some hotels work with planners so that this can be achieved by suggesting outside venues where they can cater events or offering a meal credit for a specified maximum number of functions, which gives the planner some financial flexibility and room to maneuver.

Hotels that offer no concessions run the risk of being passed over. In today's economic climate, planners can't justify spending money on meals that aren't consumed. There was a time when clients would simply write off an included meal at the venue and pick up the additional costs for holding a private function outside the property, as it was more important to them to offer their guests a variety of destination experiences. This is no longer the case. Now planners are looking to align themselves with properties that work with them to find ways to minimize expenses, and they will keep up the search until they find them. If, for example, two hotels are equal in rating—both are five-star properties with similar amenities—but one is more flexible and comes up with pricing options, they are demonstrating that they truly want your business and are willing to work with you to see how an agreement can be best achieved.

Hotel #1 may be inflexible on food and beverage menus, items and costs. Hotel #2, however, has their executive chef call and offer less costly alternatives, such as allowing a barbecue lunch menu of hamburgers and hot dogs to be used in the evening to help defray theme costs, instead of insisting on a more expensive dinner buffet selection of steak and chicken. They know that the dollars saved will go towards bar beverages and they do all they can to help the planner who is struggling to fit all event elements into the budget. They would rather work at keeping the event on property and being flexible than have the dinner moved away from the hotel to a restaurant. Showing a willingness to move beyond "no" to "let's see what we can come up with" shows that the company is one that planners will want to do business with.

In the above case, the event planner is going to choose to work with Hotel #2. Hotel #1's rigidity will come across as greed and a lack of concern with how to best meet the planner's client's needs. The planner's goal is to never put their clients in a position of feeling cheap, but at the same time bring a dose of reality to the champagne wishes with beer budgets. The planner's responsibility to their clients and suppliers also includes providing actual-cost reality checks.

A supplier's best line of defense (of why to use their product as opposed to the competition's) is to not be offensive and tear down the opposition. Education is the key. Teach planners what to look for—and look out for—in your industry in practices, procedures, pricing, terms and conditions, and contracts (without naming names) and you will be giving planners the tools to ask the right questions when another supplier is sitting in front of them.

For example, in the food and beverage industry, planners need to learn to look closely at cancellation clauses and how they differ. If an event is cancelled within 45 days of the event taking place, some facilities charge the full cost of the meal even though the food would not have been purchased by this time (as the cancellation date was outside of the date when final numbers guarantees and menus would have had to be submitted) and staff would not have been scheduled. The venue in this case is making extra profit over and above what they would have received had the event come to fruition. Had the event taken place, the only revenue the venue would have received would have been based on the difference between the actual cost of the meal and the rate they were charging. By assessing the full amount of the meal as cancellation when the food has not yet been purchased, the supplier is more than doubling what they would have made had the event come to fruition. If a similar event with another company was cancelled by the same date, another company might charge only the actual revenue (profit markup) that would have been lost and any actual expenses that may have been incurred at the time of cancellation. They are not taking unfair advantage of an event cancellation by charging for food and beverage that had not been purchased— which would have been an expense, not a profit, had the event taken place. Cancellation charges based on the full amount are fair when the event is called off as long as food and beverage guarantees have been called in and the purchases have been made. Another ethical question then arises: Does the client who is paying for the purchased food own it? Do they have the right to request to have it sent to their offices so they can distribute it or donate it to a food bank? Should the venue be able to able to resell or reuse the food they have already been fully compensated for? Industry practices regarding cancellation charges are changing. Planners need to pay close attention to contract terms and conditions, as they may be the determining factor in deciding which supplier would be best to book with. Look closely at the pros and cons, and right and wrong industry practices.

Some hotels charge in full for rooms that are guaranteed and cancelled past the attrition dates that are outlined on hotel contracts. Other hotels state in their contracts that should these rooms be re-rented, the money will be credited back to the client. Others don't. They double dip, pocketing the money from the room cancellation charges as well as the money for re-renting a guestroom. There is no compensation refunded back to the client or credits applied to on-site program costs. If the room is not re-rented, charging full value for the room is reasonable and an accepted business practice because the hotel has held the space open for your client. Arranging to have the cost of the rooms credited back should they become rented can be negotiated. If it is not already in the contract, it is up the planner to request that the supplier amend it. If a hotel is not amenable to this, and states that full cancellation charges will apply without credit, the ethical question that needs to be addressed is if the client is paying in full for the room, does the hotel not reserve the right to offer the room, for example, to their staff for personal use?

Seeing the difference in business methods allows a planner to compare apples to apples, and tells them a great deal about who they should be doing business with and whose business practices may be unethical. Draw the planner's attention to what they need to see when they are looking at other contracts, terms and conditions by walking them through how your company does business, as well as what they should be aware of. Suppliers who use this strategy will have spoken volumes without saying a negative word and naming names. The answers planners receive will allow them to make an informed decision with regard to who they want to do business with. Suppliers can do it professionally without crossing any ethical business practices and running another company into the ground. Raising your company's standards, by not putting down others, will set you apart.

One catering supplier had a habit of collecting opened bottles of wine at the end of an event, going as far as pouring the remaining dregs from guests' glasses into the bottles. The leftover wine was then used to make wine vinegar, which they then used at other events and sent out as holiday gifts. Planners hearing the stories being circulated would think twice about using that caterer's services or using any salad dressing sent over as a gift. Those types of stories will get around the industry quickly, but don't be the source or the spreader of tales. Planners will hear when someone crosses the line. Instead of telling tales, caterers can talk about what they do with unused food, such as arranging for it to be donated to homeless shelters or food banks, and they can state that their company policy is to never recycle food. The leftovers from last night's client dinner will not be served as a canapé or become the main ingredient in the soup the next day at your event. Let them know that bread that has been set out will not be packaged and become croutons, and fruit that has been used for displays is not slated to be used in making muffins, chutneys or anything else. Food safety should also be considered. Caterers who recycle food that has been sitting out, in an attempt to be economical, can put your guests' health at risk. From an ethical standpoint, clients are not paying to use leftovers, and if they are being charged in full for opened bottles of wine and uneaten food, shouldn't they be consulted on how they wish to dispose of them? That extends to floral arrangements and the like. One executive chose to have their elaborate center-pieces delivered to a local nursing home for the residents to enjoy.

Experienced planners will see what you are saying and under-stand that you are educating them about practices that have gone on in the industry. They don't need to be told specific details about who did what and when. Never speak wrong about anyone. Plan-ners unfamiliar with certain business practices will be very aware at the next event they do, or attend, when armed with new infor-mation and they will be watching very carefully what the supplier is doing with cleared or uneaten items. Industry knowledge of eth-ical and unethical business practices is what planners need to share, and that is what needs to be imparted. Educating clients about your specific company practices and procedures can win accounts.

Dazzle planners with the work your company has done. Talk to them about innovative ideas that your company has come up with. Share with planners the venues for which your company is a pre-ferred supplier. Let them know the quality of business you do. Cementing your credibility should be the focus. Planners are looking to work with suppliers they can trust, so give them reasons why they would want to have you by their side, not why they should not be using company XYZ. After all, just because they do not use compa-ny XYZ doesn't mean they will use your company; remember, there is always company ABC out their looking to secure their business as well. Always center in on your company's abilities.

Don't ask planners to share with you what your competitor is offering, how their rate compares to yours or what other conces-sions are being offered. Be prepared to go in making your best offer. Never ask to see others' quotes and be wary of those who offer to show you theirs—your proposal could be the very next one being passed around. Some planners who have been party to this unethical behavior have even gone so far as to make copies of other suppliers' proposals.

The reverse happens as well. Suppliers (and clients) come to planners' offices bearing "gifts" in the form of showing them what their competition's proposal looks like. Some planning companies not only know what other event planning companies' proposals look like, but they keep copies of them in their offices. Some make their way by ex-employees bringing samples with them when they change jobs, but others get there by other means, such as suppliers contracted by the company in the past or freelance trip or program directors who receive detailed copies of function sheets to take with them on site. One event planning company had a complete cupboard full of their competitions' proposals. When the planners knew they were up against certain companies, they would leaf through copies of these companies' proposals to see what type of facilities, themes and inclusions they were most likely to use.

One destination management company, boasting of a major event they were handling, gave a planner a detailed copy of an event's full plans that they had received from the event's planner. These were so detailed that they included client contacts, contracted prices and supplier contracts. Everything had been copied and handed over by one of the upcoming event suppliers to someone who was that event planning company's competition, and they took it back to their office and shared it with other staff members. Their event planning company had placed sacred trust in the supplier and they were not upholding it. And the event planner who willingly took the proffered information? Their company decided never to do business with that supplier again because they had shown that they could not be trusted with confidential material. But the ethics they themselves held were not high. While they professed shock at the supplier's lack of integrity, that did not stop them from taking the material and reading it. They did not let their competition know what had transpired, which would have been the honorable thing to do (they could have returned it without reading it and let them know to be on the alert because copies of their proposal were being circulated). Better still would have been refusing to take the copy when it was offered, and letting the supplier know that their actions had cost them future business.

One supplier had tendered and lost a team-building proposal because their costs were too high. The event included boat-building and they had done their homework. They had contacted marine police to find out what was needed to meet all safety standards and adhere to local permit regulations. In their costing, they had included lifeguards, an emergency medical boat, lifejackets, skilled instructors and so on. They knew that no one else had done that. They also knew that the marine police had been informed of the possible event, had marked it in their calendar and that the event could be closed down on the day it was scheduled to take place should the event planner that won the bid (perhaps because they had not included all required costs) not have everything in place. In the name of good ethical supplier sportsmanship, they called their competitor to make sure that they knew they needed to talk to the marine police and the possible repercussions that could occur if they didn't. Their intentions were honorable. They did not want an event to be placed in jeopardy without at least giving their competitor a heads-up warning. While it is up to the competition to do their homework, for this planner, in this instance, advising them of a potential problem felt like the right action to take. What they did with the information was up to them.

Don't snoop. One event planning company owner on a hotel site inspection was seen by their competition, which were holding an event at the same hotel, trying to go through confidential material at what they thought was an unattended registration desk. They were caught red-handed, flipping through binders containing what they thought were the event function sheets. Experienced event/trip directors know never to leave such material lying around and to guard it protectively. It turned out that the binders contained nothing more than the destination management restaurant menus, which they still had no right to be handling. They knew better, and their lack of ethics was clearly displayed.

Other suppliers have been known to check out what the competition who won the bid is doing. They know when and where the event is taking place and what time set up will start. They can easily be in the right place at the right time if they want to check out which suppliers are being used. Security during move in and set up is not always as tight as it is when the event is taking place, so it is easy to take a quick look around—if your business and personal ethics don't stop you from crossing that line. Some suppliers anxious to show off what they can do will even call planners and invite them to come down and take a look. These suppliers do not stop to consider what they are actually showing prospective clients—the fact that they do not honor unspoken confidentiality agreements.

Some event planners are now insisting that suppliers and their staff sign confidentiality documents forbidding them from talking about their event or taking pictures, with threats of legal action. Additional security has been hired not only for the event but also to search employees for cameras and sensitive material. Ethical breaches have occurred and information that should be considered restricted has been shared with others without thought of the consequences should that material leak out to the competition. Celebrities holding private events and clients doing product reveals to select guests are now holding event planning companies, suppliers and their staff liable for breaking confidentiality.

Suppliers need to be honest about potential conflicts of interest, both in client dealings as well as other businesses their company may own. One event planning company operates a decor rental business under a different name. Unless they are in the know, planners would not be aware that they could be doing business with one of their competitors and sharing information with them on how they do business.

T I P	When doing business with an event planning company or supplier, ask if they have related businesses.

If there is no exchange of information between the event planning company and their sister decor rental company, there is no reason not to disclose that the two are affiliated and allow the event planner to make their own decision as to whether or not to proceed. Some planning companies may in fact shy away from doing business with a company that is linked to another event planning company, but it is better for them to find out from the supplier directly before moving forward. Ethically speaking, being forthright is the right thing to do. If there is no need for concern, why would the relationship be hidden from them in the first place? This is what planners are bound to be asking once they learn—and they will learn—of the connection. Short-term profits are not worth putting at risk what could have been a long working relationship. Some planners would not perceive such a relationship as a threat and prefer doing business with someone who was direct and not attempting to hide information from them.

One event planning company owns not only a decor rental company but a sought-after venue as well. When planners call up to inquire about space, they are told who the owners are and that there is a preferred list of suppliers and caterers to work from (which is standard procedure with hotels and other venues) but that planners are not limited to using the owner's in-house decor company. All of that information is volunteered in the first five minutes of conversation, and brought up before a single question is raised. The fact that the information was so openly discussed was refreshing. That supplier obviously wanted to make sure that there was no room for misunderstanding. Planners were fully informed and the choice of whether or not to continue to do business was up to them.

STAFF

Who is working for you? Planners need to know how your business is staffed. Are your employees trusted long-term partners or made up of transient workers? With today's security climate, who you hire does have an impact on event planning decision-making. One televised show was reportedly interrupted by someone on the catering staff who had been hired on for the night. It was said that this staff member, who had been cleared by security, allegedly opened one of the back doors to let protesters in. Another event was splashed over the news when photographs from what was supposed to have been a private celebrity affair were released. The pictures had been sold to the press by someone who was involved in the event proceedings. With newspapers and magazines paying major money to scoop the world, event planners need to know that the people who have been hired to work with the suppliers can be trusted. Some companies are now running background checks, taking fingerprints and doing whatever else is required to make sure that their events are as safe as possible for guests to attend.

I know of an entertainer who brought her sister to see a high-profile event, which was taking place in a private home where the host did not know all the guests. The sister accepted champagne and was mingling with guests before it was discovered that she was not a part of the performance nor an invited participant, and she was asked to leave. Had there been backup entertainment, the entertainer should have been kicked out, too. She crossed over the business ethic line. One band invited potential wedding clients who were considering hiring them to see them perform at a private event. Happy engaged couples started arriving, only to be turned away at the door. Angry and naturally upset, they left. The band lost not only possible wedding clients but any and all business from the event planning company that had hired them to perform that night. Clients and planners need to be advised by suppliers as to exactly who will be present at an event and what their specific function will be. Everyone needs to be accounted for. Business improprieties will not be tolerated and companies can be held legally liable for infractions that occur. One company involved in major tent and staging setups stipulates that for events held at private homes, portable washrooms with running water and sinks must be provided for their staff members to use. This supplier does not want to put their company or their employees at risk of accusations of theft, property damage or any other possible charges (child endangerment, molestation, sexual harassment) by having unlimited access to family members and to the inside of the house. If staff are found inside the home, they have violated company policy and will be dismissed.

Ethical boundaries are crossed when suppliers divulge creative concepts that they see being developed for an event they have been contracted to take part in with other suppliers and even other clients. One couple planning a wedding filled with personal touches were shocked to see pictures in their local newspaper of their wedding—same venue, same color scheme, same decor, same entertainment, same wedding cake design, their own special touches. The event had been copied right down to the wedding favors. The same wedding planner had been hired to do both events, but the second one the planner contracted took place before the first. The original couple fired the planner, investigated their legal options and moved their wedding to a later date so that they would have time to design a new original wedding that was not recycled and reused.

Some suppliers put waivers on their proposals stating that they own the creative concept outlined, but it is difficult to copyright ideas. How does one company own the creative ideas to a clambake (which has been done to death) or claim creative rights for white hot chocolate as exclusively being one of their newest ideas? After all, what may be new to one planner may be an idea that has been done forever, even featured in numerous magazines over the years. Preston Bailey, a master of floral design, presented some of his ideas on a television show seen by 22 million people. Within minutes, there is no doubt that some of his creative touches found their way around the world and into supplier proposals, some of them by the very same suppliers that state that the creative ideas in the proposal belong to them. For example, the show also featured individual miniature wedding cakes set with edible pearls. As soon as the show was over many brides-to-be were on the phone to see how much edible pearls on their wedding cake would cost.

What suppliers are trying to circumvent is a planner soliciting a proposal from their company, then turning around and duplicating it on their own or with another supplier. That supplier is trying to make sure that their list of inclusions is not simply handed over to someone else to see if costs can be lowered. Suppliers receiving such a list from a planner should think twice before investing time and money developing a quote for them. If a planner holds a supplier's work in such little regard that they would hand it over to someone else, other suppliers have to know that they could be next on the list. Event planning ethics demand that creative content developed for a planner be kept confidential. While event elements may be common to the industry, how they are brought together and presented is what sets suppliers apart. For example, one caterer may suggest a traditional martini bar, while another may propose and detail creative custom ideas they have perfected for a theme martini bar. For a planner to share the exact theme martini ideas with the first supplier would be ethically wrong.

One of the event planner's roles is to orchestrate a symphony of sights, sounds, smells, taste and textures, and to accomplish this they bring in suppliers who have the right elements to develop their creative vision and turn it into reality. In turn, their suppliers add their suggestions and recommendations to the proposed concept. Past, present and future events merge and become one that has been specially designed to stir emotions and push buttons to trigger calculated responses from their client's guests. What they see as an emerging trend will be incorporated into future planning. Cirque du Soleil performers, once a new concept in entertainment, have now been used over the years to enchant guests at corporate product launches, private parties, gala fundraisers and weddings. Cirque-style entertainment has also found its way into musical videos and elaborately staged shows featuring top entertainers. The event planning world will be tuned into Celine Dion's newly created show in Las Vegas to see its much-anticipated visual inclusions and the new magic that has been brought to life. Some show elements will be re-created, merged with existing ideas to form something new or be the trigger for a fresh exciting event design almost immediately. New ideas are always being circulated around the world.

Suppliers do need to pull together and cooperate. One event planner from out of town was hitting everyone up for site inspections and to pick up their travelling costs. The supplier network came together and they kept each other informed about what was happening and the planner's latest requests. It was very obvious that this planner was trying to scam a free vacation and was looking for anyone—hotels, destination management companies, restaurants, caterers—to foot the bill. The suppliers that had been burned wanted to let other suppliers know so that they were not taken in as well.

Suppliers also band together when it comes to client history. More and more suppliers are asking to know where the group has traveled before and they will contact hotels or venues that have been used in the past to confirm facts such as the number of rooms used or final guest count. Suppliers receiving these calls are very discreet about how much information is given out because keeping client confidentiality is important. What suppliers are concerned about are clients or planners initially giving wildly improbable numbers in order to secure a better rate going in. Some clients think that if they go in with inflated numbers they will receive better rates, and should their numbers fall the suppliers may overlook the terms of the contract and allow rates based on the original numbers to stay without incurring any surcharges.

Some suppliers receive kickbacks or rebates from other suppliers for sending business to one of their associates, but this is rarely disclosed to planners. On the other hand, it is not a question planners ask their suppliers. If suppliers are receiving a referral fee, that is their business. Planners know they have complete freedom of choice to work with any suppliers from anywhere and are not limited to the ones recommended by a supplier, especially if they may be using them for only one event element. Planners object when a supplier pushes an event element—another supplier or venue—when the planner has said no. One caterer kept insisting that the local zoo would be the best place to hold a country and western- theme event, when the planner was looking at taking over a western-theme venue. The clients were all over age 65, flying in from all over the world, and taking them on a trek through a zoo for a western-theme event was not even an option. It turned out that the caterer would be paid a referral fee by the zoo for business brought in, but they weren't one of the preferred suppliers at the western venue. They were putting and pushing their interests ahead of the event. What they were proposing was inappropriate and the reasons why became very clear.

What planners may pay heed to is, for example, the name of one specialized supplier, such as lighting, that has a reputation of doing great work on major events with a particular supplier. In that case they may opt to go with that supplier as opposed to bringing in someone new and untried, and the supplier's recommendation would be very welcome.

Other suppliers never let an opportunity slip by. One hotel chain cared about not only the business a planner could send their way but also any business that would be a fit for one of their sister properties. The moment they knew of another destination being considered, they would ask the planner if they could have their associate call them. And the exact person the planner needed to speak to usually called them within an hour. In some cases the supplier would also offer to send the proposal specs out to other properties in their chain that might be able to offer a better rate due to a group cancellation if their own rates were coming in too high. The latter was an example of suppliers working together in harmony, knowing that whichever destination won the bid they had done their part to make sure that their parent company benefited. They cooperated to display a strong united front, building up each other and what they had to offer, and never tore down someone else's destination or product or uttered an unkind remark. Their company was the poster child for professional supplier business ethics. Their head office had spent time training their staff on the value of proper business decorum. No matter who you spoke to in their company they were poised, polished and proficient. Staff knew their products and all the other products their company oversaw. There was never a whisper spoken about other clients or suppliers. They were well schooled in the art of supplier discretion. If there was a conflict of interest, such as two financial companies looking at being in-house at the same time, they would advise planners that they might wish to consider alternative dates, but would never give out the name of the competing company that had booked the same requested dates. They worked in partnership with one another and their clients. Fair competition and supplier-to-supplier ethics were diligently maintained by all that worked for their organization. They practiced a principled approach to the business of special event management and this is something that all companies can attain.

3
MAINTAINING ETHICAL BOUNDARIES

BUSINESS INTERACTIONS BETWEEN EVENT PLANNERS AND CLIENTS

The role of a sales rep in an event planning company is to source new clients, build lasting relationships with existing clientele and secure business referrals. The sales rep plays an important role in the company's success and is involved in the following areas:

- Introducing the event planning company to prospective clients
- Networking by attending industry and business functions
- Taking fam trips to develop their product knowledge
- Securing bid proposals
- Qualifying the event requirements with the client
- Working on the proposal request
- Reviewing the proposal material and being fully conversant with all aspects of it
- Presenting the proposal to the client

- Following up with the client
- Contracting
- Overseeing ongoing event operations
- Making site inspections
- Orchestrating on-site events
- Making final reconciliation
- Providing year-round customer service
- Schmoozing the client

BUSINESS BONDS

People do business with people they know. There is the element of trust that develops over time between the sales rep and their client. Strong bonds can form between event planning company principals, sales reps and clients, and in some cases the relationship crosses the line from business to personal friendships, even going so far as event planners marrying their clients, being named godparents of clients' children, spending weekends together at getaway retreats and traveling the world together.

The bond between an event planning sales rep and one of her company's top revenue-producing clients became so strong that the client said if the salesperson ever considered opening her own business they would move all their company's business with them—and they did so. Their business was the foundation that the new event planning company was built on. The original event planning company was unhappy with the outcome, but had not built a non-compete clause into the sales rep's contract, so they had no recourse to legal action had they wanted to move in that direction. The non-compete clause was subsequently added to future sales rep contracts. They continued on in business, but had to work hard at recouping their losses— they had lost not only their top client but their leading salesperson in the same week. In this case, the new event planning company never forgot the valuable lesson they had learned—never become complacent and put your own company's survival at risk. From day one, the game plan of the new event planning company owner was to never put their company in a position where their business would collapse if any one of their clients decided to follow somebody else. Their mission was to secure an equal balance of clients, and they were not content to let their business be dependent on one main client and put all their eggs in one basket. After all, who should know better than the new event planning company how fast a situation can change.

With this perceived threat of loss of business in mind, some event planning company owners focus their energies on making sure that they develop a closer, tighter relationship with client decision-makers. They invite the client out socially, excluding the sales rep who brought their business to the company in the first place, schedule meetings deliberately to take place when the client's main contact is out of town on a site inspection or running a program, and inviting top clients to accompany them to VIP events where they only happen to have one additional ticket (or two spouses are included). All this is done with deliberate intent to lessen the bond that may exist between "their" client and anyone else in the company, so that the client will stay with them should their sales rep decide to move on to another company or open their own business.

Some event planning companies have sales reps and staff (both in-house and freelance) sign non-competition contracts that state that they cannot approach any companies for a period of one or more years after the company they are being hired by ceases doing actual business with them or stops being their potential supplier. The contracts are drawn up by the company lawyer, whose job it is to make sure that all relevant areas are covered. Some even go so far as to try and make sure that departing employees are prohibited from using the same suppliers or on-site staff they use for a specified number of years. Limited access to suppliers, however, is viewed as extreme in the event planning industry. Seldom has there been a supplier who has an exclusive agreement to work with only one event planning company—that would be limiting their business growth options. Freelancers, on the other hand, do sign contracts where they commit to working only for one event planning company for a specified time period, and in general they are financially compensated for their exclusivity.

Other companies work out a sliding commission fee with their sales reps, whereby they receive 30 percent commission the first year, 20 percent the following year and 10 percent the remainder of time that the client continues to book with their company. In some cases no commission is paid out in the third year, with the account then being designated a house account. Event planning companies who follow these principles are trying to make sure that their sales reps are continually creating new sources of revenue and focusing on obtaining new clients. By decreasing their sales reps' financial ties and interaction with the client, the event planning company is seeking a way to firmly establish ownership of the company doing business with them by having their in-house staff step into the sale rep's role and work more closely with the client. These companies are not rewarding their sales reps for securing the business and servicing it so well that the company chooses to remain with them. They feel that it will take the sales reps less time to service a company they have worked with over the years and therefore the commission level should be reduced. They offer the sales reps no cash incentive to stay with them after the two- to three-year period. For a large piece of business the sales representative could become better off financially by moving the client over to a new event planning company that pays a higher rate of commission with no sliding scale. A tug of war could take place between the event planning company and the sales rep over the client.

Timing can be everything with regard to when a sales rep may consider leaving a company. Some companies have a stipulation in their contracts that no money will be paid out on future business should an employee leave before the program has taken place. And often, before receiving outstanding money owed to reps at time of quitting, event companies try to have leaving sales reps sign letters to the effect that they will not sue the company for any more money. Sales reps have won lawsuits over contract clauses such as these when hundreds of thousands of dollars could be at stake. Clients can be caught directly in the middle and in the end no one wins—clients may simply opt to walk away from both the event planning company and the sales rep and take their business to someone else, rather than be caught up in unethical business practices.

Not all event planning companies operate the same way. Some believe it is unethical not to reward their company sales reps for bringing in the business and ensuring that it stays with their company, and keep the commission based at 30 percent no matter how long the account is with them. They prefer to operate their business with integrity. Should a sales rep leave, they are paid the outstanding money earned on all contracted future business, which is paid out to them once the event has taken place. Should the client choose to follow their sales rep to a new company, the account is passed over to the new company without dramatics. The client knows that their business was valued and they would be welcomed back with open arms should they ever choose to return. Planners prefer not to burn business bridges with the clients they have worked with, secure in the fact that if they conduct themselves in a professional manner the client would not leave without a bad taste in their mouth and would consider the option of returning in the future should their needs not be met by the new company handling their business.

The battle of who owns the client can become very apparent and uncomfortable for all involved. One event planning owner used to drop disparaging remarks about their salesperson to his clients. Fortunately, the clients were loyal to their salesperson and informed him of what his employer was saying behind his back. The client lost all respect for the event planning company owner and would no longer consider doing business with the company, especially since the owner was the one who hired the sales rep in the first place. They wanted no part of the unethical backstabbing that was going on. Both the salesperson and the client left. That event planning company had crossed the line of principled business practices, and the sales rep and client could not be a party to it once they were aware of how the owner was trying to manipulate their business relationship. If the event planning company would openly undermine an employee to a new business client, what unethical behavior were they keeping hidden that had not surfaced yet?

FINDING THE RIGHT MATCH
TO DO BUSINESS WITH

Clients also keep a fine ear tuned for how event planning companies talk about their other clients. Are they overly familiar? Do they share what should be confidential company secrets in the hopes of impressing them with how much their other clients reveal to them? Do they talk indiscriminately about personal transgressions that another client may have displayed? Their professional-code-of-ethics radar could be set off by a word, tone or action that they may deem an inappropriate way for the event planning company to be behaving in their presence.

Interactions between event planning companies and clients don't take place in only business settings—exotic locales, alcohol-drenched parties and people traveling without their spouses can all add fuel to the fire. In such situations, the line between business and pleasure blurs and the nature of the relationships gets cloudy. Both event planners and clients can easily step over lines of impropriety. Professional demeanors displayed sitting across the desk from each other in business attire can become unraveled when a professional attitude is hard to maintain, such as over a couple of drinks at the pool bar or splashing around in a bathing suit.

Like-minded event planning companies and clients tend to seek out and find each other. Initially a dance of discovery takes place between the two. What needs to be done to secure business can be a minefield that an event planner has to walk through with some clients. In other situations, the client is trying to interpret exactly what is being said or asked of them by the event planning company. If there are what could be determined by either side as improprieties being carefully asked or discreetly suggested by veiled innuendoes, no one wants to be placed in the position of taking a misstep and misunderstanding what is being said (unless deliberately choosing that defense method as a form of retreat).

One company lost business because they chose not to pick up on a client's very clear hints on how much they would love to go away with their family on vacation and stay at a luxurious resort. With all that had gone on with them this year, though, they simply could not afford to do so, but wouldn't it be wonderful if something could be worked out so that they could enjoy a getaway—hint hint, nudge nudge, wink wink. There was no mistake that what was being dangled before the event planner was an option—in exchange for contracting your company's services, what I am asking is for you to send my family and me away to play at your company's expense. The theme of a free vacation in exchange for their business came up repeatedly. The event planning company did not make the offer to send the client and their family members away and the customer signed with a competing company who was open to providing client freebies. These freebies are really payoffs. Event planning companies must decide whether to lose the business and feel vindicated of being involved in a client payoff, or to go with the flow, pick up the cost of the client's vacation themselves or con a supplier into providing the freebie. The client was seen shortly after, sporting a midwinter tan. Was the tan the result of a free vacation in exchange for doing business? Only the winning agency knew for sure.

Then there is the type of client mentioned earlier who asks your company to personally pick up the tab for their family vacation, but wants it billed back to their company in a way that it looks like a legitimate business expense, such as room rental charges included in hotel or venue billing. How does your company handle requests such as these if they are presented by the head of the company whose business you are seeking—the one who has the power to sign off charges without question? What if the proposition comes from someone else in a position of power, such as a senior executive or even the company owner? Do you turn away the business and say nothing, report it to higher-ups (and if it is the higher-up making the request, what then?) or become part of the conspiracy to conceal hidden expenses? In today's climate, with all the "creative costings" that have been splashed across the nation's newspapers, everyone who is in a position of financial responsibility to the company they work for is going to be poring over the books, looking for charges that seem out of line in order to make sure they have done their job properly and cannot be accused of any misdeeds by omission, neglect or silent consent on their part. They now know the penalties and the repercussions to their professional and personal reputations if they try to conceal charges that they know are wrong.

One event planning company president's direction to an employee was "this is what has to be done, but don't give me the details because if it ever goes to court I want to be in a position to say that I knew nothing about whether or not it actually took place." It was clear that if the improprieties ever came to light, the president would make the company employee, who was being instructed by their boss to do as the client asked, take the fall and bear the consequences. The president wanted to make sure that his hands were clean and that he was innocent of any possible charges that could be laid. If the employer is asking an employee to lie, cheat or do anything underhanded, that is the time to beat a hasty retreat, because their character and credibility will be called into question if they continue to work for someone without ethics. Their reputation will be tied to their employer's. In the event planning industry, colleagues, clients and suppliers are very aware of who lacks business and personal principles, and word travels fast when ethical indiscretions are uncovered. By continued association alone, your reputation will be branded by industry peers and called into question.

Event planning company owners must decide the position they are going to take on the problem of unprincipled client (and supplier) requests and instruct their staff on how to handle the situation if confronted with someone who is making such a demand. If employers are not forthcoming, employees need to address this issue with whoever they report to. Staff need to know in advance how to proceed, what to say and who to direct a request to, should one come in. Employees should not be asked to place themselves in compromising positions or to be party to something that could have serious personal, professional and legal repercussions. Knowing an employer's stand on such matters will enable an employee to know what type of company they are working for and whether or not they should stay. Employers also need to protect themselves, discuss what behavior will and will not be condoned by employees who may decide to act on a client request on their own and not inform company officials, put company policy in writing, and have employees sign off on having been informed as to what direction to take.

In other cases, staff have chosen to disassociate themselves from employers who made it a practice not to hire employees of a certain religion or cultural background, which still goes on despite human rights. Unfortunately, business ethics can be crossed on many levels and can go beyond unseemly behavior, shady practices or unscrupulous dealings. These days, more and more companies are turning to headhunters to screen potential employee candidates, choosing to post job openings on industry association Web sites or in professional magazines, or soliciting employee recommendations, as opposed to placing an ad in the local newspaper and attracting people who may not be qualified to apply for the position.

Kickbacks—both given or received—come from many sources and are not limited to corporate executives or company owners (event planning, supplier or client). Some sales reps make questionable offers to potential customers upfront and there is no confusion about they are saying. One person who was approached in such a manner reported the salesperson to his company executives, as well as to her employer. The salesperson's spouse worked for a wholesale travel agency who was able to obtain travel discounts for themselves, family and friends. The sales rep was offering to book customers they were soliciting for business as family friends. This way, the potential client would receive a substantial travel discount that they were not entitled to. There was no room for confusion or misunderstanding and the customer reported that they were being offered a bribe in exchange for contracting business services. The sales rep's employer was not aware that this was taking place. The offer of reduced travel rates was not coming from them but from the sales rep through their partner's employer (who in turn was not aware of how their employee was abusing their company policies).

Kickbacks are not limited to vacation requests, but come in many forms. Some people have mastered the art of never paying for a meal, whether in their hometown or out of the country. One such person negotiated free food and drink for himself and guests he was entertaining at a facility that his company used for business. Another client would time their unexpected "I was just passing by your office" visits to coincide with lunch or dinner, which they would always suggest doing at the classy restaurant down the street. The client invariably invited the event planning company president out, but had no intention of personally paying for their meal or expensing costs back to their company. However, the event planning company president had her own method of handling the situation and incorporated the costs for meals back into the client's final reconciliation of food and beverage costs. Her philosophy was what goes around comes around, and she felt no remorse in accepting a thank you from her client for picking up lunch or dinner and then turning around and billing it back to them.

Some clients invite event planning company owners or their sales reps to their homes or to weekend retreats for a chance to get to know one another better and review the program in a more casual atmosphere. During a stroll in the garden, event planning owners or reps may find themselves fielding queries as to what they think the electrical company that is handling their event would charge them to create some special lighting effects at home or what the staging company would charge to put in a new deck. Would the photographer they are using to capture their event be able to provide them with a special rate to film their daughter's wedding? Perhaps the event florist would be able to provide special considerations as a thank you for all they will be spending with them.

There is a subtle difference in asking for a preferred rate—which some clients do and suppliers may or may not decide to agree to—and asking for a kickback, expecting the work to be done for free. Some requests for a reduced fee are expressed merely for polite effect. The client may actually be hoping for—and fishing around for—an offer to have all costs picked up. It can be difficult to differentiate between the two. Ethically, the event planning company may not have a problem asking a supplier about their policy on special client rates and might decide to make the call on their client's behalf. If the client's intention is not to pay for the work, the client's response to a fair preferred rate offer usually sounds something like, "That is still a little too high. Do you think you could get them to do much better? After all, we are giving them so much business." At that point, event planning companies generally know that the client is asking for some form of compensation for their business. Again, this is a situation that should be anticipated being encountered someday, and company policies need to be established and reviewed with employees with direction given as to an appropriate response and how to handle such a request with business finesse.

In reverse, clients have been hit up for special rates on their products by event planning staff and their suppliers. If company policies have not been put in place and boundaries clearly outlined, event planning company heads may find their staff approaching their clients directly. For example, carpet manufacturers might receive requests for favored rates from event planning staff and electronic companies might receive numerous queries, especially at holiday gift-giving time. Some companies welcome the opportunity to increase their sales and are not opposed to making special rates available to suppliers they do business with. They will even invite event planning staff to take part in employee shopping days, opening their doors and making their guests feel welcome.

The event planning company and the client need to establish where to draw the line with requests so that professional guidelines are not broken, and make sure that employees are aware of exactly what is acceptable office behavior. Setting an example starts at the top. Employees watch what their employers do. If they see the boss has just had his new home carpeted by their client, they may feel they are not out of line making a request directly to the client when they find themselves—or a friend of a friend of a friend—in need of new carpeting. What has to be taken into consideration is how the practice of accepting perks can lead to requests for larger concessions from both sides. Companies need to decide if this is a door they want opened.

Using Business Discretion

Event planning companies often become an important extension of their client's business. They sit in on meetings where more than event inclusions, timing and logistics are being discussed. Event planning reps observe the inner workings of their customer's company and over time become very familiar with their client's corporate culture, policies, procedures and people. They can become invisible to their client's employees—part of the accepted background scenery—and confidential business and personal issues are openly discussed in their presence. They can unintentionally overhear sensitive material in office banter and offhand remarks in open discussions where their opinion on a matter is being actively sought.

The client is depending on their event planning company's sense of business integrity not to repeat anything that may be said in their presence and counting on them not to repeat office gossip, internal goings on, new product development, sales results or upcoming mergers and acquisitions. Event planners can be privy to the innermost company secrets and are being counted on for their discretion. Some of the information they hear can be classified as top secret. Clients planning a meeting, conference or product launch work closely with their event team on the creation of promotional material, audiovisual presentations and company executive speeches. Planners can spend long hours in rehearsal working on content and show flow timing with scriptwriters, audiovisual staff and their customer's head honchos. Sometimes these sessions can extend into the wee hours of the morning with a break for dinner and a couple of drinks.

Conversations can become unguarded when all become more relaxed, but clients are counting on their private discussions (and actions) staying within the four walls and not becoming office fodder that leads to potentially damaging leaks to their internal staff, competition or the media. Some harmful actions or words may end up caught on tape, and clients trust that all copies will be destroyed, handed over and not duplicated or replayed. "You didn't hear that" may be said as a joking aside, but it is not meant to be a joke. When something is said that should not have been said in the presence of company outsiders, they trust that you will forget you ever heard it. What was said is to be completely erased from everyone's memory, never to be repeated or discussed. Maintaining client confidentiality is an ethical part of doing business. What happens inside the company stays there and is not taken or talked about outside.

However, what happens when something is seen, heard or said from within that needs to be addressed with higher-ups?

HOW TO HANDLE UNETHICAL BEHAVIOR

What happens when inside client and event planner boundaries are violated? Is it ethical to withhold information? In one communication company, those planning the event heard corporate company employees speak openly about their boss in condescending terms right in front of them. They referred to him as someone who thought he was the Big Cheese and criticized him personally and professionally. They exhibited great glee when their higher-up got locked out of the building because he didn't have the brains to check to make sure the door was unlocked when he went out. Politically speaking, the event planning team was caught in the middle. They had been contracted to handle the event by the boss, but had to closely deal on a day-to-day basis with the employees. Allowing the situation to continue in front of them was unprofessional, and by saying nothing they were condoning the action. Going to the boss to let him know what was being said would have repercussions to the employees long after the staff had finished the event. Ethically they felt they could not remain quiet and had to speak up. And they felt they needed to address the issue not with the boss but with the employees themselves, explaining that seeing continued open displays of disrespect for their boss would allow them no other alternative but to address the problem with their boss. Doing so made the behavior come to a stop, and the employees got a wake-up call on the fact that they were talking in front of company outsiders and were openly showing a lack of professional regard for their company, as well as their boss.

Another situation played out differently. An event planning company owner was out for a liquid lunch (drinking) when the accounting department of one of their major clients called and left a message. When the planner heard it, he became so incensed that one of their bills was being questioned that he left a very strong and offensive voice message that was very dismissive of the accountant and the company she worked for. Upon hearing the message, the accountant was so upset she forwarded it on to the entire executive team—including the company president—so they could hear exactly what one of their "trusted" suppliers truly thought of them. They felt that client-planner ethics had been dishonored. A meeting was called with the event planning company, but no mention was made of why it was being requested. Their main contact walked into their meeting room with a tape in their hands and replayed, for all to hear, the message that had been left on the accountant's phone. Their company's team of auditors was also called in to go over the event planning company's billing to them. Major discrepancies were found. The owner of the event planning company had been "double dipping," charging them twice for items on their bills. As well, they were inflating charges, billing custom work that was merely recycled from past events and warehoused to be brought back out again. Hundreds of thousands of dollars had been falsely billed and paid by their company. Criminal charges were laid and within weeks, the event planning company no longer existed.

One corporate company had been badly burned by a supplier before and tried to be vigilant of any money scams by their suppliers. They held large events and were accustomed to paying out large deposits to their event planning company. What they asked in return was to receive a copy for their files of the cancelled checks the planning company sent to their suppliers. By doing so, they felt protected. They started to question certain inappropriate behavior—things starting to go amiss, such as charges without backup and unauthorized spending—by the event planning company and decided to make a move. They began interviewing prospective event planning companies and looking into what penalties they would face if they moved their account to another planning company. Eventually, the original company sent them a copy of a cancelled check for a hotel deposit, and the client passed this on to the new agency so they could investigate.

What they found was that the hotel did not have the full amount of the deposited check on file. The first planner had told the company that the hotel wanted more money for the deposit than it actually required. The planner paid the hotel the large sum of money, and sent the cancelled check to their client. The planning company had arranged with the hotel to receive a check back for the difference in funds (what was paid minus what was actually required to guarantee the space). The balance was not actually due until much later, and the event planning company was using the excess to invest in short-term deposits to make additional revenue. When the new agency called the hotel to find out how the funds could be transferred to their company if they took over the account, they discovered what subterfuge had taken place between the original event planner and the hotel.

The hotel in this case was innocent. They had been told that there was an internal accounting error and their company had sent the wrong amount to the hotel. That money belonged to another account. The hotel had no reason to disbelieve the event planner and no reason to hold on to the extra funds, so they quickly refunded the money. The event planning company was criminally charged. The hotel, which was completely aboveboard, was not.

Some event planning companies do charge more than they require, but not because they are looking for a way to swindle extra income from the client. Once they have signed on the dotted line on behalf of their client, they become responsible for any applicable cancellation charges. What sometimes happens is that the deposit requirements do not match the cancellation charges, and thousands of uncollected dollars can be at risk should the client cancel and decide not to pay the cancellation charges. It happens.

What event planning companies do to protect themselves and their suppliers is to ensure the payment schedule is laid out in such a manner that there is always sufficient money on hand to cover all applicable cancellation charges. The event planning company can arrange to have the funds put in trust or forward them on to the supplier. The suppliers can adjust their contracts to make sure that the requested payment amounts match the cancellation penalties. But if the event planning company chooses to send the additional funds directly on to the suppliers, they are taking away the interest the money could have earned for their client in their own bank account, and putting their client at risk should the supplier go under. It becomes an ethical catch-22.

In the first example, the original event planning company was looking to make extra income to compensate them because the client was "nickel and diming" them to death by always trying to reduce their contracted management fee, having items picked up for free, receiving promotional items at cost, looking for ways the planning company could absorb more of their expenses and trying to get the costs covered for their executives to bring spouses along on site inspections. It would have been less costly for them to have walked away from the business—they sold their integrity trying to find a way to meet the needs of a high-maintenance client who was ethically challenged when it came to a business making a fair return on services rendered. What they did was legally wrong, but why they did it was apparent to all at the new event planning company when the client then tried the same manipulative tactics on them after contracting, starting with trying to whittle down the agreed-upon management fee.

Clients rely on their event planning company ethics to manage their company's money as their own, and advise them of any potential savings and costly risks. They need to trust that their planners will steer them away from uncertain situations. For example, one client wanted to hold a once-in-a-lifetime event at a new venue, which was scheduled to open four weeks before their event was to take place. Guests would be flying in from around the world to attend this very special get-together. The venue's owners gave every assurance that the building would open on time, explaining that they had built in a two-month buffer. Experienced planners know that the best laid plans can come undone, especially when it relates to venues opening on time, and that it is advisable not to book events until at least six months after the scheduled opening date to avoid being caught in opening delays and to give the facility and staff time to overcome any growing pains. Sometimes, though, it doesn't matter how much a buffer is built in; overwhelming delays can happen. In fact, the venue had made the same promise to clients who had booked events for their original opening date—which was to have taken place 10 months earlier.

Obstacles beyond the control of the venue operators can occur, from contractor problems and labor strikes to problems getting building code or fire marshal approval. Liquor licenses may be withheld or fixtures and building materials may not be received on time. Even the historical society could step in and delay completion. That is what happened to one sports star's proposed restaurant, which was launched with great media fanfare and expense, but never became a reality. Costs to meet historic society demands, as well as structural requirements once construction began, became too prohibitive. Another major restaurant's opening was delayed because their suppliers had not been paid and they were coming to remove all the furnishings. The event was postponed. In another case, the same scenario with the contractors not being paid, a planner faced their event being closed down unless immediate restitution was made by the venue, just as guests were arriving. Luckily, the venue owner was on hand and was able to issue a check to irate suppliers.

In order to lessen client risk, event planners could request that the venue be responsible for any contracted supplier cancellation charges that could apply should the venue not open on time and dates be required to change. Many new facilities state in their contracts that they are not responsible for charges incurred should delays in opening occur. Planners should be wary if new facilities are so uncertain about the opening that they feel they have to cover themselves in the contract. Reputable venues should be willing to pay all applicable supplier cancellation charges (decor, entertainment, food and beverage, lighting, etc.). It can be done. One hotel even agreed to cover the cost of airfare cancellation for guests flying in if the hotel didn't open on time, which it did. This is when clients and planners see if a supplier will actually stand up for what they are proposing. Should an event not open on time, clients are at risk of not finding a suitable substitute with last-minute availability. Moving the dates—especially with guests flying in—is not always possible, and clients are liable for supplier charges and re-booking fees because suppliers would have held their time and services for specified dates and time.

Planners need to read contracts carefully and not be taken in by smooth-talking assurances when it comes to opening dates being met. They need to look closely at how the venue's cancellation charges are laid out. Is the venue only looking out for themselves or do they have the clients' interests at heart as well—as with the above hotel example. How ethical are their contracts and cancellation clauses? Watch for contracts that cover the supplier fully should the client cancel, but absolve them of financial responsibility if the opening date they verbally guarantee does not happen as planned.

Standard Contract Example:
Event Cancellation—By the Client:
> If the client cancels this contract for any reason, the venue shall be entitled to retain in full the first payment with all additional deposits and fees paid to the facility concerning the contract. The client concedes and agrees that the cancellation charges are not a penalty and that the charges represent an actual and reasonable pre-estimate of the losses and damages of the venue resulting from cancellation.

Here the venue is protecting itself. Should the client cancel their booking, the supplier will be compensated.

But should the venue have to cancel for any other reason, such as an an "act of God," acts of forbiddance of any government authority, fire, force majeure, strikes, civil disturbance or any other cause whatsoever beyond the control of the facility, they are not subject to any liability, loss and damage, or cancellation charges the client or others could incur if the venue is prevented from opening or operating as contracted. The building would be excused from non-performance. They would, however, return any deposits paid to them.

In this case, the venue is completely waiving themselves from any financial responsibility or cancellation charges the client could face from other suppliers should the venue not open on time or be able to perform for any of the above listed reasons, as well as any other cause beyond their control. This will be the case in most contracts. But when it comes to booking events at a new facility with a guaranteed—the key word being guaranteed—opening date, amendments to the contract should be made to reflect this. How will they stand behind their claim of a guaranteed opening? What financial risk are they prepared to take? They are asking the client to put themselves at considerable financial risk. Furnishings not arriving on time or being tied up in customs could be viewed as beyond the facility's control, as could fire marshal approval, which could prevent a venue from opening on time, or a host of other elements. The event planner has an ethical responsibility to advise their client of what they could be financially liable for should they cancel an event. But when choosing to book an event at a new venue, clients need to be made very aware of the losses they could face should anything go awry and the building not open on time. Planners need to point out the terms of the contract and explain the financial repercussions, as well as negotiate with the vendor to try and obtain a fair contract based on the venue's verbal claims and assurances regarding the opening date and have a financial penalty clause (monies that would be paid to the client) written into their contract should the venue not open on time. The code of ethics the supplier operates under will be very clear. Are they willing to risk the client's money, other suppliers' money and the event planner's money, but not their own? Buyer beware if the client chooses to move forward, but it is the event planner's principled responsibility to ensure that their client—the buyer in this case—is aware of their financial risk.

Penalty contract clauses should be added to all supplier contracts that have specific timelines that have to be met (e.g. penalty if limousines don't show up at the contracted time).

Ethics also enters into event billing and reconciliation. Clients depend on their event planners to go through every item on their final billings from suppliers to make sure that they are not being overcharged and that there are no unaccounted or unauthorized charges applied to their bills. Clients expect that an event planner's sense of ethics will have them questioning every billing discrepancy and challenging any unprincipled supplier attempts—sometimes blatant and other times cleverly buried—to charge higher fees or add on more services than were contracted for, or additional expenses approved and signed off on during the event. They trust that the event planner will go through their final billing from suppliers with a fine-tooth comb to make sure that no additional charges have been added on. For example, one caterer added the cost for their staff meals to the client's final bill. The client was being charged 30 additional full meal rates for catering staff members. Sometimes employee meals are a part of the cost of doing an event. Entertainment contracts often stipulate that meals must be provided for the performers and the same applies with technical crews. The meal requirements and the number of people they are based on are spelled out under contract terms and conditions or in contract riders. They are part of the cost of the event, factored into the costing and approved by the client. This was not the case in this example. Providing staff meals was never agreed upon or listed in the contract. The planner disputed the charges and had them removed from the final billing before proceeding with the client reconciliation. The consequences to someone in charge of staying within event budget can be severe if the event goes over budget. One corporate client had a history of firing individuals who did not come in on or under the approved event budget. Finding costing errors were crucial since people's livelihoods were dependent on it.

Event planning companies look for their clients to be ethical when it comes to meeting payment schedules and not put them at financial risk. Some companies spend hours chasing checks even though the payment schedule dates were researched and amended with suppliers to meet the client's company check runs. They rely on their clients to plan in advance to meet these dates. One company's excuse was that the signing officers were out of the office for a month and no checks could be processed until their return. The real reason was that their company was in financial distress. Failing to collect payments on time could place event planning companies in the position of being financially on the hook for higher cancellation charges by suppliers should sufficient money not be collected and the client goes bankrupt. It is the event planning company who generally signs the supplier contracts. Event planning companies try to counteract this risk by adding a clause to their contract that states that they have the right to cancel the program should a client not make payment on time. As a second precautionary action they also make sure to work a time buffer into payment schedule dates so that if there are any difficulties collecting payment on time, they have time to react and cancel the program before higher cancellation charges apply. One company, who had paid in full for their event, added all kinds of extravagant additions just before the event was to take place. The event planning company decided to bill the client for the additions at final reconciliation, which would take place after the event. They had the individual who was in charge of the event sign their approval for the additional charges. Unbeknownst to the event planning company, their client was about to declare bankruptcy the week following the event. The client knew this was about to take place and had no compunction over the position they were placing their event planning company in. They knew that there was no money to pay for the added expenditures, but they wanted to go out with a bang. Fortunately for the event planning company, the corporate president had a sense of ethics and they personally paid for the additional charges.

PART TWO

Business Etiquette

The next two chapters cover the subtleties of business etiquette, protocol and entertaining at home and out of country, as they relate specifically to the event planning industry and its significant parties—event planners, suppliers and their clients. Business etiquette is making those you do business with feel comfortable, handling business situations appropriately and eliminating barriers that hinder business. Business etiquette can make or break a career, and it is a practiced skill.

What won't be covered is proper social etiquette (which is different from business etiquette) and minding your manners. Rather, the chapters will focus entirely on event planning business etiquette in social settings.

Social etiquette is often defined as exhibiting good manners established as acceptable to society and showing consideration for others. Proper social etiquette encompasses—but is not limited to— how you should hold your spoon when eating soup, the correct way to eat a roll (broken off in bits versus cutting the roll open with a knife), which fork to use and terms of address and introduction, which in a hospitality industry profession are things that we must be proficient in. It is part of what we do in planning special events. We must know how to set a table, what silverware to have laid out and how to present it, the proper glasses to use for water, wine, champagne and the like. Planners also need to be students of the world and master proper etiquette for other countries and cultures, in order to prepare for out-of-country programs and guests attending events.

Emily Post's Etiquette (16th Edition) is one of the leading books on the subject of personal etiquette. Originally released in 1922, it has been updated by Emily Post's great-granddaughter-in-law Peggy Post.

Good personal manners are paramount to business success, and a lack of them is causing concern. Many families eat on the run today. Fast tracking, fast foods, fast lives. For many, the days when proper etiquette was taught sitting at the dinner table each night just doesn't exist. Parents work late, kids grab dinner and sit in front of the television or computer or dinner takes place in a drive thru on the way to sports practice, dancing, cheerleading or music lessons, all topped off by homework but rarely by training in etiquette. Although such lessons are on the rise—children are now being signed up for kid-etiquette workshops, which are taking place around the world and are not only geared to the upper crust. Today's graduating classes arrive on the work scene ill-equipped to master the intricacies of a business lunch when their focus is on maneuvering their way around the overwhelming display of knives, forks and spoons laid out in front of them.

Many corporate clients have recognized a need to bring dining manners up to speed and are hiring etiquette companies to come in and coach their staff on how and when to use a fish knife, the proper way to eat an artichoke or asparagus and how to work their way around the menu (for example, in some countries salad is served at the beginning of a meal, while in others it is served at the end after the main course). Some top business restaurants are making customized courses available to companies or individuals after hours in private rooms at their facility, tutoring in beverages— the different types of beer, selecting the right wine and how to choose a fine brandy. Fine cigar shops are offering courses in the differences between cigars, what equipment to buy, how to light up your own or someone else's cigar and how to store their product. Upscale hotels have made available instructed courses in how to order and dine with finesse in a professional setting, specifically for their corporate employees interested in moving up the business ladder quickly. Minding your manners is turning into big business in many ways. Fake air kisses are out and firm handshakes and eye contact are in. Casual dress and casual attitudes in business are passé. Rudeness is making way for refinement. Displays of air rage, road rage, shopping rage, e-mail rage (when your inbox overflows with spam, forwarded jokes or other time wasters), temper tantrums, meltdowns, malicious gossip and unethical behavior demonstrated at home, business or out and about are no longer being condoned, pardoned or overlooked by society.

4
BUSINESS ETIQUETTE, PROTOCOL AND ENTERTAINING

ON YOUR HOME TURF

Etiquette consultants' services are on the rise. Good manners and civility are making a comeback. Valuable lessons in civility can be found in *Choosing Civility: The Twenty-Five Rules of Considerate Conduct* (St. Martin's Press, 2002) written by P.M. Forni, a professor at The Johns Hopkins University and the co-founder of the Johns Hopkins Civility Project. Business etiquette, unlike social etiquette, is not gender related—males and females are treated equally (e.g., it would not be uncommon for a female associate to open a door and hold it open for their male counterpart, and it is not necessary for males to stand and wait for their female business partners to sit or get up each time they depart the room).

Event planning companies entertain staff, suppliers and clients in an array of formats and locations:

- Their Offices
- In Restaurants
- Out and About

- Elevated Entertainment
- Out on the Town
- Industry Events
- At Home
- Weekend Retreats
- Holiday Parties

Each situation presents a different set of business etiquette rules, protocol and procedures. Business gatherings can take place over breakfast, lunch, drinks, dinner or even over a weekend. In some instances, guests will be entertained on their own or with accompanying staff members or colleagues, and in others, their significant others will be invited to join in. Some meetings and get-togethers will be casual, while others take on a more polite social tone and are more formal.

T I P	Always confirm your meeting the day before to lessen (but not always prevent) missed appointments. Review the time, meeting place and directions. One client arrived at an office to attend a scheduled meeting they had confirmed the day before only to find out the president of the company they were calling on had forgotten to mark it down in their agenda and had left for the day. The staff remarked that this president had a reputation for being absent-minded, and senior executives met with the client instead. The meeting was not a confidence builder for the client.

T I P	Be careful of any last-minute bathroom primping if the office facilities are shared by all, especially if your expected guest is not known by sight. Arriving guests often pop in to use the washroom to give one final check before proceeding to the meeting. One guest tidying her hair observed another leave her bathroom stall and head for the exit without bothering to wash her hands. Shortly after, the guest arrived at the meeting to be greeted with the extended unwashed hand of the person they had just seen in the bathroom.

THEIR OFFICES

When a meeting with clients or suppliers will be taking place in the office, proper protocol is to send out an e-mail, voice mail or memo the day before to everyone who will be in the office that day. Office dress and demeanor over the past few years have become extremely casual, and not just on Fridays anymore. What the staff may consider playful morning office banter, such as teasing someone about their love life or lack of one, could be embarrassing if displayed before others. Advising staff that a guest will be in the office the next morning allows them to properly prepare for their arrival, and it is always advisable to let staff know as early as possible when guests are expected.

What needs to be determined is whether or not everyday dress is acceptable when clients and suppliers come calling. Just as planners advise about guests' dress codes on invitations so that they will be suitably attired, do the same for your colleagues and staff members. Let them know who will be coming to visit the office, how many will be in attendance and what the acceptable dress is for the day (for instance, for men, professional business attire means jacket and tie, business casual means an open-neck dress shirt is fine, and office dress-down casual means bluejeans).

Make sure that your office staff are prepared to dress for a successful meeting and that no one has been overlooked—nothing feels worse than walking into the office and finding out that important guests have arrived and you knew nothing about it because you were out of the office or on a program when everyone was informed. As a courtesy for those not in attendance, leave a message at their home to let them know how to dress and what to expect. That way, you never leave them exposed to a potentially embarrassing situation. If someone is left stammering and apologizing for not being in proper dress to greet customers, it reflects back to the office and how you pull together as a team.

Inform staff of any other relevant information they should be aware of, such as if the guest is an international visitor and if there is any special protocol they need to be mindful of. For example, visitors from some countries in the Orient and the Caribbean still prefer formal forms of address, such as Mr. Lee or Miss Green, as opposed to being called by their first name. Make sure someone has done the homework and knows proper terms of address, greetings and customs. How you sit, stand, speak, project yourself and even how you present your business card and accept a clients are of utmost importance. Bare arms, immodest dress or even women wearing pants in the office may make some Middle Eastern visitors uncomfortable, and talking too loudly in public is offensive to Scottish guests. Wearing shorts in the office will raise the eyebrows of guests from the Netherlands, while keeping your hands in your pockets will be considered rude to the French. In some Asian countries presenting your business card by holding it at the top two corners is considered proper business form.

What clients see in the office is a microscopic view of how their event will be managed. If the office presents itself as unorganized and unprofessional, it can't help but be an eye-opening encounter to a prospective client. Is the scene you want to project polished and professional in dress and in office surroundings? Yes, there are times when an event planning office is turned upside down because promotional items and material have come in and are in the process of being packaged and sent out. Staff may have worked around the clock for days on end meeting deadlines and are running on coffee vapors, but that is not the visual image you want to leave with your client. That is best kept behind the scenes and consideration should always be given to what is going on in the office before any in-house meetings are scheduled. If a meeting needs to take place at a busy time, it may be best to have a leisurely breakfast in that wonderful restaurant or hotel down the street as opposed to putting staff through the additional stress of making sure the office is up to company standards. Some offices try to combat this problem and limit the work disruption and untimely disturbances to employees by locating their boardrooms as close to the office front doors as possible, and having staff come meet new clients or suppliers in the boardroom instead of the host taking them on a walking tour of the office. People will respect that—they know that sensitive material that applies to an event may be out in the open and will be pleased to know that maintaining client confidentiality is an important attribute of your company—and feel more comfortable about how you will handle their account.

BREAKFAST MEETINGS IN THE OFFICE

Breakfast means different things in different countries and what may be appropriate to serve for one may not be for another. No one will be coming to a breakfast meeting that is being held in an office and expect bacon, eggs, toast, juice and coffee, which is typically defined as a "full American breakfast," but it is important to recognize cultural differences and be sensitive to what could be expected by international guests. For example, a traditional Chinese breakfast can include seafood, beef or chicken congee, a healthy rice porridge and dim sum, with sweetened soybean milk or Chinese tea as beverages. It is easy to arrange for such a feast to be served in an office and would set your company apart from others who may not make an effort to welcome guests with memorable and unique fare. And this does not apply to just matching the food to the visitor. It could be a match for a theme or destination a client is considering for an event. Serving atole, a hot Mexican beverage popular for breakfast that is mixed with milk or water, sweetened with sugar and flavored with fruit, almonds or chocolate, would give clients doing an event in Mexico or holding a Mexican theme party a taste of things to come and be much more creative than serving ordinary coffee and tea. Use caution in making sure that nothing is served that could be considered offensive to certain guests, such as meat dishes for vegetarians, beef for Hindus or pork for Muslims and Jews.

If the breakfast meeting was being held in a restaurant or hotel, the guest would be free to choose from the menu and stickhandle around food that they can't or won't eat, but in your office if the choice is not suitable, you might hear stomachs rumbling and find your client's attention is not focused on the meeting at hand. Clients with special dietary or religious meal requirements will often eat before they arrive, anticipating their needs may not be met. It is a pleasant surprise when they find out that an event planning company's attention to detail is not limited to the program they run, when provisions for soy milk for coffee or tea or nondairy spreads for bagels, croissants or muffins are provided for a vegetarian client. Brownie points (nondairy of course) will be scored for the caring and consideration that was put into something as simple as making sure that they could enjoy their breakfast repast. It would not matter if the client didn't take a single bite. They would still be able to see firsthand the effort made and the little touches that can set your company apart from your competition.

It is all in the planning and preparation. With all the food allergies and medical conditions, such as diabetes, that require careful consideration, planners are very aware of the importance of finding

out if there are any special meal requests for events they are planning. A discreet call to a client's administrative assistant to find out
if there are any food or beverage preferences is always recommended. The more in tune you can be when meeting all of your
client's needs, the better. You do not have to make it a big production or delve into personal history, just avoid an unexpected surprise by making a simple request to find out what would be suitable to serve. If it is not possible to find out if there are any food
concerns, always make sure that a variety of food is available. For
example, don't serve only breakfast pastries that contain nuts or
are covered in chocolate in case the client is allergic to them. If you
are serving a continental-style breakfast, have a display of simple
selections such as whole-grain specialty breads and an assortment
of toppings at hand, as well as fresh juices, and an interesting
assortment of cheeses or whole nuts—but not peanuts in case anyone might have a severe reaction. In fact, for someone with diabetes, cheese, nuts or whole-grain products would be better than
anything made from white flour.

If your guest is a fitness buff, think about what you would serve
for a mid-morning health break during a meeting and adapt some
of the food choices into your breakfast food presentation. Selections could include fruit-flavored, fat-free and even dairy-free
yogurts with toppings such as seasonal berries, granola, nuts and
dried fruit; granola bars; raisins; whole fruit; fruit juice; sodas and
mineral waters; regular and decaffeinated coffee; and regular and
herbal tea. Use this chance to show more creativity than just bringing in a box of donuts. After all, what you do as a company is take
an event and make it special, and what you serve and how you present it will reflect on your company.

Arrange to have the food delivered well in advance or catered.
Invest in good company dishes or rent them for the occasion to further showcase your creativity with the food and presentation style.
Always ensure that you have proper serving utensils and accompa-
niments. In an office, manners can sometimes be casual, but never
display that side in front of guests. Practice graciousness at all
times and not just when guests are around.

Do anything but be bland. One event planning company served
their prospective clients tea and coffee in plastic foam cups, with
packages of sugar, artificial creamer, stir sticks, ordinary paper
napkins and packaged cookies set out on a paper plate. Is this the

company you are going to entrust to plan an elegant formal dinner party or imaginative theme event, when they have shown no sense of occasion in their own office? If a company does not extend itself to impress its invited guests, clients will be asking themselves, as they pass the jar of artificial creamer, if they can be sure that the company will go the distance with their event. Cups should be fine china, sugar served in cubes with tongs, crystallized sugar sticks or raw brown sugar and milk and cream served in proper containers—crystal or silver—not directly from the carton or little plastic sealed servings. Napkins can be paper, but should not be run-of-the-mill. If a theme breakfast is the scene you want to set, be imaginative with the tableware, cutlery, serving dishes and utensils, as well as the food. For example, for a Caribbean feel, banana leaves can be used as placemats, sugar cane sticks add an exotic touch to a glass of fresh island juice and a whole pineapple halved and hollowed out makes a colorful container for a tropical fruit salad. Coconut bread shows more flair than serving ordinary croissants or bagels and steaming hot Blue Mountain Coffee from Jamaica will help set the tone. Again, take the opportunity to show your company's creativity and never settle for the basics. This applies to any office meeting where there will be food and beverage.

Plan for your guests' arrival as you would any event—have everything ready and in place and schedule staff to be in early in case of early arrivals. Make sure that someone will be at reception to welcome the arrivals, assist with hanging up any outerwear (make sure that you have sufficient hangers on hand) and be on hand to staff the telephones. Put the telephone in the meeting room on do not disturb. Ensure that the coffee and whatever food is being served is prepared and ready to be set out. In the event planning industry it looks decidedly unprofessional to be caught running around last minute in a flap due to traffic delays or stopping for one more call before putting the coffee on. If the meeting is your priority, make it exactly that.

Should the guests arrive before the host, bring them to the boardroom. Do not leave them alone in a private office where items that they should not have access to may be lying around on a desk. People are masters of reading documents upside down. Bring them the beverage of their choice and assign someone to sit with them and make pleasant chitchat until the official host arrives. The key is to make the client feel welcome and that their early arrival is not an imposition. Your office has to project that it has not been caught unaware and is prepared to handle unexpectedly early guests and put them at ease. Have sufficient staff on hand to make sure that you will not be interrupted by business telephone calls, couriers, letter carriers or any other foreseeable interference.

Ensure that everyone in the office is aware that a meeting is going on and that they should refrain from calling across the office to one another in loud voices, using speaker phones or stopping to have a group discussion outside the meeting room doors. It is easy to forget you have guests when they are tucked away behind closed doors. One very personal conversation about working conditions between employees with very identifiable voices was overheard by an office manager and their guests, who were being directed to the office washrooms located down the hall. Conversations from inside the bathroom could be heard clearly up and down the corridor when voices were raised and inappropriate comments about various staff members' abilities were being loudly made. Good business behavior does not stop or start at the office door.

It is not necessary to take guests on an office walkabout at the end of the meeting, especially if key personnel have been brought in to meet one another face to face. Some liken it to being shown every hotel room possible on a site inspection, when often an overview is all that is required. But if the tour is deemed necessary, ensure that anything that should not be seen is not left out in the open. Do an office sweep before guests arrive, or better still the night before, make sure that everything that *needs* to be tucked away is tucked away. Schedule the cleaning staff to come in the night before an office visit to bring the bathrooms up to par, vacuum, empty garbage and remove any fingerprints from tabletops or windows. Some company owners like to show off their top-of-the-line office equipment and the number of staff they have on hand to let customers see they are more than capable of handling their business.

If an office tour will be of value, it is important to keep it brief. Planners will be hesitant to make business calls while a client or supplier is standing nearby, and when deadlines are pressing, every business moment counts. What sometimes happens during an office tour is that the guest and the host get caught up in a conversation with each other and remain in a central area talking without thinking about the impact their presence may be having on the rest of the office.

Make sure that you have sufficient food on hand to serve both the company and attending staff. One event planning company had a standard office rule—FHB. Short for "family hold back," it meant that it was important to make sure that the guests are served first. After the guests have departed, any leftovers are generally set out for the rest of the office to enjoy.

If a breakfast meeting is scheduled to take place in a restaurant or hotel, make sure that it is open before recommending it. There is nothing worse than pulling up in front of a closed restaurant, having to confer in cars and set out for another location. Restaurant site inspections are par for the course, and arriving at a closed facility should not happen to someone in the industry. Skilled planners know to check beforehand. One customer was involved in playing "follow that car" as their host set out to find an open restaurant for breakfast in a commercial area. They ended up at a greasy spoon after pulling into a number of places that did not open until lunch. Remember, some restaurants are closed on Mondays.

Always take note of your parking spot. One supplier hosting an out-of-town event planner to breakfast and a walk-through of a large entertainment complex forgot where he had parked their car. The event planner had left noting where they parked up to the resident expert. Much time was spent embarrassingly walking up and down aisles until they could spot the car. Keep in mind that this was a supplier the event planner was counting on to get her guests from place to place without getting lost.

IN RESTAURANTS

The business lunch is often a battle of wills, most of which goes on before you set one foot out the door:

- What Part of Town Will We Meet In?
- What Type of Food Will We Eat?
- What Class of Restaurant Will Be Best?
- Whose Connections Will Get Us Better Seating?
- What Time Will Lunch Take Place?
- Who Will Make the Reservations?
- How Long Will Lunch Take?
- Will We Order Drinks?
- Who Will Pick Up the Check?

WHAT PART OF TOWN WILL WE MEET IN?

Try to be considerate of your guest. While it may be more convenient and eat up less time to have them come to lunch close to where you do business, what will work best for them? Some people commute to and from the downtown core by bus, bike, car pool or train, and do not necessarily have access to a car during the day. Lunch meetings that are easy to get to by taxi or public transit are usually appreciated. As the host, if you are coming from some distance and the return trip could take several hours, it may be advisable to meet somewhere in the middle. When returning to the office is not feasible, some people prefer to schedule a late lunch and directly afterwards leave to go home, and look to choose a restaurant where they will not be tied up in rush-hour traffic.

If the lunch is an important get-together and not just an informal chat, make sure not to schedule back-to-back appointments too tightly. You want to avoid continually looking at your watch or trying to catch the waitstaff's eye to hurry lunch along so that you can make your next meeting. If you are heading to a specific area where more than one client or supplier is located, it is tempting to line them all up in a row and work your way through them one by one in a day. But meetings can become engrossing, key topics may be brought up that need to be discussed and focus needs to be on content, not on how fast you can wrap up this meeting and move on to the next. Buffers need to be built in so that you don't overextend your commitments. Someone is going to end up feeling slighted, rushed or pushed aside if meetings are scheduled back to back.

Allow ample time to find parking. Suggesting lunch at a five-star business hotel with a great restaurant and valet parking can be a great time-saver because you don't have to circle the block looking for a parking spot and the service is usually impeccably geared to the business crowd. Lunching in the latest hot restaurant has its drawbacks. Owners are looking to turn tables over quickly, so line-ups and delays can occur. To them you are just one of the crowd. What is recommended is that you become a regular at a top restaurant known for their finesse in handling the business crowd, where your reservations will be honored and the maître d' knows that you prefer table number three when you dine there.

Parking on the street in some cities, especially in late afternoon, can be dangerous because tow trucks are standing at the ready to remove any cars that are illegally parked once designated rush hour commences. A trip down to the car pound to pick up your car is very expensive and not the way you want to end your luncheon. Some people use the valet services of a hotel and walk or catch a taxi to their lunch location in order to make sure that they get there easily and promptly.

WHAT TYPE OF FOOD WILL WE EAT?

Don't be wishy-washy when it comes to making a suggestion. Event planners, suppliers and clients are so used to dining out and being accommodating that many hesitate to name a preferred cuisine or recommend a favorite dining spot. A great opportunity is lost if, for example, both host and guest love Thai food, but play it safe and suggest Italian. A chance to relax over a favorite meal and discuss the merits of red versus green curry dishes has been lost. It would have been an added bonding bonus if the host could have suggested a suitable Thai restaurant up to business standards, not family dining, that would have been of liking to both individuals.

It is always better to check out a restaurant before you recommend it. Inspect it as you would any other venue you were considering using. Check out the bathrooms and the level of cleanliness, and make sure nothing is moving that shouldn't be. Sample the cooking. See how professional the service is. One Japanese restaurant was initially in demand because of their great prices, sushi selection and food preparation, but the service was at best surly. For a group office lunch it was fine if you were willing as a group to exchange convenience and good food and close your eyes to the service (most offices in the area switched to ordering their lunch in as opposed to dining in their restaurant), but for a business lunch the service was unacceptable.

WHAT CLASS OF RESTAURANT WILL BE BEST?

More important than the class of restaurant is good food, good service and tables set apart from one another. There is nothing worse than choosing a restaurant for a private business discussion and finding that the next table over is practically sitting on your lap. That may be fine for casual greetings over coffee but if anything is truly going to be discussed over lunch, care must be given to the proximity of the tables and the noise level. How easily you can talk and be heard is important. You never know who is sitting around you. Who knows who and how what you say can be misconstrued or possibly taken out of context. A reporter overheard the director of communications for Canada's prime minister refer to one of the world's leaders as a "moron" in what they assumed was a private conversation. The comment made headlines around the world—breaching both work ethics and business etiquette.

One casual remark about agency overide payments (additional commission paid in return for meeting and exceeding business quotas) over coffee in a mall by two company employees was overheard by the mall manager. Their rent was based on revenue and what they discovered was that the override payments were not being included in the figures they were receiving. Accountants were brought in, the company books were reviewed, and they were then billed on the money owing on the "hidden" override profits. This is not to say that all business conversations taking place over lunch are about illegal goings on, inappropriate name calling or the like, but talks of mergers, promotions, dismissals, sales projections, new product development and other matters that could be damaging if overheard by the general public often take place with little regard about who might be sitting within earshot. Discretion is required, and ensuring that the restaurant you recommend is conducive to business conversations is imperative.

Concern is not only limited to how close the tables are. Some restaurant ceilings are miked over VIP table locations. One lighting company installing special effects for an event being held in a top restaurant was shocked to find microphones hidden in the ceiling decor. Higher-ups could monitor their waitstaff to make sure that their standards were being maintained, but if they could do that then they also had the capability to monitor table conversations. In some large upscale restaurants, there is even a "control center" where general managers can watch specific tables on a television monitor, as well as listen to waitstaff. They use the monitoring system to see when they should start to prepare or bring out the next course. This can't be avoided but knowing that you could be overheard in what seems to be a private setting is important. Issues that are best left discussed in the privacy of your office need to be redirected if they come up in conversation.

Use care and be aware of where you are and what you are saying. If sensitive subjects are being discussed, a working lunch in the office where privacy will be easier to maintain may be more advisable, although even then it is not always assured. But even office space is not sacred. One client used to leave suppliers on their own in the boardroom—their staff were instructed to leave the room on one pretense or another at the same time. What suppliers didn't know was the boardroom was bugged and conversations between the remaining suppliers could be monitored by the client. One company owner used to monitor meetings without their executive staff being aware they were being eavesdropped on. She would sit in her office and hit the intercom buzzer for the telephone that was situated in the boardroom or office where the meeting was being conducted. Engrossed in the meeting, few would notice one tiny, steady, lit-up red light on the telephone in the midst of all the other flashes of incoming calls as the president. This occurred not only when outsiders were in the office but during internal staff meetings as well. This was discovered when one key employee hit do not disturb on the telephone to make sure that their meeting would not be interrupted by paging. The president's assistant, who was aware of what was being done and often listened in to the private conversations as well, came storming into the office to insist that the do not disturb button be taken off. Puzzled, the employee complied, but noticed that as they did so the intercom light came on. One plus one equaled two. The employees did not confront the company president because many were already on the verge of quitting; instead, they passed the word around the office so that all staff members were aware of what was taking place and took care to schedule meetings in early mornings or late afternoons when the president was out of the office. This same company president used to tape client incoming calls—without telling them—and replay them for their sales representatives and executives to hear. She also used to place a tape recorder in her open briefcase, which she placed on her desk or credenza when she wanted to catch private conversations.

If an event planner was setting up a meeting in a hotel that had airwall dividers that separated the room, one of the first steps he or she would take would be to test the meeting space to see what could be heard on the other side. The same rule applies when you are holding a meeting in the office or in a private room at a restaurant. Test to see how loudly voices carry. Can your conversations be heard by people walking by the closed door or from an adjoining office? Many times, offices are selected and considered superior because of the view, but little thought is given to whose office is next to whose and how much they can actually hear when the office door is opened or closed. One top executive who was having marital spats that overflowed to the office discovered that every word could be heard from arguments they thought were behind closed doors. For all the privacy their closed office door gave them, the conversations might as well have been taking place in the middle of the office.

WHOSE CONNECTIONS WILL GET US BETTER SEATING?

Some business meetings take place in private clubs or in restaurants where one of the parties is well known or has a business association that can ensure a great table. If you are the host you may still wish to make the reservation, but make sure that the facility knows who you will be dining with if your guest is one of their regulars. The restaurant will appreciate knowing that so they can suggest a suitable table that will meet both your needs and the preferences of their regular client. However, it is essential to clearly establish that your party will be dining there as your guest so that there is no confusion over check presentation.

WHAT TIME WILL LUNCH TAKE PLACE?

Check operating times with the restaurant and how many meals they serve over the lunch hour. Also find out if their restaurant closes down between lunch and dinner service. You want to suggest a time when the meal and service will not be rushed and when lingering over coffee will be possible. Some people prefer to schedule an early lunch hoping to avoid having to wait in line or at the bar while a table is being cleared. They may like to arrive in advance of the restaurant opening, as early as 11:00 or 11:30 a.m. By the time these people arrive at the office and allow time for the drive to the restaurant, find parking and be there in advance of their guest, there isn't much time left in the morning to get anything done except to go through the mail and return a few telephone calls.

Many businesspeople prefer the later seating so that they can get a good start on their day before breaking for lunch, and leave their afternoon unscheduled in case an extended lunch is warranted. If the lunch meeting is taking place at a location midway between the two parties, it is probably not feasible to wrap up the meeting back in the office. If the restaurant is closing between lunch and dinner, ask in advance about a good spot to retire to so you can continue the meeting. Don't be left standing outside the restaurant's front door looking for somewhere to head to. Planners and suppliers would never leave that to chance during a program, so apply what you do professionally to everyday life and run your luncheon as you would an event. If the lunch is scheduled to take place in a business hotel, there is usually a quiet lounge your party can move to.

Who Will Make the Reservations?

Usually the host or their assistant would make the reservation. Use this opportunity to find out about the house specialties, special orders and meal requests. Perhaps the restaurant is known for their chocolate soufflés and the guest you are hosting is a chocolate lover. Find out if you have to order certain items in advance. Some restaurants want to know beforehand or at least at the beginning of the meal, so that they have time to properly prepare your dishes.

How Long Will Lunch Take?

Allow for more than just one hour for the actual lunch to take place. You don't want to give the appearance of being rushed. It is better to postpone a meeting and schedule it at a more opportune time than to leave a guest with the impression they have only been squeezed in and are not really your priority. Don't talk about how busy you are, how much you have to do back at the office and how many overtime hours you are putting in. Focus on why you called the lunch meeting.

Take time to relax before jumping right into business and remember that the art of conversation has two parts—listening and talking. One guest had just returned from vacation and was meeting her host upon her return. The host immediately jumped into his list of complaints and discussion on how much had gone wrong during her absence without stopping to ask if she enjoyed her trip. The guest felt under attack by a barrage of harsh words being thrown at her and felt as though she needed a shield to protect herself from injury. She quietly asked her host, "Would it have hurt to have taken five minutes to ask me how my trip was before blasting me with everything that went wrong in my absence?" Her comments gave her companion pause and he realized how inconsiderate he had been.

Never presume to ask personal questions, but make polite two-way conversation. Make sure there is give and take and the discussion is not one-sided. Don't immediately launch into a mound of negatives at the start of the meeting. Consider what you are about to say and how you broach the subject. A simple greeting can put guests at ease: "Welcome back. We missed you. Did you have a good time on your vacation? You look wonderful. What was Fiji like? I've always wanted to visit. What did you like best about it?" "We missed you" is a tip-off that something may have gone amiss during her absence, but not a full-out attack, and a hint that the conversation will eventually come around to discussing any areas that may need their attention now that she has returned.

A meeting over a meal should never be allowed to degenerate into a tattletale session. Ask about the destination, but not who they traveled with or where they stayed, because this could be seen as stepping into personal territory. Should they choose to divulge information it will be generated from them and not by probing questions. Luncheon meetings are not always private tête-à-têtes and a guest may feel uncomfortable divulging to their colleague, business associate or employee that they stayed in an exclusive, expensive hotel or retreat, whereas the destination they traveled to may be well-known.

WILL WE ORDER DRINKS?

To drink or not to drink over lunch, that is the question that must be answered individually. As the host you will have reconfirmed the reservation a day earlier, and timed your arrival so that you will be there before your guest, have time to make sure that the table is to your liking, and impart any special instructions to waitstaff. It will also give you time to settle in, and check your cell phone for any messages (in case your guest has been unavoidably delayed) before turning it off when your guest arrives. In most cases, you will be asked if you would like a drink while you are waiting. Is it advisable to order an alcoholic drink while waiting for your guest? It depends. One client was taken aback to see what they thought was their host sitting with an open bottle of wine on their table as they were being seated. They made a comment about starting to drink before them, only to discover that what they thought was a wine bottle was in actuality a flavored olive oil for dipping their bread in.

What is important to note is that the arriving guest does notice what you have ordered and whether or not they admit it, they will keep track of how many drinks are consumed. What image do you want to project? How do you want to be perceived in the industry? Event planning is a social industry and alcohol plays a part in most events. We have all witnessed what a few drinks can do—loose lips allow business slips—and how it can affect professional behavior. Some prefer to take their lead from their guest.

Letting their guests order first, the host is then free to choose their own options. If a guest chooses not to drink, the host may follow suit—feeling uncomfortable being the only one to order a drink in a business setting. If the invitee orders an alcoholic libation, the host does not have to order the same. They could order an altogether different beverage, or they could order a non-alcoholic version of the guest's drink. It is not necessary to justify their beverage choice, or make the guest feel awkward if they ordered an alcoholic drink. "I'm driving," "I'm allergic," "I'm on cold medication," or "Drinking gives me a headache"—are all valid reasons for choosing to sidestep the issue. Remarks like "doctor's orders" lead to the possibility of personal questions being asked about medical conditions that could impact how they do business with you. Look how Hollywood stars shy away from saying they have been sick, had heart surgery or otherwise, because they know that studios may hesitate when it comes to thinking about contracting them if they are perceived to be in poor health.

WHO WILL PICK UP THE CHECK?

Day after day in countless cities around the world, the battle of the bills and wills is carried out. It is an inevitable conclusion to the meal. Neither side wishes to appear cheap, but in reality it's most likely that neither one is personally paying for the meal. It is generally expensed back to the office, or as with some event planners, folded right back into the program costs under some innocent, meaningless category, such as communications, or elsewhere where it may not be identified. Actually, the client is paying for both their own and the host's meals, but appearances would have it look otherwise (the same may apply to gifts). One way to circumvent this ritual is to prepare for it ahead of time. Call in your credit card number or present it upon arrival to the maître d' with tipping instructions (e.g., have 15–20 percent added to the subtotal, excluding taxes, as a tip for their assistance). Sign the receipt in advance and request that the bill not be presented at the table. The maître d' can slip your signed receipt in a sealed envelope to you upon departure. Subtlety is the key to handling the situation with tact. Of course, you only want to do this at an establishment you can trust with a pre-signed credit card receipt. Not all restaurants have pre-printed receipts (some have electronically generated bills that can't be pre-signed) so check with the maître d' about how to discreetly sign the receipt away from the table.

> **T**
> **I**
> **P**
>
> Find a restaurant in a suitable price range. Some clients are uncomfortable being taken to expensive establishments where a steak can run over $50 and side dishes are an additional $10, with perhaps an additional charge for rolls and butter. Some establishments offer their guests menus without prices, which could trigger concerns because most clients try to be respectful of costs and are conscious about not wanting to be perceived as being bought. The exception is when a client is being taken to lunch to sample something that is the talk of the town, such as Kobe beef burgers. While such meals are extraordinarily expensive, clients may overlook that as there is a certain excitement to having tried something that few others have.

> **T**
> **I**
> **P**
>
> One executive who took a client to a well-tried and tested upscale business restaurant for lunch was heard to remark that they both came away hungry after a five-course meal. The restaurant prices were at the high end of the spectrum, while the portions were miniscule—one main entrée consisted of three tiny scallops. As well, service was not up to business standard. Restaurants—management, styles and level of service—will change, so be on top of current reviews and referrals. Always try a restaurant out before suggesting it for a business meeting.

What can also be tricky is colleagues—business peers going to lunch together where everyone will be responsible for their own bill. Many restaurants prefer not to issue separate checks, but this is a reasonable request to make if the meal is going to be an individual business expense for which backup bills are required to be submitted. Find out the restaurant's policy in advance. Some people will prefer to simply split the bill equally, but that is usually a suggestion made by the individual who is ordering before-meal drinks, an appetizer, a salad, an entrée, wine or beer with the meal, dessert and coffee, and maybe a cigar—not by the person ordering only soup and salad, and bottled water. It is an unfair practice, be it a personal or professional lunch.

If it is a business lunch, say, during a seminar, only one person will have a receipt to submit if the cost of the meal is going to be reimbursed by the office. Some companies have a maximum meal allowance and any excess is paid by the employee, who may not be in a financial position to do so. Individuals may not want to look cheap, but the colleague who is dining on the company's expense is in a different position than the one who may be paying for their meal personally. It is ethics meets etiquette. Some questionable practices do take place and you need to be careful how a solution is presented. Some solutions are honorable and some are not, and sometimes it is difficult to tell which is which.

One of the guests, if the bill is being divided, may not have brought enough cash and may request that if everyone pays them they will put the total bill on their credit card. Firstly, all restaurants are capable of billing on a credit card only what the individual owes. It is not necessary for the individual to put the entire amount for the group on their credit card. Secondly, if the guest does put the full amount on their credit card, then they now have a receipt for a large amount that could be billed back to the office and not raise any questions, depending on how it is presented. The employee received the cash from those dining with them and will be paid a second time by the company reimbursing them for a business lunch if it is submitted as a legitimate expense. It happens. And just because it is colleagues dining together and not the boss doesn't mean that expenses will be light.

If the bill is divvied up—equally or otherwise—with everyone paying cash, there still can be delicate issues to deal with. For an industry where budget preparation and management is key, it is surprising that people who should be on top of current taxes and appropriate tipping forget to include them when calculating how much they owe. There is always someone who "forgets" the third glass of wine, the tax or the tip. They know better but choose not to do better. Someone—unless there is an outspoken member of the group—is usually left making up the difference. A query, if the cash comes up short, asking whether or not everyone remembered to calculate taxes and tips at X percent may be the gentle reminder someone needs to rethink their cash contribution. One employee who worked in event operations and final reconciliations was never shy about bringing out her calculator and working individual bills out to the last penny. Under her watchful eye, everyone paid what everyone owed. That is not what you want see take place in a business meeting. Make sure that you come equipped with credit cards, debit cards, or cash in various denominations so that you are prepared to handle payment smoothly without any undo fuss.

> **T**
> **I**
> **P**
> When making the reservation, always check to see what forms of payment are acceptable and whether of not separate checks can be issued. If you are paying for the meal with your company credit card, check with accounting in advance to make sure you are under your credit limit, and allow enough time for a payment to go through if necessary to clear additional funds. This may be important if you are going to be hosting a large number of guests at an expensive venue. You don't want to be placed in an unpleasant situation and have everyone scrambling to find ways to pay if your credit card is refused.

OUT AND ABOUT

Meeting for drinks in a bar, restaurant or lounge after work is giving way to other forms of getting together. Enjoying high tea is making a comeback. In the spring, summer and fall, golfers are gathering at putting greens to practice their swing or to take in a quick round of golf before having a drink at their favorite club. (Some even begin their day with a 6:00 a.m. start on the golf course, followed by breakfast in the clubhouse with their customers.) Baseball fans are slipping out early to catch a game with their client in the company's private box. People are combining an activity with a reason to be together, preferring an informal setting that may be more conducive to the business of getting to better know their customers than a formal restaurant setting. Seeing personal behavior out of an office or traditional surroundings can be telling.

ELEVATED ENTERTAINMENT

Some sales or company representatives who are looking for new ideas to provide fresh and memorable ways to entertain business associates are considering personal corporate entertaining to take advantage of one of the best-kept secrets of the wealthy society and business crowd. Major corporate players have discovered—as sponsors and patrons—how supporting the arts and non-profit and research organizations in their fund-raising efforts benefits not only the organization but the individual as well, both personally and professionally. Whatever the motive, everyone comes out a winner.

"You can get a million dollars of free publicity by underwriting a party for $10,000," Ian Schrager said in a *New York Times* article by Meryl Gordon. Ian Schrager is the man who started Studio 54 and who presides over a dozen high-style hotels in New York, Miami, Los Angeles and London. The right match between the underwriting sponsor (you or your company) and the event can serve to establish the individual or corporate branding in a very subtle way. One individual reaped incredible press coverage from this type of arrangement for as little as a $5,000 investment. You don't have to underwrite a party in full or in part—that is just one of the methods that can be employed in "value added" entertaining. The ways and the means vary.

Another approach is to purchase "giving" memberships in support of the arts. These can be surprisingly inexpensive and bring with them numerous benefits, including entry into exclusive events. By choosing the right event (something original or suited to your guests), the purchase of a corporate table or individual tickets to a gala fund-raiser can be a great way to host business clients.

There are wonderful causes individuals or companies can lend support to by attending their events. These can include everything from masquerade balls and exclusive wine and food tastings to fashion shows, art exhibits, celebrity golf tournaments or tennis matches, polo matches, film festivals, movie premieres, or rollerblading or biking on a highway that is being closed solely for the event. While anyone can purchase a ticket to a sought-after show, those in the event planning industry know the value of inviting guests to a once-in-a-lifetime night of theater, music or dance. A client who is a true movie buff will remember being invited to a sneak preview of an upcoming film at a private screening featuring a guest appearance by the director, much more than steak served up at a local restaurant. The get-together is a winner, the charity is a winner and the event is a taxable receipt, so the corporation wins as well.

Entertaining has come full circle. Event planning industry individuals and corporations are able to give back and support others in their entertaining endeavors. No longer do you have passive audiences in their seats, but audiences who actively participate in raising funds for a host of worthy causes in an environment that lends itself to successful personal and business entertaining.

OUT ON THE TOWN

Entertainment events in the evening generally include companions or spouses. Dinner followed by the theater, an exclusive concert or recital or a dinner cruise timed to see a special firework competition are several suggested business events suitable for couples to enjoy. When planning evening events, pay attention to the same considerations you would if you were planning any event. Time the event to take place when both parties can easily get to the location. Make it accessible. Partners may work in opposite ends of town, or one may be coming from home. In some cases, your guests may share a car or not want to be in the position of having to take two cars. If your invitees are traveling home by commuter train, make sure that the evening is timed to end before a mad dash to the station is required. Be conscious of babysitters on a school night—your guests may not be able to stay out late on a weeknight, and will be concerned about having to go to work the next day if the event is not scheduled to take place over the weekend. Don't talk shop all night; one of the parties will go home either stressed or simply bored.

Schedule a cocktail hour as a buffer to gather guests together before dinner. If an evening of entertainment at a theater is to follow dinner, check to see what VIP upgrades can be purchased for your party. Some theaters have special reception rooms that add a special touch for guests during intermission, specifically for VIP ticket holders.

Look for ways to use your event planning skills—creativity, timing and logistics—to set your event apart, even if it is just for a party of four. Some restaurants in the downtown core offer parking passes at nearby parking facilities. It is a nice touch to present them to your guests at the end of the evening with a parting evening memento. Arrangements can be made in advance at some theaters to have CDs from a musical performance personally signed by the performers and given to your guests as a thoughtful take-home gift. Loot bags of retro candy provide an element of fun conversation during a show production of *Hairspray*, *Grease* or *The Graduate*.

INDUSTRY EVENTS

Most of the time, industry suppliers such as hoteliers, tourist boards or airlines do not bring together corporate clients and the event planning industry. It can put the corporate client who does business with more than one event planning company in an awkward position. If the event planning companies involved are feeling possessive, they may circle the client all night and fend off competing sales reps who want to use the opportunity to introduce themselves and their company to potential clients.

If the two—corporate clients and planning companies—are brought together, it is best not to commit yourself to driving together to evening functions. Some sales reps believe it gives them an edge with their clients, demonstrates the bond between their companies to would-be competition and gives them one-on-one time with the client during the ride to and from the event. But driving a client to an event or offering a ride home after an event is definitely a no-no. Sometimes you can find yourself in a compromising position or fending off unwelcome advances at the end of the evening. One client asked her very attractive sales representative to drive her home after an industry event. The sales representative was married, but she was not. The client knew that the sales representative's wife was out of town, and after being driven home, she deliberately forgot to take her briefcase from the back of the car. Shortly after, she called the sales representative on his cell phone and asked him to bring the briefcase to her condo. When sales representative presented himself at her door, the client had switched into a silk wrapper and had two glasses of wine poured. What the client did was staged, but it did not net her the results she wanted. The sales representative, when telling the story the next day in the office, said he left so fast that he left tire marks in the driveway. He recognized that he had placed himself in a professional and personal position of risk by trying to be accommodating, although not as accommodating as his client would have liked.

As well as personal risk, such as putting yourself in a situation of entrapment with rape charges (real or not), there was also company risk. We live in a litigious society. What if an accident had occurred on company time while the employee was driving a client home? I know of a hairdresser driving a client home after an appointment who was involved in an accident. The client was injured and reportedly sued her hairdresser and her company for $100 million. The same thing could have happened to a sales representative driving his client on business. And if alcohol were involved in any way, the charges and consequences—personally and professionally—could be much higher.

> **T**
> **I**
> **P**
>
> "Let me call a cab for you and charge it on the company credit card," may be what staff could be instructed to say if placed in an awkward situation by a client requesting a ride home. But would legal liabilities apply if the taxi were involved in an accident on the way home, since the cab company and charges were being handled under the banner of company business? Clear instructions as to how to protect themselves and the company must be reviewed with employees. They need to know in advance how to protect personal and professional boundaries from being crossed and how to do it without putting anyone at legal risk.

In another case, a female supplier accepted an offer of a ride home from a client. Her strategy was to thank the client for the ride and quickly hop out of the car. His strategy was to insist that he would not be a gentleman if he did not escort her to her front door (and see if he could maneuver his way inside). At the front door, he attempted to kiss her good night and although she was able to fend him off initially, the client actually placed his foot in the door, preventing her from closing it, and tried to talk his way into her home.

One company president who was hosting an event volunteered to walk a female guest home on his way to the subway to catch the commuter train. The company president asked if he could step in to use her bathroom facilities before his long journey home. Trekking home was not on his mind once he stepped inside. The guest would never invite a stranger into her home, but knowing someone in the industry by name, by sight or by having done business with that person can have you lowering your guard and trusting someone you really don't know, and putting yourself in a situation that could be dangerous.

AT HOME

Some company owners like to entertain guests and employees at their home. Think about the repercussions that could come from entertaining guests on your property.

One event planning company owner, who pirated software for the company computers, which often crashed, and copied and returned sales tapes because "they couldn't afford to buy them," invited staff to his home for a get-together. The owner's wife took everyone on a tour of the house, pointing out all their special gadgets and toys, their new second car in the driveway and their brand-new deck. The wife went on and on about how many times they had redecorated the bathroom as well as the rest of the house, and the fireplaces they had added to the kitchen, bedroom and bathroom. The employees were made aware of how little was put into the office and the ethical standards their company owner was operating under. It was an awakening that may not have come about as quickly as it would have had the event taken place in the office, not at the owner's home. After dinner, employees and the partners were invited to enjoy their backyard hot tub. A quarrel broke out between a couple when a staff member's husband decided to go into the hot tub sans bathing suit and the owner's wife thought it was a great idea. The employee left the party and her spouse stayed, becoming too hands-on friendly with another employee in the hot tub. The employee and her husband ended their relationship as a result of the incident. The style of party was not suitable as an employee spousal event, for which the only activities were sitting around drinking, being taken on a tour of the lavish house and ending up in a hot tub. This style of party is more suitable for entertaining close friends and family members. The company manager had advised against it, but the owner's wife was determined to show off her house regardless of the cost to employee morale. The employees, who worked long hours, and dealt each day with outdated equipment and even took on the office cleaning responsibilities on top of their regular workload when a cleaning company could no longer be afforded, or so they were told, could clearly see what had more value to their employer—and it wasn't pulling together as a team to build a better company.

One event planning company owner liked to use her home to impress clients and would have them gather there for a cocktail reception prior to whisking them away in limousines for an evening out. Guests would return to a lavish spread, complete with waitstaff and bartenders. Meeting downtown in the client's offices or in a private room at an upscale supper club located close to the theater district would actually have been more convenient for the guests, and cocktails, limousines and an after-party spread could still have been done in the same manner. Pulling the guests to the owner's home served no purpose—except to showcase the owner's lifestyle and home.

> **T**
> **I**
> **P**
>
> For private events at home or in the office, check out liquor permits (depending on the size of event they may be required), event insurance, noise bylaws and parking (on some residential streets the maximum parking limit before being ticketed or towed could be one to three hours).

WEEKEND RETREATS

Some companies like to invite clients and suppliers to their weekend retreats in the hopes of building a stronger bond with their guests. They hope that by deliberately moving their business relationship to a friendship they will influence negotiations and contract decisions, and put them in a stronger position than their competition—loyalty in exchange for weekends away by the lake. Some owners do it as a way to break the bond between client and sales representative, so that if the sales representative ever leaves the client will stay with them. These weekend getaways would include the clients and their partners, but exclude sales representatives and their partners. The sales representatives would be very aware that their relationships with their clients were being undermined by their employer.

Use caution when bringing your business life into your personal life. Do you really want clients to have access to your personal lifestyle, possibly going through your bathroom medicine cabinet, peering uninvited into family closets (that happened to one host touring her guests), checking out how your refrigerator is stocked and what brand names you buy, putting mental price tags on your belongings and wondering how much of your home and lifestyle their company has provided? Examine the real reasons you are considering inviting clients, suppliers, peers and employees into your home, and in some cases, into your hot tub. Is it to move the relationship from business and social entertaining (with established professional boundaries) to personal home entertaining (inviting familiarity and breaking barriers), to impress them, or to define a position of power or possibly intimidation? It is not a cost-saving measure because creative business alternatives would come in at about the same dollars. If the reasons are not valid, it could backfire and cost you business, not build it.

HOLIDAY PARTIES

Giving holiday parties a meaningful theme works toward raising the bar of good behavior, not putting staff in the situation of raising one too many glasses at the bar and demonstrating how their musical underwear plays a seasonal tune. One leading financial institution makes its exchange of staff holiday gifts meaningful by adding a twist. Staff members draw names and are asked to bring an unwrapped toy or other gift that best represents their coworker. Each gift comes with a message attached from their secret Santa as to why this gift was selected (to be written in the spirit of the season). One person's gift was a set of juggling balls to represent how wonderfully they seemed to juggle a multitude of tasks each day, at home and at work. Another gift was a cheery children's sweater with matching hat, scarf and mittens. The message was about the warmth and good cheer that person brings to the office. At the end of the event, the gifts were donated to a children's charity. For the employees, their true gift was the messages they received about how they were perceived in their workplace. They were also able to contribute to a worthy cause instead of spending money on trinkets or joke gifts that may not be used.

Another company sells tickets for a chance to win their professionally decorated company Christmas tree. The tree is delivered right to the winner's door after the holiday party. Some employees have donated their winning tree to a local nursing home or women's shelter. The money raised is donated to a needy charity, such as a food bank. Local merchants and professional decorators have been known to donate the tree, ornaments and their talent. It is an opportunity for them to showcase their talent and wares (in exchange for discreet signage saying thank you), as well as to do something good for the community. A Christmas tree is just one example that can be used. Companies need to be respectful of all their employees religions, holidays, beliefs, and traditions.

Yet another company decided to hold a private, catered, holiday Sunday brunch at the office with horses and sleigh shuttles to an afternoon silent auction for charity (tickets were purchased in advance). This was a great opportunity to do some holiday shopping while benefiting a great cause. Employees were thrilled with the items that were offered for bid. One guest at the event bid and won a bouquet of roses delivered to his mother once a month for a year, a gift that would be too expensive at full retail cost. When the employees returned back to the office, an array of decadent holiday treats awaited them.

For a final example, another company I know of adopted needy families as part of their holiday celebration. Each department was assigned a family and a list of what would make their holiday special. Food, warm clothing and gifts for all members of the family, not just the children, were being given in lieu of exchanging office gifts with one another.

Use what you know how to do best to your benefit. Don't let your guard down when entertaining at home for business or pleasure. Treat every interaction as an opportunity to show how you conduct yourself when overseeing an event. Don't lower your standards to anything less than your best.

T
I
P

Make sure that provisions are in place for guests to get home safely from any event if they have been drinking. If the event has been hosted by you or your company, you could be liable for any injuries. Have taxi numbers or vouchers handy or special overnight rates arranged at a local hotel. Be careful of asking one or more people, or being asked yourself, to take responsibility for seeing another person home. Make sure no one is being placed in a position in which they could be charged for improper conduct or driving while under the influence or be the recipient of unwanted advances by someone who may have had too much to drink.

5
BUSINESS ETIQUETTE, PROTOCOL AND ENTERTAINING

OUT OF TOWN OR COUNTRY

There are three scenarios when planners, clients and suppliers are entertaining or are entertained socially out of town or out of the country:

- Familiarization Trips (Fam Trips)
- Site Inspections
- Personal Travel

When an event is actually in progress, the dynamics between entertaining planners, clients and suppliers changes from business schmoozing to serious business, which will be discussed in Part Three of this book, which deals with codes of conduct.

Business etiquette, protocol and the how-to of entertaining can be different in each case. No longer are just the eyes of your peers on you, but so are the eyes of the world. In this day and age of e-mail and instant text messaging, what you do or say can circle the globe in a matter of minutes. When asked about a trip to Washington, one planner asked her colleague, "How did you know I went there? My own mother doesn't know I was away." Another business acquaintance, staying at the same hotel while on a site inspection, had seen the planner there and mentioned to a friend of a friend that the competition was checking out one of their hotel discoveries.

FAMILIARIZATION TRIPS

Familiarization trips (fam trips, as they are called in the industry) can take place locally or around the world. Local weekend getaway resorts often invite planners to enjoy a mini vacation so that they can fully appreciate the hotel's amenities and guest experience. They can be as short as an overnight stay or take place over an extended time period, although they seldom exceed two weeks. The fam trip is usually coordinated by a group of suppliers representing different sectors of the event planning industry, who come together to put a program in place that will show off their properties and services to a group of event planners or corporate clients, but never to both at the same time. Some familiarization trips are complimentary—at no charge—while others charge a minimum fee to attend (usually well under what it would cost to visit on your own). A fam trip is different from a site inspection. The request for a site inspection is initiated by individual planning companies either to have a member of their staff check out a specific new venue for further consideration or post-proposal presentation, or for contracting purposes when the client travels with the planning company representative and is taken to see all the included program event elements.

Who is hosting—picking up costs or donating complimentary product, overnight stays, transportation, meals and beverages and gifts—will determine what guests get to see or do. If an airline and tourist board are joining together and inviting guests to see a specific destination, it is in their best interests to show the planner as much as possible. Come prepared, with comfortable shoes, and pack a good attitude because you could end up seeing every hotel, restaurant and venue that could possibly be a consideration. Tourist boards cannot play favorites. They represent their destination as a whole and support all of their properties equally. They know that planners and clients come with an array of different needs, budgets and expectations, and they want to show them how their destination can be put together with a variety of elements to best meet their requirements.

If a hotel and an airline (as opposed to a tourist board) is paying for the fam trip, some hoteliers may be possessive about time and frown on guests straying away from their itinerary to check out the competition or be wined and dined by others on their dime. Other hotels feel secure about their product and know that no matter how tightly they schedule the program inclusions, a determined planner will always find a way to check out other properties, and they are more relaxed because they know what will happen. It is a given: Planners will not travel (in some cases halfway around the world or further) to a destination they have never been to and not check out the hotel that is down the street. They know their client will be asking them how their proposed hotel compares to the others. Visiting another hotel's property can be done up front—graciously and discreetly—with the host's unspoken permission during scheduled "time at leisure." It can also be done with great subterfuge by returning from a jam-packed day and evening out, saying their good nights to their hosts—who have been determined to thwart plans to check out other hotels by leaving no unscheduled moments from the moment their guests are picked up at the airport until the are delivered safely back there for departure—and banding together to grab a taxi to another property for a "nightcap" (also known as checking out the competition) on their own time, even if it is 3:00 a.m.) What is not acceptable behavior is skipping out on a scheduled event or activity, arriving late because you were held up touring another property or taking time away from your host by detailing your findings about another hotel to the rest of the group at a time when everyone's attention needs to be focused on where you are now. That is disrespectful to your host.

Some event planning companies choose not to be obligated to any one airline, hotel, tourist board or other facility, and instead of having their employees take part in an organized fam trip they prefer to pay upfront and send planners where needed with no commitments to any affiliations. Their individualized fam trip (or site inspection) may include their employees staying at more than one hotel during their visit so that they can truly check the room amenities and service, as opposed to seeing them on a quick walkthrough. Planners can focus their time on what products, venues and inclusions fit the needs of individual current or potential clients in addition to checking out what they perceive to be up-and-coming destinations and properties. They prefer their planners to see quality of product (as it relates to their office requirements) as opposed to quantity, and don't want their staff wasting time seeing or taking part in activities that would not be suitable to their clients' needs. Their time might be better spent checking out a venue or activity that could be included on their program, such as a hot air balloon ride, rather than touring a local tourist attraction, which their clients could do on their own if they choose. Savvy planners customize the fam trip to meet their company's individual needs.

Not all attending are on fam trips for professional reasons. Sometimes a fam trip is used as a reward for office staff who may not typically get to travel on site (accountants, receptionists, mail clerks), as a gift to family and friends of the owners or an inexpensive personal vacation for someone, with an emphasis on play, not on the product. Some planning companies have sent staff away to destinations that they would never consider using themselves, just because someone in the office has asked if they could go. Suppliers come away feeling that they have been "fam scammed." It is unethical to take freebies under false circumstances. True, the purpose of a fam trip is to put "heads into beds," but suppliers are hoping to entice planners to recommend their product above all others. They are looking to have people on the trip who are in a position to influence the buyer and will be able to discern what their property has to offer. The cost to put on a fam trip can be considerable, and suppliers can come away feeling used and abused by their industry colleagues. "Fool me once, shame on you. Fool me twice, shame on me" becomes their modus operandi when considering who to invite on future fam trips. Word does get around the industry about fam scams.

Some planners will not take part in a fam trip unless single accommodation is guaranteed. There have been too many stories in the industry of what can take place when an exotic locale, alcohol and people traveling on their own come together. One planner walked into her hotel room to discover a party of two going on and she couldn't gain access to her bedroom for a number of hours. Her designated roommate for the trip was someone she thought she knew, and it was an uncomfortable situation. Another planner felt he had been assigned added duty as a babysitter when his roommate continued to overindulge each night, and it became his responsibility to make sure that he made it safely back to the room each night.

Fams need to be designed with care. Professionals in the industry who choose to avail themselves of fam trips want to be assured that they will come home with their reputation intact. They don't want to be a party to drunken debauchery, to have to fend off unwelcomed advances or to be put in compromising positions. One supplier took a stand and was supported by the rest of the attendees—and sent one guest home mid-fam trip. She was making a spectacle of herself and embarrassing everyone by her bratty and demanding behavior, unseemly dress and excessive drinking. Another supplier, driven to exasperation by the antics of one "couple" on their trip, drove off and left them behind at an out-of-the-way tourist spot the group had stopped to see. They were more focused on finding nooks to rendezvous in than viewing the sights. Their goings on had gone too far and the rest of the group was uncomfortable. Something had to be done. A very public display of inappropriate intimate conduct was the final straw. Private admonishments had had no effect. They were both sent home, and a bill for full charges was sent to each of their respective offices.

But it can't be one-sided. Respect and demonstrating high standards has to come not only from the supplier but from the planner as well. Some airlines upgrade fam trip guests to business class or first class in order to make their flight more enjoyable (although it is better for planners to experience exactly what their client's guests will experience), and in return expect good behavior, appropriate attire and that they do not broadcast around the cabin that they are flying free and offend the full-paying passengers. The same applies for hotels. Often they host their guests in upgraded suites, and they expect suitable dress and conduct from their invited guests while on property.

SITE INSPECTIONS

A site inspection is different from a familiarization trip. While a familiarization trip may be made up of planners or corporate clients being hosted by a supplier, a site inspection is the client, planner and supplier coming together to do a full review of a contracted—pending site inspection approval—piece of business. The site inspection is where all event inclusions are finalized.

The cost of the site inspection is generally included in the proposal cost summary breakdown and is usually based on one event planning company executive and one client representative attending. Some clients insist that any charges be the financial responsibility of the event planning company as a cost of doing business, and may be one of their terms and conditions. Some companies stand firm and will not pick up costs other than for their own employees. Others comply on the surface, but find ways through "creative costing" at final reconciliation to bill back actual costs. Those whose sense of business ethics include honoring what they say don't look for ways to recoup costs. If they agree to be responsible for all site inspection costs as part of contracting, that is exactly what should happen. They should not be looking for a means to bury costs. What planners do need to be aware of is the cost of doing business. If a planner's management fees are going to be eroded by client demands that excessive costs be picked up, reduced or waived, this may not be a client the planner should consider doing business with since it will only get worse as the event progresses. The event could conceivably run at a loss for the planning company if hours are spent going back and forth over terms that had been agreed upon initially when the business was awarded, but balked at when time comes to sign the contract. On the other hand, clients should beware of signing with event planning companies that begin to add on costs that should have appeared in their cost summary breakdown. It may mean they have not done due diligence—the process of investigation—into actual event costs and may not have verified all event requirements in their "estimated" cost summary breakdown. The time to decide whether to move forward is before both parties sign on the dotted line and are legally bound to produce the event.

At times, a client may request that more than one representative attend, and if the site is complex, or if there are extenuating circumstances, an event planning company may send along another company member to assist, advance the program inclusions or serve as reputation protection. One sales rep knew he would be facing a difficult time if he traveled to the site inspection with a client who had openly expressed interest in him, so another company representative was sent ahead to just "happen" to be on another site inspection at the same time. He would team up with them at the destination. This was not discussed with the client in advance, nor would the extra charges to bring down another in-house company rep be applied to the program costs. The client had expressly said that only the sales representative was to accompany her, which when combined with past actions (silk wrap and wine—see Chapter 4) left the event planning company concerned as to the client's possible motives. The ploy worked and the client, although not happy about the situation, bought the coincidence.

Depending on the location, site inspections can be one to eight days in duration. They rarely exceed that length of stay because the object is not a full program at a leisurely pace but a blitz to cover as many event elements as possible in as short a time as doable. For example, a planner checking out a seven-night cruise where all the events are taking place onboard the ship may not necessarily stay for the full duration if the purpose is to check out the ship. The planner may choose, depending on his or her schedule, to instead fly into port, tour the ship and fly out the same day, or board the ship, sail for a couple of days and schedule a return flight from one of the ports of call. If a client is looking at doing special events in each port of call, they may choose to stay aboard ship for the full duration or split the site inspection and sail for a couple of days and then fly to each port as opposed to losing time at sea.

Some unethical event planning owners, looking at taking advantage of a client's thinly veiled hints to bring his or her companion along on the trip, may look at a site inspection as an opportunity to bring their own spouses along, with costs for both partners being buried in the client's billing along with the other personal expenses on the trip. A tactic commonly used is to suggest that it would be good idea to get the other (female or male) perspective on event inclusions, enabling the client to justify in their mind (not necessarily his or her company's mind, or even knowledge) the prospect of bringing their respective spouses along.

On a site inspection trip, the client expects to be looked after from beginning to end, usually starting with a limousine to the airport if their event is being held in an out-of-country location. The client's expectations can include the arrangement of passes to the first-class lounge, being upgraded from economy to business or first class and never having to put their hands in their pocket to tip, pay a bill or make a purchase. For some clients there is no limit to their expectations and they anticipate being wined and dined at only the best restaurants—at his or her company's expense. Those traveling with clients on site inspections need to discuss with their office in advance what boundaries need to be put in place, and how they should handle situations and perhaps expenses that are getting out of hand, for example, a client wanting to go scuba diving daily in the Caribbean when scuba diving is not included in the list of program event inclusions, requesting to sample expensive brandies at over US$100 a serving or golfing at exclusive courses. What is acceptable behavior and what is not and when and where does their responsibility to the client end? Some clients on site inspections view their event planning company rep as their personal party playmate into the early morning, and expect them to accompany them to questionable venues, for example, strip clubs or the local red light district, and even provide them with paid companionship.

Corporate clients also need to put guidelines in place for acceptable behavior and expenses with their designated site inspection staff. For example, an event planning company may decide to pick up the cost of one scuba diving excursion and host the client as their guest, but when a request for another outing is made, their representative may be instructed to ask his or her client how they would like to have the payment handled. Would he or she like to have it billed to their personal credit card or billed and itemized on the site inspection reconciliation? With regard to staying out late to play, the planner can always politely excuse themselves from further evening adventures by informing his or her client that they need to firm up their plans for the next day and send in an updated site inspection report so that their office can begin to implement event changes and additions.

Bad business behavior is not limited to the evening. One client, thoroughly enjoying her site inspection of Mexico, was inhaling tequila at an alarming rate. The combination of hot noonday sun and power drinking was loosening her inhibitions, but efforts to get her to stop or at least slow down were met with resistance. The client was settled in at a local cantina and had no intention of leaving before she was ready. The bartender was quietly instructed by the sales representative to bring the client only virgin margaritas as her steps were rapidly becoming wobbly and her speech becoming slurred. The woman was the corporate client's wife, who was sent on the site inspection to review the program, and she was enjoying the attention of two local gentlemen who were encouraging her to drink and dance with them. The sales rep had not suggested this cantina stop, but her client had insisted on dropping in for a drink and did not want to return to the hotel quietly. The planner, with the help of her driver and local destination management representative, was able to assist the client back to the car on the pretext of returning to the hotel to pick up messages and freshen up, and then going to an even more popular locale. Both the planner and the destination management company knew that the client was going to be going no further than her guestroom once they arrived back at the hotel. The client was returned to the safety of her room and put to bed. The sales rep maintained careful watch over the client, checking on her condition constantly. Then the inevitable happened—the client became ill and proceeded to pass out again. The sales representative called back to head office, partially for advice as to how to proceed with the next step and partially to find out where her responsibility ended. The event planning company owner advised the sales rep not to call in medical assistance or to notify the hotel and ask for help—which was the sales rep's plan of action—as the owner wanted to protect the client's reputation. The sales rep was requested to assist the client to the shower and help her clean up, have her clothes sent to the laundry, order coffee and so on. After showering and changing her clothes, the client wanted only to go back to sleep and be left alone.

Could legal action have been taken if the client had choked again when she was unconscious or if she had developed alcohol poisoning and medical attention had not been sought earlier? What if the client, in her intoxicated state, slipped in the bathroom or decided to jump in the pool to clear her head and was permanently injured? Depending on what transpired, yes, there could be legal action. And who would be responsible? The employee who saw the need but didn't call in professional help and instead followed company direction? Or the event planning company for not authorizing that medical care be sought? The event planner had only had verbal—not written—confirmation on how to proceed, which could be denied if the matter went to court, leaving the event planning company rep personally open to legal liabilities and criminal charges should anything have come to pass.

Event planning companies pride themselves on making sure that their clients never place themselves at risk, personally or professionally, when organizing their events. They make sure the clients consult their company lawyers and have them prepare waivers to be signed by their guests before allowing them to take part in a trip or participate in various activities, waiving responsibility for future claims. But rarely do event planning companies make sure that they protect themselves or their staff from legal liabilities that could occur on a site inspection, which can take place before a contract is signed, and have their clients sign a waiver. Event planning offices need to provide strict guidelines and procedures that must be followed should their employees find themselves on dangerous ground. And these guidelines and procedures need to be reviewed before the staff sets foot out of the office door. When you are in the middle of a major crisis, there is not always time to stop and make a telephone call to find out the next step.

There are times clients get drunk. There are times they turn belligerent. These are not isolated cases. People get carried away—sometimes literally. One client's behavior was so bad stepping off a dinner cruise in the Caribbean that the sales rep asked permission "to give him a quick tap—he won't know what hit him." Racist remarks and challenges to fight everyone on the dock were just the beginning of what was taking place, and the client had to be removed from the explosive situation immediately. Can a sales rep put their hands on clients, and physically restrain them for their own safety? What can you do—legally—and not step too far beyond the etiquette and ethical behavior line? Punching a client out is not a permissible solution to the problem at hand, but drinking excessively and placing you in a dangerous, potentially life-threatening situation as a direct result is not acceptable behavior on the client's part. Event planning company representatives are on site inspection trips in a professional capacity, and not there to act as babysitters or moral barometers for the clients. They are there to do their job, hold themselves to high standards, and lead by example, but not to party. Their clients are there professionally as well, but some don't hold themselves to as strict a code of conduct. Those are the ones who view site inspections as mini vacations—a time to work and a time to play—and sometimes they play very hard.

Client indiscretions on a site inspection should not become the topic of general conversation or gossip back in the office, but situations should be reviewed without naming names. Suppliers who witness client indiscretions are held to the same standards. Sales reps do not expect to arrive back in his or her office with everyone knowing from their suppliers what has transpired. It is the event planning company's owner's responsibility to address any issues directly with the client, and the discussion should stay between them. Tactics—ways how not to let a situation escalate out of control and how to handle it if they do—should be discussed with staff. Nobody wants to see his or her client refused boarding for having had too much to drink, or led off to a local jail. It is the site escorts' job to manage the visit and manage their client as best they can, and the tools to do so need to be taught back in the office.

> **T**
> **I**
> **P**
>
> Every event planning company needs to talk to their company lawyers to set company policies in place. It is recommended that you invite the company lawyer to come speak directly to staff and advise them as to how they, as the company's legal representative, should encourage controlling situations that could have personal and company implications. Employees should be allowed to contribute, because they may have personal experiences to share that may not have been considered. Company policy can then be prepared, distributed and signed off, having been reviewed by all involved.

What happens if the client sets off into the night with a stranger? (One travel journalist on a Caribbean site inspection, who should have known better, still has not been found.) Sometimes there is little you can do to stop such a course of action. But staff representatives do need to know what to do if clients are missing the next day. Planners need to know company policy on how to handle clients' "special" requests, such as visits to the red light districts in Amsterdam, Thailand or Nevada, where prostitution is legal, or strip clubs their clients may have heard about and wish to visit. Are sales reps expected to accompany their client? Or do they assist them in making special arrangements through their supplier for a car and driver to go with them, with the explicit instructions to the driver/bodyguard not to leave them on their own? Does the event planning company and the corporate client they are handling—not the individual on the site inspection—condone that behavior? Is the event planning company putting itself at legal risk or jeopardizing its relationship with its client by making the arrangements for the corporate company's representative, or leaving the client to his or her own devices to find their way to and from what could be dangerous territory?

If a supplier gets out of line—is rude, makes suggestive remarks or exhibits unprofessional behavior—this issue must be addressed immediately. You cannot afford to wait until you get back in the office to rectify the situation. An alternative can be requested, or a new supplier can be found. Both supplier and planner are there to do a job.

Trust can be too freely given, not earned, in the event planning industry. The people the hospitality industry attracts are often social in nature. Many assumptions are formed because people are "in the business" and people's guards are not always up. One hotel general manager invited an event planner to dinner after the site inspection had concluded and the client had departed for home. The planner was staying on for a couple of days to make program changes. A hotel general manager taking an event planning rep to dinner or lunch is a normal occurrence and raises no red flags. Neither does setting a meeting time and place in the hotel lobby, although meeting at a specified hotel restaurant or lounge is usually the norm as opposed to meeting in the hotel lobby.

This being the Middle East and the event planner a woman traveling on business on her own, it was reasonable to think that it may be more in keeping with local customs for an unaccompanied woman to be escorted to dinner. What was unexpected—and should have sounded warning bells—was to be told upon arrival in the hotel lobby that the general manager's car and driver were waiting for her. Dining off property had not been discussed. Inside the car were seated two women dressed in traditional clothes. The driver said that he would be taking them as well to meet with the general manager. Settling into the car, the planner gathered that one woman was someone's intended (assuming the general manager's) and that the person accompanying her was her mother acting as chaperon.

The planner relaxed and thought that the general manager was putting in place steps that would protect both of their reputations (perhaps the general manager dining with an unaccompanied woman would have raised eyebrows at the hotel, and that bringing his personal life (and intended wife) into the hotel was not something that he felt comfortable with.) But dinner at a public place was not on the menu. Everyone was driven to the general manager's house where a dinner, catered by the hotel, had been arranged. Another man joined the group and he was introduced as the woman's intended husband, which left the event planner as the general manager's date, with no chaperon to protect her reputation. Wine was flowing freely, which was unusual because the general manager had said in an earlier meeting that he did not drink because of religious reasons.

Immediately following dinner, the party of three excused themselves and left with the driver. The event planner, wary by this time, was ready to depart as well, but there was no room in the car for her now since the man who had arrived on his own took her place. The event planner was told the driver would be returning shortly to take her back to the hotel, but for now, she was left on her own with the hotel general manager—not in a public place but in his home, alone with no one aware of her whereabouts. It soon became apparent that the driver would not be returning, as unwanted advances were being made by a host who had clearly had too much to drink and had no intention of sending his guest home that evening.

The event planner had put herself in a position of high risk by simply accepting what was second nature at home—dinner with what she thought was a trusted business associate. Had an invitation to dine at the general manager's home been offered originally, she would have refused as it crossed the line from business to personal. Circumstances led to her being alone in an unfamiliar area and in a position that was circumspect. Only when the event planner tried to find her way back to the hotel on her own was a cab sent for her. The next day, the general manager sent a huge bouquet of roses to the planner's room with an apology, blaming his actions on the wine with an invitation to dinner again that night at a restaurant outside the hotel after a visit to the top of the mountain to see a spectacular view that should not be missed. Inside or outside the hotel, the event planner would not go, certainly not on her own, to the top of an isolated mountain with a man who had violated business ethics. A valuable lesson had been learned about trusting fellow associates too freely.

> **T**
> **I**
> **P**
>
> Never place yourself in a vulnerable position or high-risk situation with a client or supplier, and do everything possible to avoid having a client or supplier placed in a compromising position. Make sure—back in the office—that rookie sales staff and event planners are fully apprised of the different situations they can encounter along the way, how to sidestep them with grace, and what needs to be done to protect their personal reputation and the company they represent.

All guests need to be respectful of customs and protocol when they are visiting, and planners need to prepare themselves, advise their clients accordingly and lead by example. One sales rep on a site inspection in the Caribbean showed up for a meeting with top hotel officials in clothes more suited to the beach, and was sent back to change into something more suitable. The clients, on the other hand, came to the meeting dressed in business casual, which was more fitting for the occasion than the flip flops, shorts and short-sleeve, open shirt worn by the planning company representative. Event planning companies need to establish expected dress codes for site inspections and make sure that they are adhered to. How their representatives conduct themselves on site—including dress—reflects back to head office.

Suppliers must be mindful of the customs and proper etiquette for their incoming guest, and this includes forms of address, greetings and expected dress. One female supplier showed up in what was deemed immodest dress, which was offensive to Asian clients on a site inspection. Her excuse was that this was actually her day off and as soon as the meeting was concluded, she would be off to enjoy the day. Of course, that is not an acceptable excuse. If a business meeting is scheduled, professional business attire is expected.

It is the event planning company's responsibility to prepare suppliers properly as to what to expect, brief them on protocol and advise them that if they are in doubt about anything, they should refer the question back to the event planner.

On a site inspection, suppliers also need to be told what is permissible to discuss with the client. Some event planning companies prefer that suppliers not talk about pricing or special concessions in front of their clients. Others get uneasy when clients and suppliers exchange business cards because they don't want the supplier or the client calling each other directly, which they know can happen. There are many reasons for this. First, in the event planning company's eyes, they—the event planning company—are the supplier's client. The event planning company's client is not. They are the end user to the supplier. Second, the event planner needs to be in charge of all event planning elements, and if a client adds or deletes items directly with the supplier without informing the event planning company, they will lose control of the program and costly errors could be made. Last, the event planning company may not be comfortable opening the door to the client and supplier developing a closer relationship, fearing that they may be removed from the equation next time, with the client going directly to the supplier to book their event. The event planning company wants the client bond to remain with them. A simple, "I'm out of cards but X has my number," may be preferred. A venue that is owned by an event planning company that owns a decor company as well—depending on their level of business ethics—may be tempted during a site inspection to let that slip out in conversation or have material featuring their other services included in the client's packet. The event planner may not have chosen their decor company to handle the business and the supplier could try to sway business their way. If the information parcel is slipped to the client in a sealed enveloped addressed to the client, it is going to raise more suspicions than if two identical kits are handed to the event planning sales rep to give to the client. Both may contain material outlining the company's other services (which should never be done—it is unethical—and would be perceived by the event planning company as an underhanded attempt to secure more business), but when done in an open manner instead of with deliberate subterfuge, the sales representative will know exactly what the client has received. If it did contain material that breached business ethics, the sales rep would not be likely to recommend using this venue in the future. If an event planner is bringing in a client, it is very short-term thinking on the supplier's part to try and solicit business away from the planner. A client may do only one event, while an event planning company can provide an ongoing source of revenue. Suppliers who cross that ethical line become known in the relatively small industry fairly quickly.

But it is not always the supplier who is at fault. One client who had been on a site inspection requested that the supplier send a copy of the contract directly to the client to review. The supplier was then placed in an awkward spot. Should he do as the client requested and say nothing to the event planner, or call the event planner and inform her what their client requested and ask how to handle it? Regardless of what may be going on between the client and event planner at this point, the supplier has maintained his business integrity by being upfront with the person or company that introduced the client to his facility. The event planning company is then put on the alert that the client it is dealing with is not exhibiting ethical business behavior and may be going behind its back looking to make deals directly with suppliers, or may be questioning their integrity. The event planning company can then decide on how it wants to proceed.

What also needs to be discussed with suppliers prior to the site inspection is who will be picking up the bill for meals and drinks as the site inspection progresses. Regardless of who pays in the short term, it is all eventually charged back to the client file, but sorting out in advance who will physically be picking up the tab when out with the client allows for a smoother transaction. The supplier, who will have made many of the site inspection arrangements, may prefer to have all charges billed to his or her company and then submit the charges to the event planning company for payment.

When on site, planners and sales reps need to ensure that they bring sufficient cash and have an adequate line of credit available to meet any unexpected charges. There is no set amount since each destination and site inspection visit has different requirements. Planners need to thoroughly research site inspection costs the same way they do a proposal and walk through each day's possibilities. For example, will they be driving their own car, escorted by the supplier, having a private driver or jumping in and out of taxis? Each scenario requires that different cost considerations be factored in. They should do this well in advance of departure in case their local bank needs time to arrange to bring in foreign funds. Many times, it becomes a mad dash to the bank the day before departure to pick up traveler's checks and cash (in small bills for tipping). For the event planning company's protection, make sure that the majority of the money taken is in traveler's checks, unless there are extenuating circumstances. One event included a very special meeting for corporate VIPs, where a large cash "donation" to be paid in U.S. funds, not local currency, was part of the terms and conditions. The event planning company had to look at the legal amount of money each person was allowed to bring into a country before distributing the traveler's checks among the staff traveling with the group. The event planners on the program cashed in their traveler's checks when they arrived in the destination and made sure the money was divided up further among the staff so that if anything should happen, the lump sum was not at risk. As to whether it was ethical or legal to be paying cash "donations," that is a separate issue.

Special Note:

Don't be naïve. Naïveté has landed people in jail, on the witness stand and in personal and professional peril. Planners need to make sure that what they are doing or are asking others to do is legal, ethical and moral.

In another case, a very experienced planner took a large amount in cash instead of traveler's checks and put it in the hotel's safety deposit box as soon as he arrived in the hotel to ensure its safety. His bank had been out of traveler's checks in the currency he required, he was pressed for time and he did not want to make a trip to another bank, so he opted to take cash instead. When he went to retrieve the funds from the safety deposit box, they were missing and he had no proof that his money had been put in the safe. The hotel does not know what people are depositing or not depositing in their security box. They only control who signs in and out for the box. In this case, there were no other signatures. Had the money been in traveler's checks, the risk would have been limited and the funds easily replaced.

PERSONAL TRAVEL

When planners travel personally, they need to determine the merits of requesting a discount at a supplier's property against being truly on vacation with no strings attached. Some hotels are thrilled to offer special rates to those in the industry. They know that once they have you on the property, in return for certain concessions they may have granted, business etiquette demands that in exchange, they receive some of your time to tour the property, meet their staff and possibly join them (or they join you) for breakfast, lunch, drinks or dinner. It can seem to be never ending as they or their staff stop by to see how you are enjoying your stay, or ask if there is anything you need or something they can do, as you attempt to put business behind you and relax. Some vacations can turn into full-fledged site inspections unless planners practiced in the art of pink panther moves are able to maneuver through the lobby and hotel public areas without being seen. But there are still voice mail messages to contend with. In addition, vacation or not, good business behavior is still expected since you are not traveling incognito.

Some people prefer that their personal vacation remain exactly that and do not approach their suppliers for special rates, upgraded rooms, assistance with dinner or ticket reservations or advice on what to see and do while they are on the property. The cost is too high a price to pay. They prefer to be able to put business aside for the duration of their stay. Others prefer receiving the benefits of the profession as opposed to privacy and will take the time to tour the facility in exchange for an upgraded suite with a view, welcome gift in the room and a hosted dinner. Seasoned travelers make their presence known to their hotel contacts on the last day, limiting the amount of personal time they have to invest. They are introducing themselves as a professional courtesy, but they did not put themselves in a position of owing the hotel anything—future business or otherwise.

There are ethical considerations in asking for a discount. Company policy should dictate what can be asked of suppliers by their staff. It is not up to the individual. However, deciding whether or not to accept an approved company discount is up to the individual. Event planning companies need to have ground rules about what employees are permitted to request. In exchange for special concessions, suppliers will be looking to receive special consideration from the company, not necessarily the individual, when it comes to being included in a proposal.

Staff needs to be advised on company policy about how to handle client requests for personal travel as well. It is the company, not their client, that is requesting the favor from the supplier, and that goes right back to whether or not making such a request is deemed ethical by the event planning company. There are also other aspects to consider. Do planners want suppliers wining and dining their clients on their own or having their client's vacation inter-rupted by well-meaning staff continually checking on their stay or trying to set up a tour of the property? Do the clients want to be put in a position of feeling obligated to (or bought by) a specific property if they choose the same hotel or chain they vacationed at for a company event? Business and pleasure may be best kept apart.

Business entertaining is a dance between partners, and toes get stepped on, steps are missed and people stumble as they carefully try not to break protocol or rules of business etiquette. Each part of the whole—planners, clients and suppliers—need to know exactly what their company policies and personal values will permit them to do, and be prepared to take a stand. Crossing business and per-sonal ethical limits in exchange for a sale may not be a part of the equation.

PART THREE

Codes of Conduct

Improprieties have taken place in offices from the White House and royal palaces on down to ordinary suites at home and around the globe. There was the case of the mayor who allegedly had a girlfriend and wanted to bring her to events at their workplace, which also happened to be where his other half worked. Interns are having intimate private parties for two, where meetings of another kind are taking place across a boardroom table. Newspapers reported a governor leaving his wife and family on Thanksgiving Day to spend it with another woman—divorce is on the horizon. The world is changing. Everything is out in the open for everyone to read about over their morning coffee or as they gather by the water cooler. Sex happens in business, in airplane washrooms (the infamous Mile High Club) and even during an evening out. More and more upscale restaurants are adding bathroom attendants whose duties include more than making sure their bathroom facilities are kept up to par. They are also there to make sure that nothing inappropriate or illegal (drugs) takes place in their bathroom stalls. Affairs are carried on in the office, people have too much to drink and are overly familiar with guests in social settings, books are being cooked, lies are being told, people are being indiscreet and it is all being done right in the open, in the news and on TV.

White-collar crimes are being committed and top business executives are being led off in handcuffs or appearing on front pages of newpapers. Advertisers, clients and suppliers are shying away from having their product or company linked by association to theirs. Ethics have become lax, standards have been lowered and raising the bar and setting and maintaining codes of conduct at home and in the office has become challenging. No longer is life lived by example.

The pendulum has swung too far and now companies and individuals are stepping in and stepping up professional and personal standards in their lives and workplaces. Bad behavior is no longer excused and people are being held accountable to personal and business codes of conduct. On September 11, 2001 and the days that followed, the world saw people pulling together and cooperating with one another in a new way. Heroes were everyday people doing their best for their families, friends and others, and no longer were celebrities who exhibited behavior unbecoming their position tolerated.

How people behave out in the world, in their homes and at their offices will be open to intense scrutiny. More and more people will be asking "Would I do business with you personally?" and "Why should I do business with your company?" The company your company keeps and the behavior your suppliers and staff exhibit reflect back not only on you and your company but on the client's business ventures as well. People have seen firsthand on the front pages how one company's image has pulled down another's by business and personal association. One multimedia corporation talked publicly about the great financial losses they incurred when their company head was being investigated for insider trading. Advertisers did not want their company to be linked to their product.

Alliances, endorsements and referrals will take on new meaning and strength, with companies being very careful about who they choose to do business with in the future. Companies will be looking to do business with event planning companies that can create excitement, not indictment, and vice versa. Old relationships will be reviewed, and some will be renewed while others will be discarded. Business behavior will play a big part—and clients looking for the best deal will be wary if they feel it comes with unethical strings attached. They would rather initially pay more than pay a higher cost personally and professionally somewhere down the line if business is not going to be conducted aboveboard. People know it is their credibility and their reputation that is at stake. Employees will no longer take a personal risk to save or make their company money if they are being asked to do anything that smacks of being unethical, unseemly or unprofessional, and they will be quick to disassociate themselves from the action and the company they work for or do business with. From former president Bill Clinton to Enron, lack of honesty is seen as a problem everywhere. Everyone is being held up to a higher code of conduct in this changing world.

6
CODES OF CONDUCT IN THE OFFICE

CLIENTS, SUPPLIERS AND PLANNERS

Codes of conduct in the office need to be clearly defined. We all know from former president Bill Clinton's statement, "I did not have sex with that person," how important a clear definition is. It must leave room for no misunderstandings, misinterpretation or misbehavior and must be firmly established. Your colleagues, employers, employees, suppliers and clients will be watching with new eyes to see how business is being conducted and how individuals are presenting themselves and interacting with others. It is time for "plain speak" not social niceties when codes of conduct are being laid out, defined and addressed. Let there be no room for confusion. The world is very clear when President George W. Bush speaks about what actions, behavior and people he considers "good" and who in his books is "evil." Everyone knows exactly where he stands on certain issues and what he believes to be true.

Many companies are busy dealing with pressing day-to-day issues and do not take the time to set out company responsibility, office policies and procedures, let alone review or update them. Now setting out codes of conduct and professional principles are added to the mix of what is expected. In the past, some companies were lax on training, cautious about investing time and money in employees in case they left. In many cases, staff were thrown into situations to sink or swim. Some followed bad habits of fellow employees simply because no one taught them the office rules of what is and is not permissible. One company's envelopes have "Official Business Penalty for Private Use $300" imprinted on the outside. One can only guess about what has gone on in that company to get to a place where warnings of misuse are printed on office stationery. An office's profits can be quietly eroded by employees using company supplies—pencils, pens, paper clips, paper, tape, sticky notes, file folders, push pins, markers, envelopes, stamps and equipment (e.g., photocopiers, computers and printers)—for personal use. What can seem inconsequential adds up rapidly if not checked. Employees often take their lead about what is permissible from their bosses. If the boss takes home company supplies, it may be OK for everyone else to do so, but there is little consideration that it could be legally considered petty theft.

Time is something else that is often stolen from companies. Fifteen minutes here on a personal call, another 20 minutes there on friendly chitchat, stepping outside for a cigarette, running personal errands on company time, playing computer games, sending and receiving personal e-mails and so it goes throughout the day while the work sits undone.

One company that offered flexible hours to their employees had one who misused the system. She would arrive into work each day at 6:00 a.m. or shortly after, proceed to go to the employee lunchroom to get coffee (which could have been picked up on her way in) and then sit back and chat on the telephone to her mother for a good half hour. She would then commence to eat breakfast at her desk, flipping through the daily newspaper. Time would then be spent catching up on office gossip with the receptionist when she made her mail deliveries at 7:00 a.m. This would go on for about 45 minutes. As other employees arrived to start their day, there would be more chitchat and more coffee fetched, Internet surfing until 9:00 a.m., when the employee would then actually start to work because management was now in. An early lunch hour would be taken and then they were off for home at 2:00 p.m.—their workday was officially over. This scene was played out in the office day after day.

There were no systems in place for monitoring how much work was being done and whether any company policies were being abused unless a witness spoke up. Companies expect some personal calls to be made on company time, as well as some doctor and dentist appointments, and there are always requests to leave early to attend school recitals and the like. It is generally a matter of give and take. Scorecards are not kept and personal respect is given. They know employees often work overtime or through their lunch hours to meet deadlines. There are companies that give, in addition to holidays, a specified number of personal days that staff can book off in advance or use if they or a member of their family is ill or they require them for personal use. There is mutual respect and appreciation on both sides.

But some companies have been forced to use protective measures because of employee misuse. They monitor telephone calls, e-mails, instant text messaging, documents and Internet use. Employees can be fired for misuse of office-owned materials, visiting porn sites on the Web or other inappropriate behavior. Companies are spying on their employees as a security measure, and also to protect themselves from loss of staff productivity, misbehavior, client leaks, breaches of company confidentiality and legal liabilities. Disclosure of what is being done and clear guidelines of accepted business practices in the office are key.

Attempts are made to control costs and determine what can be billed back to client accounts as communication costs, and systems are put in place to track the charges, but employees freely give out their passwords for long-distance calls, faxes and photocopiers to visiting suppliers and clients who need to use the telephone, send a fax or make a copy with little regard as to who else might be listening and might use the code for their own personal gain.

In some companies, obscene e-mail jokes are sent through the office and time is spent playing computer games with the sound turned off so as not to attract attention to how their time is actually being spent. Some people could care less, and play games right in the open until management is seen on the horizon. Company cell phones are being used for non-business calls and employers are having to spend time monitoring the numbers being dialed. Most employers expect to see some personal family calls and will absorb them if they are within reason. However, if an employee exceeds reasonable use the employer will charge them for the calls. Event planning is not a 9-to-5 job. There are times when 14-, 16- and

20-hour days are the norm and family members do need to be able to reach one another. There are times on site where it would not be recommended to leave cell phones turned on, such as in the middle of the client's presentation, but cell phones do come with vibrating options and hotel staff can find people in an emergency if the hotel operator is advised to put calls through to the registration desk, which is typically staffed and located near the room the event is being held in.

But in addition to monitoring how the company cell phone is being used, companies now need to set limits as to when the company cell phone can be used. Cases are before the courts and legal liabilities being reviewed to determine who can be charged if an employee causes an accident while conducting business on a company cell phone (i.e., talking while driving). The company could face charges. The same applies to personal injury. If an employee is injured while their attention is focused on text messaging or picking up e-mails in their line of work, they may be eligible for workman's compensation.

Some employers consider nothing off-limits in the office and will go through employee desks before staff arrive, after hours or even while they are in the office. One employee in an office meeting glanced up to see his employer going through his desk and remarked, "I hate it when she goes through my personal stuff." It was no secret to anyone in the office that their desks, as well as their garbage, were being searched. The owner did make sure that that never happened to her by always locking her office door. After all, who better than she to know how easily people can go through your desk if left unattended.

While some may consider their desks sacred sanctuaries, their personal lives are not held in the same regard. Intimate home life and dating details are often discussed in the office when they are best left at the office front door. There is often little thought given to who else may be around—confidential personal matters are discussed in front of suppliers and clients, and casual flippant behavior is demonstrated. It lowers the tone of the office and can lead to inappropriate behavior from others.

One client would arrive in an office and drop himself into the lap of one of the female employees, whoever happened to be seated. This client had been privy to talks about the employees' love lives and would jokingly (to him) announce his availability. Their lack of proper office code of conduct had led the client to believe that whatever he did would be acceptable. A polished and professional demeanor does not usually invite clients to take personal liberties in the office, although there are exceptions. And then the question remains of how to handle client's hands-on familiarity with employees. Event planning can be a huggy-kissy social industry.

Employers looking to employees not to abuse their company ethics or provisions need to do the same in kind. Some companies ask employees to put business expenses such as airline tickets, client lunches, long-distance calls and even office purchases on their personal credit cards or calling cards and submit the bills for payment. Should delays occur, such as the accountant is on vacation and forgot to leave signed checks, or the company may be in financial straits, it is the employees who are putting themselves at risk of being charged interest, not being repaid or even damaging their personal credit record.

In an attempt to save moving costs, an event planning company owner asked employees to help move heavy boxes and take down fixtures. One employee ended up in the hospital after being injured from lifting. The owner herself was not involved in the move due to ongoing back problems from old injuries. She was asking her staff to put themselves at physical risk, which she herself would not do, so that the company could save money. Injuries can have a quality-of-life impact for the individual and their family. Think twice about risking long-term injuries and your family's future to save someone a few dollars. Know what insurance coverage is offered by the company you work for. A commissioned salesperson slipped, fell and hurt her back helping move something at the office. Unfortunately, in this office, commissioned salespeople were not covered under the company's insurance policy. The employer's response was too bad, so sad, but there would be no compensation unless legal action was taken. Employers and employees need to have a clear understanding of what can be asked or expected, and their legal liabilities and insurance coverage should they become injured in the office or on related office business such as client meetings, site inspections, company-requested familiarization trips or during events.

Fair business practices is a code of conduct both employers and employees are looking for. The conduct of some owners regarding commissioned sales staff is questionable. Many commissioned salespeople are kept in the dark with regard to what their commission checks have been based on. Often there is not—from the salesperson's standpoint—full disclosure. While commission rates may differ, for the most part, their check is based on a negotiated percentage of the management fee, less all applicable expenses. What expenses are applicable is not always clearly defined. Client business lunches, gifts and other personal expenses may be deducted from the gross amount, as opposed to coming from a company promotional budget, with the commissioned salesperson picking up the full cost as opposed to costs being split between them and the office.

Many outside commissioned sales representatives do not have a problem with client-related expenses being subtracted, but do request a say in the type of client gift purchased and the dollar amount being spent. Client gifts are generally signed from the entire office and not just the sales rep. In some cases sales reps suspect that the company is not being upfront because the costs for client meals, gifts, etc., are sometimes billed back to the client under communication or promotional charges and are therefore not a business expense to be deduced from the bottom line. Some sales staff are kept from seeing how the actual final billings from suppliers compares to what is being charged to the client. They are aware that in some cases not all savings are passed back to the client, but the company is not making all information transparent for everyone to see.

The sales staff may also be concerned that if an owner has taken members of his or her family on the program, they are in fact paying for the owner's family to go. They may suspect that the costs to bring the family along was at least partially subtracted from their commission checks. And in some cases, they would be correct. It is a practice that has gone on in the industry.

Trustworthy conduct is important in the office. More time is spent in the office or on site with fellow employees than with family and friends, and trusting that the office will pull together to work as a team is very important—although not always demonstrated. One employee, working through the holidays to complete a deadline while the balance of the office was off, was devastated to find that her employer had come by the office and left again without stopping to see if she needed anything or if he could lend a hand. He had crept in using the back door and left the same way, but she had seen his car pull up right next to hers. The planner had small children at home waiting to be with her, and a boss who could not interrupt his day to acknowledge her commitment and give something back. One event planning company owner would rather hire staff to stuff envelopes than pitch in and help when there was a tight deadline and every spare pair of hands would be expected to work. This staff could not expect that their employer would be there if ever needed in a pinch.

Another event planning company owner operated under a different code of conduct. If he was needed, he was there. Stuffing envelopes, sending out for pizza when staff were working down to the wire, and if need be on program helping to make sure that their client's guests were being looked after. Staff turnaround in that office was minimal and staff members who did leave often asked to come back. Employee spouses were also supportive of the company. They pitched in when needed and were paid for their efforts, and were often invited on large programs to assist behind the scenes and not left behind. Company bonuses were paid and the owner would take the time to counsel junior employees on the merits of taking lump-sum income, such as company bonuses, and investing in growth areas rather than frittering it away here and there. The boss's boss had done that for him and it had enabled him to start up his own business. He was just passing on the gift of education that he had received to the people who worked for him.

One company was so intent on producing their own in-house event promoting their trust, caring and commitment to their staff that they forgot to show it. They scheduled the meeting to take place out of the office between 11:00 a.m. and 2:00 p.m. and the buses began transferring employees starting at 10:30 a.m. The office cafeteria did not open until 11:30 a.m. and closed again at 2:00 p.m., and the staff understandably assumed that if the meeting was taking place over lunch they would be looked after at their company pep rally. No coffee was available. No tea. Not even water. No hospitality, but we appreciate you as a company, please trust us to grow the company with your support, and thank you for doing a wonderful job. The whole impact of the meeting was lost. What was said was not shown. The employees were then shuttled back to work disgusted and disgruntled. They had seen the lavish food displays that management brought in over the years to serve to guests, but they didn't even get water. The conduct that the company showed was not one of caring, trust and commitment to their employees' well-being.

Titles, company cars and the like can sometimes tempt employees to move on and change companies, but these are meaningless if the company is not managed by a team of professionals. One employee loved her company, her work and servicing their clients, and resisted all offers to woo her elsewhere, even turning down opportunities to manage in the office she was in. What she wanted most of all was to stay with the company she worked for, doing the work that she loved, with some raises in income and to work occasionally from home so that she could be with her three small children. She wanted to manage her own time, productivity and income. Her desire was to manage her own business, not other people's—that held no appeal. She approached her employer with a plan. She wanted to bring on a personal assistant at her own expense to handle some of her paperwork, freeing her up to focus on sales and giving her a service backup. She requested a computer at home be linked to the office network. Her employer was receptive to the idea and it paid off big time for both the employer and the employee, so much so that the employee soon needed two personal assistants to manage the business she was producing. She didn't ask her employer to pay for the assistants because she wanted to be the only one to have full access to their time. She believed in herself and the employer believed in her enough to give something a little out of the ordinary a chance.

Openness to growth—personal as well as business—is conduct becoming an employer. They did not fear losing their employee or look for ways to bind them to the company. The computer at home became a gift, not a company loaner.

TIP Company cars are loaners, not gifts, and are often presented as a reward, but their true purpose can be to tie an employee to a company because when you leave, the car stays. It can be difficult to discern the true motive when it comes wrapped in a shiny package, but be wary of what you could be accepting along with the car keys.

One employer was content only when their management team was in the office or traveling on business. When it came time to schedule a senior executive's vacation time, there was always a reason it had to be put off. When time was finally given, urgent calls would be placed to return immediately due to work emergencies that they could not handle. The same work ethics—total commitment and dedication—that they demanded of staff did not apply to the employer. The company owner, rarely in the office, was often in the local pub down the street or "doing business" on the golf course, which can be a valid sales tool except that the owner was bringing in no new business and played only with golfing buddies. When he was in the office, he was gone every day by 2:00 p.m. No good-byes, just a quiet disappearing act. He would pack up the family, including kids and in-laws, and travel on all out-of-country company events. This behavior was not professional in the office or on program. Sales reps had difficulty with extended family members and children being present at their corporate client's events and were often left to explain why the owner's family was accompanying them and not there as a part of the working event team. Clients also wanted to know exactly who was picking up the cost of having them there. The sales reps who objected were told if they did not like it, they were free to leave. Many did, not wanting to continue to work there and risk their professional reputation by association.

A simple statement can demonstrate company standards. An unfailing "one moment please" sets a supplier's company apart from their peers' abrupt "hold on." "It would be my pleasure" or "How may I help you?" is how one hotel has instructed their staff to answer the telephone. What it shows incoming callers—clients and suppliers—is that business practices are in place and maintained, and that their employees are accountable for how they answer the telephone and treat incoming callers. This is critical because these incoming calls are often a prospective client's first interaction with the company.

Manners are no longer a thing of the past and are on the return. One company president makes it a policy to return all telephone calls within 24 hours. If she is out of town, a staff member returns her messages. It is done without fail. Clients notice. You don't want the planners, suppliers and even clients you deal with to have to resort to using special phone features to hide their company name from call display in the hopes of being able to speak to an actual person after messages go unanswered. It is better and less time consuming to deal with a caller on the spot once than to avoid numerous calls or voice messages.

Teach colleagues, suppliers and clients that time consideration is an important code of conduct to your company. One employee spent 20 minutes going on to another about the lack of consideration that a client had shown for their time, and then moved on to the next employee in their path voicing the same complaint. They did not stop to take a breath or consider their own actions—that they were stealing time away from another employee as well as their company. They were guilty of the same thing they were accusing their client of.

A sales rep loved to call staff on her way to work so she could begin her day, catching up on news while she was tied up in rush hour traffic. Employees, in early to get a jump start on their own day or working to get caught up, dreaded taking her incessant calls. They did not have time to engage in office gossip or politics, keeping someone amused so they would not be bored in traffic. They had their own work to do. The sales rep was demonstrating a lack of regard for others and the work they were in early specifically to complete. Rather than come in early or leave late to avoid being stuck in traffic, she preferred to sit in traffic and eat up valuable minutes of another employee's day. The situation couldn't continue, was addressed and was put to a stop.

Time, personal and business, is a precious commodity and needs to be treated with respect. Constant thought disruption, junk e-mails, forwarded jokes or other messages you're being copied on but that are not relevant to the work that is being done, and telephone calls where you know you are being used as "filler" to fill someone else's time while they are driving to work, in line-ups or waiting for a meeting—are not productive to the workday, office or individual. One sales rep, who did not have to punch a company time clock or put in a certain number of hours, would simply say to staff, "I'm off to a meeting. I'll call in for messages." Sometimes the meeting was with her hairdresser or manicurist, but she burdened no one with meaningless details. She wasted no one's time including her own.

TIP

When transferring calls to other extensions, be careful what is being said aloud in case the transfer connection did not go through. One client heard a staff member talking about them and what a pain they were to deal with. The staff member was horrified to see that the call had not gone to the other person's voice mail and that the client was still on the line. They tried to redeem themselves by saying the comments they made referred to another client, but they only dug the hole deeper. Either way, the client knew that the company standards did not include being respectful of clients.

Confidentiality is another code of conduct that can go missing in offices between staff, suppliers and clients. E-mails are freely forwarded and some are blind carbon copied to others without the recipient being aware of it. Discussions are held in the middle of the office when discretion should have been going on instead. In the middle of doing a final reconciliation one employee announced to the office that client XYZ had charged X-rated movies to the hotel bill. They could tell by the hotel coding which movies were family viewing and which ones were not. Another discussion that should have taken place in a private office was how to handle a client who wanted to change his flights and travel separately from the group, and instead of flying business class purchase two economy tickets instead—one for him and the other for his friend—while still billing the company for business class and pocketing any differences. Remember, names can be dropped easily and you don't always know who knows who is listening. Answering the telephone, an employee was startled to hear her next-door neighbor's voice on the line, and wondered how they knew to reach her at work. The neighbor was calling because she was now the agency's newest client. The employee had been unaware of where her neighbor worked and tried to recall what they might have said within her earshot about her company, working conditions, the staff and their business practices. Couriers, repairmen, delivery clerks and letter carriers come and go, and they are all someone's neighbor. The world is getting smaller each day and employees need to be careful what they say, where they say it and how they say it. The six degrees of separation theory does not always hold true. Sometimes you're not so far separated; sometimes the other person is right next door.

Blind carbon copy (bcc) when sending an e-mail to multiple business clients, contacts and suppliers because they may prefer to limit who has access to their e-mail address. Remember that business e-mails should be handled in a professional manner—spell checked, no smiley faces, not typed in capital letters (signifies yelling) and no e-mail shortform codes like LOL (short for lots of love or lots of laughs or laughing out loud).

Professional leadership and behavior are codes of conduct that employers, employees, clients and suppliers look for, and the first place they look is in the office. They are looking for companies who:

- Demonstrate high levels of ethical behavior at all times
- Exhibit professional conduct both inside and outside the office
- Have event planning proficiency—people who are experts in their field
- Do business with integrity and with no conflicts of interest
- Cultivate a climate of respect
- Hold client confidentiality in high regard
- Conduct business with transparency—full disclosure
- Value their employees and the contribution they make to building working relationships
- Encourage educational growth

7
CODES OF CONDUCT
ON SITE

CLIENTS, SUPPLIERS
AND PLANNERS

A chain of on-site command needs to be established between clients, suppliers and planners. There's a reason why an orchestra has only one conductor. Everyone involved is playing an important part in the overall production, but the conductor is responsible for directing when and how different sections will be brought in and for overseeing the entire performance. All those who have been assembled together to perform for the event will have their eyes focused on the conductor, waiting for instruction. In the case of an event, a designated lead planner is selected to be the conductor. Typically, the client contacts the event planning company to design their event and their planner brings in the right players (suppliers) to create an event that will meet all of the client's needs and objectives. Event planners work with an array of suppliers—not a limited palette. They custom design every event and are very careful about who they contract to handle various aspects of the event.

For example, in addition to doing sound and creating the actual audiovisual performance, an AV company may also do lighting. An event planner may choose, however, to bring them in for only one component and use another supplier to handle the lighting in order to obtain a very special effect they are expert at making. Two companies that are technically competitors could end up working on the same event for the event planner. The event planner is not doing this to bring about conflict, but to achieve a certain effect. Their high business ethics and company code of conduct may not allow them to duplicate the lighting company's creative ideas just to keep everything under one umbrella and make it easier for a single supplier. Doing that would not necessarily serve the client's interests. The event planner may have also come to know and trust the work of one supplier and will fly them in if necessary, rather than risk bringing less than the best to the client. Planners may try out new suppliers, but unless they have seen them operating first-hand elsewhere they usually start them in areas that are not crucial to the event's success. Event planners are sensitive to supplier confidentiality and what is revealed to the supplier's competition; there are times when they themselves are in the same position.

One corporate client hired a planning company to take care of all aspects of their event (travel arrangements, housing, food and beverage, entertainment and off-property activities) with the exception of the audiovisual production (what takes place on the stage) for their new product launch. For that, they were using the services of a communications house, which, like many such companies, had an event planning company division as part of its organization. The communications house wanted to handle both event components as well as the stage production, but in this case the client chose to go with a known-to-them event planning company for the event portion. Event planning companies that do not have a communications arm can have the capability to design audiovisual shows and stage production numbers by affiliating with an associate and subcontracting their services, which could limit creative options. The pro to an event planning company aligning themselves with a communications company is that it is one-stop shopping. The con is that by working with only one communications company, the diverse needs of all of the event planning company's clients may not be met. It would be the same as the planner only using one caterer to handle all of their events and having the caterer try to adapt their style of food preparation and presentation to fit any occasion when, in the case of a Japanese theme event, for instance, the skills and showmanship of a knife-wielding master sushi chef are required. Another alternative for the event planner is hiring different independent suppliers—audiovisual, lighting, staging and special effect companies—to create something exclusively for their client using the planning company's vision of how the event should look, feel and unfold.

In this example, the communications company fought the event planner every step of the way by delaying critical information such as show content, timing and logistics. They hoped to prove that their services were superior to the event planner's and to secure both parts of the business the following year. They banned the event planning company from their meetings with the client, and on site they attempted to bar the event planner from the meeting room when their show was being staged, even though the event planner was responsible for everything else that was taking place in the room. The client had to step in and resolve the issue, but it was clear that it was a one-sided war. The following year the client did award both parts of the program to one supplier—the event planning company who had maintained their professionalism throughout the whole ordeal and worked hard to not make the client feel caught in between.

Clearly, a single conductor would have been helpful. If everyone is off doing their own thing, the end result will be chaos and confusion and the integrity of the event will have been compromised. Egos are not supposed to be part of the equation, but often are. As the event moves closer, stress levels rise, tempers fray and power struggles come into being, with everything coming to a head in the form of an explosion of bad business behavior, as demonstrated in the above example.

When an event is about to take place, there are three stages when two or more of the parties involved—clients, suppliers and planners—will come together to finalize the plan of action. These stages are:

- Pre-Event Meetings (Pre-Cons, short for Pre-Convention or Pre-Conference)
- On-Site Event Orchestration
- Post-Event Celebrations

PRE-EVENT MEETINGS (PRE-CONS)

A pre-con is a meeting that takes place before the event. It's a dry run of what has to be done. First-draft detailed event function sheets—on which all event elements, inclusions, timing and logistics are outlined in great detail so that all involved have a clear understanding of what will be taking place, where it will take place and, under the event planner's direction, when and how they should all come together—will have been sent out to the client and to the various suppliers in advance of the pre-con. Advanced circulation of these sheets allows the client and the various suppliers sufficient time for review, and allows the planner time to make any changes and prepare the final copy. For more information on function sheets please refer to *Event Planning: The Ultimate Guide to Successful Meetings, Corporate Events, Fundraising Galas, Conferences, Conventions, Incentives and Other Special Events* (John Wiley & Sons, 2000), which includes sample function sheets, and *The Business of Event Planning: Behind-the-Scenes Secrets of Successful Special Events* (John Wiley & Sons, 2002).

Once the first draft has been reviewed, and changes incorporated, a final draft is prepared. The final draft will be sent out before the meeting to the planner and the various suppliers taking part in the event . This gives suppliers time to review any additions or deletions and prepare a list of questions or suggestions to discuss at the meeting.

There are two pre-cons. One takes place between the client and the event planner to finalize any outstanding details such as event additions and deletions. For instance, if an event is coming in on or under budget, a client may opt to add extras at this time, such as hosting an open bar as opposed to only having wine served at the table. A separate pre-con is held between the event planner and their suppliers. The supplier pre-con meeting can often be a changing of the guards, because upper management, rather than the operational staff that have been working on the file, will attend, and items that have been previously agreed upon may need to be negotiated once again.

Event planning staff go into both pre-cons fully prepared. In the case of a hotel supplier pre-con the event planner can be addressing what appears to be a cast of thousands—one hotel pre-con had over 50 people in attendance. Sometimes the review is delayed because the senior representatives who sit in on the pre-con meetings are not necessarily always up to speed with the event planning function sheets. Difficulties can also arise when one department has authorized something another department disagrees with, such as setting up a private satellite check-in for the guests. For some representatives it may be the first time they are seeing the event planning function sheets as opposed to their own in-house version, and there may be points that have been agreed on, signed off on by operations managers and are now under dispute.

Key issues that have been resolved may surface again in the pre-con, and the event planning staff needs to expect that and be prepared to handle sticky situations. For example, one Asian company insisted that no guest of their event be assigned a guestroom on the same floor or on a higher floor than the company president; this was a matter of great cultural and corporate concern to them. The issue had been resolved with the rooms manager and was one of the terms of the signed contract. The company president was to be assigned a suite in one of the hotel's two towers, while their guests would be housed in the other tower. The front desk manager that would be on duty that day objected. He wanted to assign whichever rooms became available first to guests, regardless of which tower they were in.

The event planner is sometimes caught in the middle of internal power struggles and office politics. Power struggles have no business being brought into the meeting room during the pre-con, but too often occur. Instead of walking into a review of event details, planners may find themselves caught in the throes of a heated debate between division heads. While the division heads' code of conduct is unacceptable, it should be anticipated and prepared for back in the office. Event planning staff need to be taught how to lead a meeting (and not let the supplier attempt that), make sure they follow their meeting agenda (and not the suppliers'), take control of the meeting if it gets out of hand and to hold firm to what has been contractually guaranteed.

There is strength in numbers. If the supplier is sending a contingent of 50, the event planning company will need to send in at least one additional representative to take notes and be aware of what is going on in the room while the other company representative addresses the meeting. Generally the lead event planner and the event planning sales rep attend the supplier pre-con—they are the ones who know the event requirements inside and out—and they should be free to focus on the meeting. Adding one more staff member whose role is strictly to make observations and record any changes is recommended.

Planners need to know in advance exactly who will be attending the pre-con meeting so that they can ensure everyone has received their own copy of the final set of function sheets in advance of getting together for last-minute instructions. Many planners don't like to limit the number of supplier attendees because the more people who know what will be expected of them and the manner in which it is to be done, the better informed the people reporting to them will be and the event will run smoother.

T I P	When scheduling a supplier pre-con meeting, confirm in advance who will be attending (name, title, department), see if they have received a copy of the event planning company's function sheets and check to see if any key operational contacts will be on vacation, on a seminar or not attending the pre-con for any other reason.

One operations manager, who knew that there were going to be many surprises awaiting the event planning staff when they arrived, scheduled her vacation for the important dates, including the advance move in. She told no one in the event planning company's operation department that she would be out of the country over that time period even though she spoke to them the day before her vacation, which was also the day the planner was scheduled to arrive (although the company president did track her down). Fortunately, the event planning company was fully prepared for unforeseen emergencies, and brought copies of all operational correspondence and signed contracts. These proved to be invaluable because the function space that had been contracted had been double-booked and the other client had already set up their heavy equipment display in the ballroom. It looked like they were going to be moved to less desirable space. Because the event planning staff had backup in writing, they were able to have everything resolved to their satisfaction with the help of the hotel president's help. A luxurious private villa was secured for the event, catered by the hotel, and added features such as an extended cocktail party were thrown in, all at no cost to the client. The villa was one that was well known and guests were impressed with their host's selection. They were never aware that a change of venue—for the better and initially not in the client's price range—had been made.

Both the event planning company and their suppliers need to hold themselves to a professional code of conduct during the pre-con. It must be clearly established that anything affecting the event must be cleared through the lead event planner. For example, rooms cannot be upgraded or substituted at the supplier's discretion. Event planning sign-off and approval must be obtained without exception. It is a non-negotiable issue. In another case sales staff made room substitution changes before the group arrived that were not as per the company's contract. The poolside rooms that the group had blocked had been assigned to another group. Their rooms were now being assigned hillside, which were not as contracted or acceptable. The hotel ended up upgrading all rooms at no charge, providing special concessions and waiving the cost of all rooms for the duration of the group's stay—all because what had been legally signed and contracted was not going to be provided. Oceanfront rooms were given to all participants in the end.

ON-SITE EVENT ORCHESTRATION

The codes of conduct areas between clients, suppliers and event planners that need to be defined before the function sheets are prepared and outlined in them include:

- Client Expectation
- Interaction of Client, Planner and Suppliers
- Dress Codes
- Behavior
- Teamwork
- Eating and Drinking
- Schlepping
- Personal Expenses
- Add-On Charges
- Respect

CLIENT EXPECTATION

Event planning sales reps and staff need to determine client expectations, which are very different from client event expectations and event objectives (these, along with strategic planning techniques to achieve them, are covered in depth in *The Business of Event Planning: Behind-the-Scenes Secrets of Successful Special Events* (John Wiley & Sons, 2002). The client's expectations include trusting those planners and suppliers working on their event to keep client confidentiality and to be discreet when they are speaking directly to the client's own internal staff by not passing on tidbits of office gossip and goings on they may have been privy to. Clients also expect that those they hire to plan their events will embrace their corporate culture and be able to work within cultural framework. For example, while times are changing, in some cultures it is still very important to do business only with men, and one event planning company got into hot water over this point. The corporate client president and his management team were furious to find out that their male event planning sales rep was not going to be present at their event because the rep had scheduled his vacation at that time. As well, the planning company president had not planned on attending in the sales rep's stead. The client was not told in advance about this breach—to them—of business etiquette. In the end, the planning company president had to fly in for the day to apologize for this lapse of professional judgment. It was known that to this client, utmost importance was placed on having a male counterpart attend. Any of the female event planning staff could be standing right beside the male representative, but the client would not speak directly to them. They would speak only to the male, who would then turn and direct the female staff to do their client's bidding. It was their culture, their way of doing business, and it was their expectation to have male representatives be on site. Ethically speaking, the event planning company should have either turned down this job, declined the sales rep's request to go on vacation during the event or made alternative arrangements to have another male representative on hand during the event (and introduced to the clients well in advance of their event taking place) since they knew the client's cultural attitude.

Client expectations can take other forms. One client wanted an event planning staff member assigned exclusively to look after her daughters and to personally accompany them when they went out.

The time to find this out is well before the event takes place, so that additional staff can be brought on site to look after very specific requests. Event planning orchestration is tightly structured and every person has a job to do. To unexpectedly lose a skilled person and member of the team so that they can play babysitter can impact the quality of the event. Client expectation and special needs must be determined in advance.

Interaction of Client, Planner and Suppliers

On site, the chain of command is such that usually the supplier and their staff report to their client, which is the event planner. The event planner's staff keep the lead event planner apprised of all matters, and it is he or she and their event planning sales rep who obtain client approval for any changes or additions. The suppliers do not go directly to the event planner's client. That is not an accepted business code of conduct. After all, the supplier was not hired by the corporate client. They were chosen and contracted by the event planning company. People say you should never get between a bear cub and its mother—they obviously have not witnessed the reaction of a planner whose supplier goes directly to the corporate client! If a supplier works to circumvent the planner, they are violating the accepted event planning code of conduct. The same applies if an event planning company tries to go around their own sales rep to the client without keeping the sales rep updated. The sales rep is not an independent entity as the supplier is, and is equally possessive of their role—having brought the client to the event planning company—and should not be excluded. Sales reps prefer that the planners apprise them if any decisions need to be made, and it is their place to discuss the matter directly with their client. Once trust has been broken, it is not easily—and may never be—repaired, as there will always be doubt about true intentions.

Supplier suggestions are always welcome, but should be made to the planner and not directly to the client. More and more suppliers have crossed that ethical business boundary hoping to have a client book directly with them the next time. Event planning companies can thwart suppliers' suggestions along the way as they work to strategically meet their clients' objectives—and for suppliers with hidden agendas it is easier for them to meet their own personal objectives if an event planning company is not in the middle.

For instance, a caterer may recommend venues that are not necessarily right for the client, but are right for them. The caterer may be an approved supplier at one venue but not at the one that is the perfect fit for achieving the big picture results—the purpose of holding the event. Their hidden agenda may be to have the event held at a venue they can cater at and receive a referral fee for recommending. Caterers care about the food, the service and the presentation, but that is just one small event element. To the professional event planner the food is an event inclusion to get them to a specific objective. If the venue is the absolute right fit but the caterer is not on their approval list, the event planner will stay with the venue and work to have catering approval granted, which can sometimes be done at a surcharge. If costs to bring in the caterer become prohibitive, the event planner will go with what best fits their client's needs, not the caterer's.

On site there is a new element thrown into the mix—the client's guests. Usually the guests interact with the event planning staff, and supplier access to the client's guests is limited. Individual event planning companies will have their own in-house code of conduct about client, guest and staff interaction, which defines acceptable behavior. The event planning company must review their standard procedure with their client and see what adjustments need to be made to issues of dress codes, staff meals and staff participation. Every client is different. For example, one client holding a meeting on a cruise wanted the event planning staff to dine with them every night at their tables, while another company wanted the event planning staff to eat at the same time as their guests but to sit separately and be accessible to them should they need them during dinner. Yet another company preferred the staff to eat dinner before their guests, so that they would be available to go to the lounge and hold group seating for the VIPs.

Clients' code of conduct is not an area to be left to chance. One corporate company president physically pulled an event planning staff member off the dance floor after she had been asked to dance by a senior executive. He was angry that the planning staff was mixing with their guests since all the staff were there to work, not play. In fact, the planning company's policy was no dancing with guests, but the event planning staff felt this could be an exception because it was not with a guest but one of the client's senior corporate executives. Put in a similar situation, another event planning staff member excused himself politely and left the scene on the pretext of having an urgent matter to attend to. In another instance, one of the client's guests had had far too much to drink and was harassing one of the female staff members. Fortunately, this event planning company had a policy at events where liquor was flowing freely of teaming staff in a "buddy system," so that if one was in trouble the other could come to their aid. Their female staff members were never placed in a dangerous or compromising position. As the event planning buddy came to the rescue, so did members from the corporate client's executive team. They took control of their wayward staff member and led him away from the party and back to his room. The corporate client had a buddy system in place as well, making sure that their staff were taking care of one another. They defused the situation by engaging their colleague in jovial banter—allowing the female staff member to graciously make her escape—and suggested that maybe it was time for them all to call it a night and they would walk him back to his room to make sure that he safely got there.

It is a sign of the times that it is not only the females that need to be on their guard and have a buddy safety system in place. Male staff members have also been sexually harassed by female guests. One female guest came on to a male staff member openly in front of her husband and not just once but several times during the course of the evening, attempting to touch him and inviting him to dance. A fight was close to brewing. Female event planning staff came to their male staff member's rescue asking if they could have his help with a request from the company president, and whisked him away from a potentially harmful situation. Hearing the company president's name gently reminded the husband that he was at his office function and that better business behavior needed to be displayed by both his wife and himself.

One event planning sales rep crossed company policy codes of conduct by accepting an invitation to join the client's guests in an impromptu midnight skinny-dip at a resort. The event planning company lost that account because of this inappropriate action. Ensuring guest safety was also an issue—guests had been heavily drinking, and were swimming without lifeguard supervision in a pool that was closed to the public. The sales rep witnessed this and took no safety action. The only action he took was to take off his clothes and join in. Questionable guest conduct is not for the event planners to judge and certainly not to join in with. If the planning company has concerns, they need to deal with them with the client's company heads, and in cases where guests' safety is an issue these concerns need to be dealt with immediately. Had an accident occurred and a guest been seriously injured, the event planning company could have been held accountable because a member of their staff was present when the incident was taking place.

Guests are not always on their best behavior. After all, they are there to party and play in most cases. Bars are hosted (and complimentary) and drinks are plentiful. Event planning staff need to be prepared to handle adult situations, such as guests drinking to excess, drinking and driving, sexual misconduct, fighting, drugs and even death by natural or preventable causes.

Events can get wild. It is not an everyday occurrence, but it can and does happen. One event planning staff member remarked that she would have been better off having a bowl of condoms on the registration desk as opposed to candy. An incident at one event resulted in rape charges being brought forward. In another, the sheriff was called and a guest who had tried to push his boss through a plate glass window was led away in handcuffs. Clients have died during events. One client attending a farewell event in the Caribbean said their goodnights, went back to their guestroom, and never woke up. In another, a deadly car crash claimed a client's life during a road rally event. One emergency took place at a children's party, which was being held in the day in a nightclub. A small child picked up something she found on the floor and put it in her mouth. It was a drug—Ecstasy—left over from the night before and missed in cleanup. The mother was able to retrieve half of the pill and the child was raced to emergency care. The facility is reportedly being sued for negligence.

Event planners need to be aware, be prepared and have a plan of action to handle all possible situations. They need to have a policy on what to do if a guest invites himself or herself unaccompanied into another's hotel room, for instance. One event planning staff member was to go to a hotel to see a celebrity guest off in the morning. The guest said that he hated to have breakfast alone and asked her to join him for coffee in the lounge before he left for the airport. The event planner agreed to what seemed an acceptable request. The next morning she arrived at the hotel but the guest was not in the lobby as planned. Calling his room, she was informed that he had taken the liberty of having breakfast ordered to the room for both of them. That was the only liberty he was going to be taking. The staff member thanked him but said that she would meet him in the lobby when he was finished and that in the meantime she would send a bellman to his room to pick up his luggage and make sure that the limousine was waiting out front. The event planner did the job she was there to do and did not put herself at personal or professional risk.

DRESS CODES

Event planners need to set dress policy for their staff and suppliers in accordance with standards set by them and their clients. For example, is it permissible for the suppliers to be in clothing with their company logo on it or does the client prefer to provide all staff with shirts bearing their corporate identification? These issues need to be discussed.

Can staff, on a cruise for example, dress for dinner or do they need to be in company uniform the entire time? If dressing for dinner is acceptable, what specific articles of clothing are acceptable? A backless dress might not be in accordance with the standards of both the event planning company and the client. One customer was turned off by an event planning employee wearing a fanny pack on a beach activity day. He did not think that it looked professional. Some clients will allow their staff to wear shorts in tropical destinations, while others prefer to see them in more formal attire. Staff need to know what to bring on site.

Standards also need to be set for when staff are at leisure. If at a hotel, the planning staff are permitted to enjoy the facilities when they are not scheduled to work, are bikinis or thongs permitted on the beach or by the pool? Can the men wear T-shirts, shorts and sandals as they walk through the hotel in off-hours? Proper attire also applies to the staffs' off time when they are still visable to the clients and guests. Have company standards been set and made clear to employees? There is also the issue of what event planning staff are allowed to do when on site. If they are on their own time and spending their own money, can they visit the resort's spa? Or would the client have objections to seeing a working staff member taking the timeslot that could have been made available to one of their guests? An event planning company's standards may be high, but they still need to review them with their client to see if they agree on what is and is not acceptable dress for work and off time, as well as what staff may be permitted to do when they are not scheduled to work.

BEHAVIOR

Professional behavior between event planners and suppliers is expected at all times. If there is an area of conflict, take it away from guests and the rest of the staff and resolve the matter away from the eyes and ears of others.

Event planning standards, how clients want things done, and supplier operating procedures may differ. It can be a simple thing, such as how cups and saucers are to be displayed at a food station. The facility's day-to-day setup style may be to stack the cups and saucers together but in separate piles, while the event planner may have stipulated in his or her function sheets that they wish the cups to be placed on the saucers and then stacked to make it easier for guests to pick them up. This may be a client or company preference for a more polished presentation. A battle of wills will take place if the supplier's staff reverts to form and will not set the table as requested.

The event planning staff will not depart until everything is exactly as requested, confirmed and reviewed in the pre-con, and if need be they will physically correct the situation themselves. Of course, that can upset the supplier's staff. But planners will not settle for less than the best for their clients. Countless hotels have said in the beginning that they don't do private check-ins and that all guests must register at the front desk and stand in line with the others. For meeting planners and incentive houses this is not acceptable option—they want the guests to feel like VIPs, who do not have to stand in line. They will prefer to set up a private group check-in, and will move through the hotel chain of command to ensure what they need will be accommodated. Sometimes they will go directly to the top, which can cause hard feelings among those they have bypassed. Event planners will train the hotel staff on what they know needs to be done, as in the case of private check–ins, if the hotel is unfamiliar with the procedures of how to do it easily and effortlessly.

Supplier staff often underestimate the determination or lengths an event planning staff member will go to in order to have a flawless event execution. One event planner called top government officials to handle a dispute over moving unsightly cement trucks off of event property. They had been brought in on the Friday before an event for construction that was not taking place until Monday. Instead of a view overlooking the ocean, guests would be seeing a line of trucks blocking the view. The hotel could not get the construction owner to move the trucks off their property, but government officials valuing tourist dollars being spent in their country succeeded. The event planning company and their client were happy, but the hotel senior staff were not as they could be facing reprimands and repercussions on Monday for not having found a way to solve the problem on their own. Event planners need to be very aware of this, and ensure that they handle their part diplomatically. They are gone come Monday, but the people they leave in their wake could suffer consequences.

Planners know that problems will occur because the supplier staff that are working the event have not been a part of the planning, operational or pre-con process, and have simply been brought in on the day of the event to work. What could be viewed as a display of defiance may simply be an employee following their normal daily routine, determined to do their job as they have been instructed to in the past. Not all suppliers fully prep their staff about changes in procedures. Experienced event planners anticipate this and build in buffer time when advancing a setup. Time has to be factored in to be able to handle any last-minute glitches. Displays of tempers on either side won't solve the problem and will be seen as unprofessional behavior.

Demonstrating professional behavior does not stop at the end of an assigned work shift. Proper business decorum must be shown throughout the day and the night regardless if an employee is scheduled to work or not. What behavior is deemed acceptable must be bluntly laid out back in the office. Out of town, on-site event directors and supplier staff have been caught up in one-night stands and ongoing affairs, not necessarily with each other but with clients' guests and local staff. One event planner was allowing local staff entry to her bedroom through her ground floor patio doors, hoping to avoid being caught. One of the client's guests reported the incident. That kind of behavior reflects on the company as a whole.

Sometimes true love, not lust, can be ignited on an event program, but budding romance or not professional business levels must be maintained. Back at home, if you decide to pursue an interest, know in advance your office policy about company or client dating. What happens if the romance continues and the client's employee then wants to take their new companion as their guest to the next event or out-of-town trip? When setting office policies and procedures, make sure that the art of visualization that is used when planning an event is used to see the far-reaching impacts.

TEAMWORK

Never leave a fellow employee stranded. Remember to take care of your own. One event planning company owner gathered those of his troops who were not scheduled to work to have dinner with him. Everyone relaxed and had so good a time that they completely forgot about their working colleagues. The other staff members were tired and hungry after long shifts and no one had notified them where everyone was headed. Walkie-talkies had been turned off during the meal, leaving the other staff to handle whatever came up. A hotel staff member was dispatched on a hunt and seek mission to find their wayward staff and remind them that a program was going on and they needed to be responsible not only to the client but also to their fellow staff members. The working staff never abandoned their posts but felt abandoned by their peers. An event is set up as a relay team with each person depending on the next to be there, ready and waiting to take the baton and run with it when the responsibilities are handed off. They are counting on each member of the team to do their part.

EATING AND DRINKING

Event planners must establish codes of conduct for their staff members and suppliers with regard to drinking (not just alcoholic beverages) and eating on the job, and it is always a good idea to check in with the client to see if the two are in sync on such policies. Can coffee, tea, soda or water be consumed at the registration or hospitality desk? Is it OK to set the beverage out in the open or should it be tucked discreetly out of sight (which is much more professional)? Will staff be eating in the same room with guests or in a separate area away from the event? Is staff permitted to drink alcohol while off duty? What about while on duty? Some event planning companies permit it. Clients and their guests—caught up in the moment—have been known to bring their sales rep a beer during an afternoon sporting activity or tell planning staff to help themselves at the bar at an evening event.

The issue of whether it is permissible for planning staff or their suppliers to drink while on or off duty is one that needs to be established by the event planning company, not the client. It's best not to drink. It is important to remember that in the event of an emergency, everyone needs to be ready to perform at a moment's notice. There could be legal ramifications if something goes wrong and staff have been drinking. How are staff members supposed to handle a corporate client president's invitation to have a drink? What is the preferred behavior and response? A polite "Thank you. I'd love some juice, a soda or water once I'm finished working" (not a beer, glass of wine or alcoholic drink) or a simple "I'm fine, thank you" is sufficient—depending on the event planning company's policy.

One event planning staff member accepted the offer of a drink from a company president and when asked what she would like to drink replied, "Champagne." Taken aback, the company president, who was out of line as was the employee, answered, "You are not worth the price of champagne." This exchange took place in front of the client's guests, who were then placed in an embarrassing spot. One guest joked that he'd pick up her tab in the hopes of dispelling the tension, but that only served to make it worse. Ice wine, which is rather expensive by the glass, was the beverage of choice for a planner at another event. The client was surprised by her request for the beverage. Firstly, it was not something that was even being offered to their guests, and secondly, it was never their intention to offer the staff member an alcoholic drink—a beverage, yes, an alcoholic one, no. But they hadn't clarified their offer. In both cases, the event planning staff felt accepting an alcoholic beverage, not requesting a soda or juice, did not overstep the code of conduct while working. Boundaries had never been set out by the event planning office and they had never been instructed to politely say that they didn't drink, and therefore presumed it was their choice. Some event planning companies would never assume that even if they did permit their staff to accept an offer for a drink that their staff's choice would be alcoholic, and that their employees would take liberties and ask for champagne or ice wine. Set office guidelines as well as boundaries.

One client who was serving champagne at an event wanted to keep costs down but ensure that her guests who would appreciate a fine glass of champagne weren't disappointed. The client requested that her planner order champagne at two different price points. The less expensive champagne was free flowing and passed on silver trays to the majority of the guests. The bar was instructed to open a bottle of the best champagne only for the hostess, who would go to the bar personally to pick it up. The hostess would then take the opened bottle and top up the glasses of their guests seated at their VIP tables with the better champagne. The other guests, seeing the brand of champagne being poured (the brand was easily identifiable by the shape of the bottle), thought they too were being served only the best, which was the hostess's intention but not a cost she wanted to bear. The host was not being ethical. She was being economical. She wanted to create the illusion of being thought of by her guests, and be written up in the media, as a lavish big spender. Allusions as to her character and the code of conduct she entertained guests under would have been destroyed had the truth ever come out how her guests had been intentionally misled.

Schlepping

Some clients think that hiring event planners means that they will include in their duties the schlepping of goods to and from the event. Some event planning companies try to use their suppliers in this way. This is wrong. People should be hired for their expertise, not to be on call to fetch and carry.

At the end of their client pre-con meeting, one event planning company found themselves being loaded down by their clients with material they wanted them to be responsible for and carry. The planning company had already provided the client with information on the best ways to ship material to the event, the timelines, the customs guidelines, delivery instructions and reminders of shipping deadlines—all of which the client had chosen to ignore. The client thought they could save money by having the planning staff bring the materials with them. The event planning company's policy was that they would gladly help their clients make arrangements to send goods such as printed material to the event and have it shipped back afterwards, but their staff could not be responsible for carrying anything with them personally or checking client material in under their name at airports. In the end, the client decided to divide up the material for their own staff members to carry down rather than pay overnight shipping costs. The client's staff should have been concerned regarding any health risks. If any of the staff members became injured by lifting heavy items on company business and suffered long-term disability as a result, they may or may not be covered by insurance. For out-of-country events, were they placing themselves at any personal risk by transporting goods across borders? The answer is yes.

Event planning staff who travel the world need to make sure that they do nothing to trigger an entry under their name that could cause entry delays at customs and immigration, or refusals of entry, such as by being suspected of unlawfully importing goods without a license or goods that have been produced in a country that is not acceptable (because of trade agreements) to the country they are being brought into. Some companies, in the interest of saving dollars, foolishly go against the advice of their planning company and purchase goods that would be illegal to have shipped to a specific destination. For example, T-shirts with company logos with labels showing they were made in a country whose goods are not permitted in.

After September 11, 2001, it became even more important that no one carry anything on airplanes or other modes of transportation other than their personal belongings, which they packed themselves. There are delivery companies, ground transportation companies, porters at airports and bellmen with trolleys at the hotel to offer assistance to move items, and their charges and tips must be included in the program as a cost of doing the event. Event planning staff and their suppliers are not personal assistants to be used at a client's whim to save them money by fetching, carrying or performing menial tasks. The client's policy, and their staff's stance on what they are being asked to do, is between the client and their employees. One company president requested their planning staff be available to personally schlep for them, to draw their bath each night, lay out their clothes and pick up after them. That business code of conduct is not acceptable. It is not what the event planning company has been contracted to do. Their focus and attention must be devoted to the event at hand, and they cannot take time away from their responsibilities to act as a personal assistant. In this case the employee ended up having his own staff draw his bath and attend to his personal needs. A professional butler can be contracted worldwide (visit www.butlersguild.com) for a short-term event should services such as these be required. (For an incentive program, a personal butler can be provided for all of guests, only for the VIPs or for a specific event.) The event planning company can only offer their recommendations and provide direction. They can't afford to put their staff, their company or their supplier's staff or company at physical or personal risk or in a compromising position, and can only counsel their client to do the same. There are legal liabilities in many areas that companies need to consider.

PERSONAL EXPENSES

Event planning companies handle personal expenses and meal allowances in a variety of ways. Some companies pay staff a flat per diem regardless of what will be taking place, while others subtract meals from their per diem when provisions have been made to feed the staff. Other companies set a guideline for meal costs and have staff sign all meals to their guestrooms or to the master account. The system that is used is up to the individual office. Clients will sometimes have input, since in the end they are the ones paying for staff expenses, but what definitely needs to be decided is whether or not receipts must be provided as backup for a per diem.

Is it up to the individual to decide what they want to spend the set amount of money on? Some staff members may prefer food for the soul offered by a yoga session when they are off, and have a simple meal that would still allow them to remain within the meal per diem guidelines. Others may prefer to kick back and have a quiet meal in a quality restaurant away from the group, while some may prefer to recharge in their rooms with room service. What event planning companies can't afford to do is have their staff running on empty and restricted to a one-star meal allowance at a five-star resort. The staff do not have time to go off property in search of inexpensive meals, and cheap fast food or local grocery stores are not usually found in walking distance of top facilities.

Forgetting to factor taxes and tips into the meal cost can make it difficult for their staff as well. During an event everyone gives their all. Staff members do not hold employers to an eight-hour day; they are there until the job gets done. But they need to know that they are being looked after and they don't have to worry about whether or not they can afford to eat both breakfast and lunch on their per diem. One event planning company sent their staff off with a US $32 daily meal allowance in a hotel where that amount would not even cover breakfast, let alone breakfast with taxes and tipping. That sort of thing indicates poor homework and bad planning. The situation was resolved by having the staff sign all of their meals to the master account. If an event is taking place on a cruise ship, a meal allowance still needs to be costed in for beverages but it does not have to be excessive and could be based on four to six nonalcoholic beverages (sodas or specialty drinks such as a latte or cappuccino at the ship's coffee bar) per day. Of course, at an all-inclusive resort, a meal or beverage allowance would not be required.

ADD-ON CHARGES

When clients add event elements on site, these add-on charges are sometimes treated as "gotcha" charges and marked up exorbitantly by suppliers and event planners. They know that they have the client caught in a moment of emotion when they are likely to approve any expenditure. In the middle of a beach barbecue the client may authorize picking up the cost for all their guests to enjoy waterskiing, banana boat rides, personal watercraft and the like. At that moment, they do not care what it costs because their guests are having a wonderful time and they want to make it even better. The event planner may have suggested this add-on in their original proposal and had it refused as too expensive, but knowing human nature the planner realized that this was something the client was likely going to want when they were on site.

Done in advance, event planners would have worked with preferred suppliers, negotiated rates and prepared company liability waivers. In the middle of the event, however, planners have to work with their destination management company to secure the services of reputable local vendors on the spot, obtain their rates and waivers and deal with the concern that some guests may have already had a drink or two and should not be operating the equipment. One client was so insistent on including the motorized water sports at their party they had the event planning staff contact the hotel to have someone bring them over thousands of dollars in cash to pay the vendors so their guests could play. The client had already had a couple of drinks himself and would not be thwarted from his mission and was prepared to sign for any amount. Unethical suppliers and event planning companies may use this opportunity to inflate prices with items such as a rush charge, which may or may not be valid, and boost costs with hidden charges or profit markups.

Planners need to come to the event with prepared authorization forms for add-on charges, know who is authorized to sign them and have the client sign their approval of additional costs before moving forward. The forms should clearly detail the day the add-on took place, exactly what the activity was, the cost, who requested it, the supplier who provided it and the company executive who authorized it. It should be signed by the authorized client, planning company and supplier representative. Failure to obtain the proper signature from an employee who has signing authority could result in the event planning company being financially responsible for any additional charges, or could leave suppliers on the hook if there are any disputes at final reconciliation.

Another add-on charge that event planners try to prepare their clients for is their top executives being put in the position of picking up tabs for drinks, meals, sporting activities, sightseeing, taxis, tipping and other guest charges, or asking the on-site staff to handle it on their behalf and have it billed to the master account. Not all of the items, such as ice cream for everyone from local beach vendors, can be backed up with receipts. The client should be reminded to get handwritten receipts for backup if nothing else is available. Planners should try to note any expenditures they see taking place and keep a record of costs should the client have any questions with expenses their staff may have submitted.

Respect

Never should an individual help another break one of their own company rules. One event planning staff member on site at an all-inclusive resort was supplying a hotel employee with cigarettes and other amenities that were free to guests. Aiding and abetting someone to be dishonest is not acceptable or professional behavior. The event planner employee could reason it away—I don't smoke and the cigarettes are there free for guests, so I am only passing on what would have been my share if I smoked. But that doesn't cut it. The policy of the hotel is that their staff is not permitted to ask for or accept items from guests. To the hotel these items are in a sense office supplies, and misuse eats up their bottom line. In short it is stealing from their company. Company rules and regulations set by others must be respected by clients, suppliers and event planners.

POST-EVENT CELEBRATIONS

Post-event celebrations should take place back in the office when the event has come to an official conclusion, not right after the last guest leaves the event. There is still teardown and move out to be responsible for, loose ends to be tied up, master bills to be reviewed and signed off, and for out-of-country or overnight events, distribution of departure notices to be ensured, guestroom bills to be examined for unauthorized charges, baggage handling and morning breakfast to be overseen, transportation to be dispatched and client material being shipped back to their office to be gathered, packed and sealed by their staff. All this needs to be checked to see that all is in order. The time to let down your guard, relax over drinks and take a breath has not come until all guests have safely returned, luggage has been accounted for and everyone and everything has been looked after.

Generally, the first day back in the office is a time of reflection and review with the staff that were on site and those who remained behind staffing the office. Returning staff do little more than check voice mails, e-mails and incoming mail, and take the day to regroup and recharge. After an event there is always a certain sense of letdown, exhaustion, completion and event separation anxiety. What has been of primary importance for so long is now done, except for the final reconciliation, client, office and supplier review, and packing away of files. That will come when everyone has had a chance to settle back in. First days back are often a good time to schedule a celebratory lunch, gather thoughts, discuss the event but not individual guest, supplier or staff bad behavior (it's not a permissible code of on-site conduct to return telling tales and naming names) with the staff, make notes and share and savor the success—and the knowledge of how to make the next event even better—with the rest of the team. Any staff disciplinary action is done one-on-one and in private. If new office policies need to be put in place, that can be done and reviewed at a more appropriate time. In a few days, event reviews will be set up with both clients and suppliers.

CLIENT, SUPPLIER AND PLANNER CODES OF CONDUCT

Clients, suppliers and planners all need to determine their own individual codes of conduct and professional standards on site, and then compare them with the others to see if they are in accordance. Each company has to decide how far it will bend their rules for their client. For example, if an event planning company's policy is to have their staff dressed professionally in uniforms so that they are easily identifiable to guests and local staff, while the client would prefer a more casual look that will blend in and not appear so rigid, an advance discussion will determine if there are areas of compromise. The event planning company may decide to have staff dressed in uniform only on arrival and departure days for out-of-town events and allow them a more relaxed, but professional, dress code when they are overseeing other event elements. When establishing codes of conduct on site, some questions each client and supplier need to ask are:

Clients

- How do I want my staff interacting with the event planning staff?
- How do I want my guests interacting with my staff?
- How do I want my guests interacting with the event planning staff?
- How do I want my staff to dress on site?
- How do I want event planning staff and their suppliers to dress on site?
- What are my company's policies with regard to staff drinking or smoking during the event?
- What are my company's policies with regard to event planning staff and their suppliers drinking or smoking during the event?
- What are my company's policies regarding event planning staff meals? Do I want them to eat with us or on their own?
- When my staff is not scheduled to work, how should they be conducting themselves?
- When the event planning staff are not scheduled to work, do I want them by the pool or on the beach with my guests, or dropping by the event?

- Do I want my staff dancing with guests or other staff members?
- How do I want the event planning staff and their suppliers to conduct themselves if a guest or a staff member asks them to dance?
- Who does the event planning staff report to on site, apprising them of any program changes or areas of concern?
- Who on site from my staff will have authorization to make changes or approve additional charges?
- Who do I need to assign expense dollars, company credit card authorization and long-distance calling cards for the event?
- How much additional cash should I bring on site?
- What expenditures do I want billed back to the master account?
- What client-planner-supplier boundaries should not be crossed?
- Have I done everything to ensure that my company is fully insured and protected from legal liabilities that could be incurred on site?
- What conduct and business behavior do I expect to see from my staff, guests, planning company and their suppliers?
- What strategies do I need to put in place should any staff member or guest step out of line, drink too much, cause any damage or place themselves in compromising positions with other guests, company staff members or suppliers?

Suppliers

- What are my on-site behavior expectations for my staff?
- How do I want my staff to address the client, their guests and the event planning staff?
- What will be appropriate attire for the duration of the event?
- Do I want my staff eating meals with the event planning staff or do I prefer to have them dine separately so that we can use that time to touch base, talk privately regarding any event concerns and make any necessary program adjustments?
- Who am I delegating to authorize any changes and cost increases?
- How do I want my staff to handle any offers to dance, drink or mingle with the guests?

- What do I need to do to protect my company and my staff from any legal action or being placed in any situations that could be personally or professionally damaging to their reputations? Have I received the originals and made copies of all required permits, such as for parking, building and safety inspectors (e.g., tent setup), special effects (e.g., pyrotechnics), liquor and other licenses, insurance and fire marshal approval, from the venue?

Planners

- How do I want my staff interacting with the client and their guests?
- How do I want my staff interacting with the suppliers?
- How do I want my suppliers interacting with the client and their guests?
- How do I want my staff to dress on site?
- How do I want my suppliers to dress on site?
- What are my company's policies with regard to staff drinking or smoking during the event?
- What are my company's policies with regard to supplier's staff drinking or smoking during the event?
- What are my company's policies regarding event planning staff meals? Do I want us to eat with the clients if they invite us, or on our own to use the time to our advantage?
- How will meals be handled? Included? A per diem? Other?
- How should expense accounts be handled so that they are not abused?
- When my staff are not scheduled to be working, do I want them by the pool or on the beach with the client and their guests, or dropping by the event?
- When my supplier's staff is not scheduled to work, how should they be conducting themselves?
- With regard to dancing, do I want my staff dancing with guests or my clients if asked to take part in the festivities?
- How do I want the supplier's staff to conduct themselves should a guest or a client staff member ask them to dance?

- Who does the supplier's staff report to on site, apprising us of any program changes or areas of concern?

- Who on site from my staff will have authorization to make changes or approve additional charges?

- Who do I need to assign expense dollars, company credit card authorization and long-distance calling cards for the event?

- How much additional cash should I bring on site?

- What expenditures should I be prepared for?

- Have on-site additional charge form authorization sheets be prepared?

- What client-planner-supplier boundaries should not be crossed?

- Have I done everything to ensure that my company is fully insured and protected from legal liabilities that could be incurred on site? Have I received copies of all required permits, such as for parking, building and safety inspectors (e.g., tent setup), special effects (e.g., pyrotechnics), liquor and other licenses, insurance and fire marshal approval, from the venue and the suppliers?

- What conduct and business behavior do I expect to see from my suppliers, my staff, my client and their guests?

- What strategies do we need to put in place should any staff member, client, guest or supplier step out of line, drink too much, cause any damage or place themselves in compromising positions with the client, their company staff members, the guests or suppliers?

8
CODES OF CONDUCT ON SITE

EVENT PLANNING
CRISIS MANAGEMENT

Event planners need to be prepared to handle any emergency. In the past, event planners were concerned with being able to respond quickly and ethically, exhibiting proper business behavior and conduct to:

GUEST SAFETY AND SECURITY

- Fire
- Theft
- Personal Injury
- Drinking
- Drugs
- Rape Charges
- Fighting
- Death
- Legal Liabilities

EVENT FULFILMENT, SAFETY AND SECURITY

- Delays
- Strikes
- Permits
- Terms and Conditions
- Staffing
- Legal Liabilities

Today, terrorism and supplier bankruptcy have been thrown into the equation. The concern of supplier bankruptcy has risen in recent years. Business dramatically declined in the event planning and hospitality industry immediately following September 11, 2001, placing some event planning companies, suppliers and airlines in serious financial jeopardy. Will the supplier you are contracting and depositing with today still be in business when the event planned for a year from now takes place? This is now an area of serious concern.

Event planners need to consider not only the menu but their plan of action in a serious crisis when holding a simple dinner theater event. After a Moscow theater was held hostage by terrorists, this is a reality. There could easily be copycat hostage-takings in other parts of the world. Even after September 11, 2001 and heightened airport security, breaches have occurred. During the American Thanksgiving 2002 holiday crush, 15,982 pocketknives, 98 box cutters, six guns and a brick were confiscated at airports in the United States.

Now there is the additional concern of pilots not being permitted to fly because they have been drinking. It has been a long tradition of pilots not drinking and flying. Each airline has their own policy, rules and regulations in place regarding the number of hours that must elapse between a pilot drinking and flying an aircraft, for example, 10 to 12 hours. While pilots may have violated this in the past, it was not in the news as much as it is today. When an infraction occurs it is on television, on the radio, in newspapers and flashed across the Internet in minutes. Airline passengers are now greatly concerned. People flying are becoming diligent about reporting broken codes of conduct to authorities, not overlooking them. Passengers will not hesitate to take action on an aircraft if the crew needs assistance subduing another passenger.

People have been killed and seriously injured in hotels (Kenya), nightclubs (Bali) and even in McDonald's (Indonesia and India), movie theaters (Russia) and a circus show (Bangladesh) thanks to bombs, explosions and deliberately set fires. There were mysterious outbreaks aboard several cruise ships and large numbers of passengers became ill. It is questioned whether there was a common cause, such as viruses or terrorism, on the numerous infected ships.

Event planners must be prepared to handle these unexpected or uncontrollable events. Planning staff must be fully versed in emergency procedures, customs and protocol. With regard to customs and protocol, security checks may require removing shoes, veils and headwear, which may cross some guests' religious beliefs. Planners need to make sure that guests know what to expect and must be prepared should they encounter areas of resistance (e.g., one woman refused to remove her veil for a male photographer taking photo ID). Event safety and security, and multicultural and foreign event planning sensitivity are covered in detail in the second book in my Event Planning trilogy, *The Business of Event Planning: Behind-the-Scenes Secrets of Successful Special Events* (John Wiley & Sons, 2002).

Training is of paramount importance. Schools are now training children what to do if they see a gunman on property, disabled people are signing up for martial arts classes designed especially for them and airline personal are being trained to handle hijackers. Event planners must be prepared. They are managing and responsible for not only an event but guest security and safety.

Event planning crisis management is different from a force majeure (unexpected and uncontrollable event) occurrence. A force majeure is beyond their immediate control. It can be classified as an act of nature (such as hurricanes, earthquakes or flooding), of terrorism or of war. A crisis in event planning is a problem that has come to a head. For example, the florist sends the wrong flowers or doesn't show up on time. To an event planner, that is an event planning crisis. They are producing a live show and everything must go as planned without mishap. Some event planning crises are easy to fix. Others take more ingenuity. For example, suppose that during installation a tenting company drives a stake into a water main that was not marked during an inspection and the lawn is flooded. The event planning company and the tenting company had both done their jobs. Water officials had been called in to inspect and clearly marked the property for water lines, pipes, sprinklers and the pool system. The cable, gas and electrical companies had been in as well. What needed to be done had been done. Figuring out how something had been overlooked and finding someone to blame is not what needs to be done. An immediate solution has to be found. Playing the blame game is not going to resolve the problem when your new objective is finding a way to avoid having the guests attend the event in their galoshes. Planners need to kick immediately into event planning crisis management mode. Fixing the problem right away is the priority. Afterwards it is important to review what went wrong so that it won't happen again.

A major event planning crisis would be something along the lines of a medical emergency, death on site, fire or guest arrest—unexpected but still not a force majeure. Planners need to know how to handle each level of crisis and the conduct they, their staff and suppliers will be expected to exhibit.

Crisis management mode—expected business behavior in an event planning emergency crisis—consists of three parts. These three stages can be defined as the ABCs of event planning crisis management. They are:

- Plan A—Anticipation
- Plan B—Backup
- Plan C—Crisis Management Mode (code of conduct and expected business behavior in a take-charge crisis situation)

ABCs OF EVENT PLANNING CRISIS MANAGEMENT

There is more to event design than planning and preparation, and it is as easy as ABC. An essential element in producing a successful event and being able to handle anything Murphy throws at you is to always have Plan A—Anticipation. You need to ask yourself what could go wrong. What can we do to avert it? If this occurred despite our attempts to avert it, what would be the next step that we would need to take? That would be Plan B—Backup. Like the Boy Scouts, be prepared. At one gala theatrical opening, an unexpected storm came up in the middle of the night, and the tent—one of the largest available—blew away just one day before the scheduled event. The tent had not been securely fastened, but rather than point fingers the event planners scoured the country, located another tent, and had it flown in. Had security been factored into the event plan to make sure that no harm came to the tent or contents, there would have been someone to call for emergency help before the tent sailed away, and the event planning company would have been aware of what was taking place immediately instead of finding out the following morning when the crew showed up. Plan B—Backup, which in this case was having security on hand to monitor the situation, was not in place. The event planning company had to move immediately into Plan C—Crisis Management Mode.

The British press was outraged when Queen Elizabeth and Prince Philip were set adrift on the Red River in Manitoba, Canada when the boat they were traveling in broke down. Plan A—Anticipation had been thought of. The boat was towed to shore by a water taxi that had been trailing it. The question of what if the boat breaks down had been asked, and Plan B—Backup was in place. Plan C—Crisis Management Mode came into play because the weather had not been factored into the what ifs. The Queen and Prince were left waiting in the freezing cold without the benefit of a blanket and the Queen was reportedly ashen faced after her rescue from the river. Warm lap blankets, stored out of sight just in case, to ensure the royal couple's comfort should have been part of Plan B. If an event planner was doing a horse and carriage ride for guests as part of an event in New York in the fall, lap blankets to keep guests cozy would be an important thing to include so that the guests could enjoy the ride in comfort. A customized blanket could be included and be both serviceable and serve as a take home memento of the day. In other destinations outdoor heaters are usually recommended for guests' comfort when events are scheduled to take place outside where there could be cool winds off the ocean or the night air could be chilly. Weather considerations have to be included in Plan B. In the case of the Queen and Prince, having missed a step in Plan B meant that Plan C—Crisis Management Mode would include having warm blankets waiting when the water taxi docked to help lessen the effect of being left sitting in the cold (better still would have been to have had an emergency run, taking blankets to members of the couple's security detail for final deposit with the Royals at the boat) and assisting the Royal handlers to secure thermoses of hot tea to have ready for the Queen and her Prince.

Business behavior, when operating in crisis management mode, dictates that the only people who are aware that a problem has arisen are the on-site event planning team and their suppliers. Guests, wherever possible, are not to be made aware that something has gone amiss with the scheduled plan of events. The problem needs to be identified quickly, the proper people informed and action taken without causing a commotion. If chaos is about to break loose, the last thing planners need are their own internal staff adding to it. What guests see on the outside is a situation under control, with no obvious signs that the event planning crew is about to have a meltdown because something major—in the case of the Queen and the blankets—has been overlooked and they are aware that the press is going to have a field day and their professional reputation is going to be bruised. In the case of the burst water main, all that could have been done to prevent it was done, and what remained was to fix the problem. The situation that was created was something beyond the event planner's control, but fixing the situation as quickly, unobtrusively, and with as few distractions as possible was under their control. The mini or major event hitch is just another event element to be managed professionally and with poise, with everyone calm and composed.

But event planners must also be prepared to think and act fast. A chain of command and an action plan must be set up and reviewed with the on-site team in advance. If what has been anticipated becomes reality, everyone knows what the backup plan is, knows exactly what they are required to do and not a moment is lost. Should the situation escalate and move into crisis management mode, the action plan is taken to the next level.

An example of a successful crisis management operation was reported in the news. It involved a fun family outing that turned into a serious situation where many lives could have been lost if not for the quick actions of the event planning team who were fully trained and prepared to handle it. One hundred and sixty bales of hay were used to construct a maze for a family event. Mazes for the general public can often be found at Halloween exhibits, Christmas tree farms and produce farms created from highly flammable cornfields or stacked bales of hay. Mazes for corporate events can be used as team building events and have become popularized on shows such as Survivor, where competing teams must find their way through the maze, gathering items and exiting as quickly as possible. While families with small children were in the maze, a fire broke out and quickly engulfed it. Families had to scramble to get to safety. In minutes, the area where the fire broke out had flames over 15 feet high. The minute that danger was spotted, designated staff, as instructed to do in an emergency, mounted the bales and directed guests to the exits. Other staff members pulled families to safety, while still others broke through walls of the maze and created more exits. Key personnel called emergency services and staffed fire extinguishers. Loudspeakers were used to keep the crowd informed and calm. No lives were lost and no injuries occurred. Guests were shaken but safe. A youth who had started the fire with a pocket lighter was charged with arson.

T
I
P

In an emergency situation, it is important for staff to remain calm so that guests do not become panicked and hinder rescue operations. People need to be kept informed without becoming alarmed. They need to know that the situation has been reported and that help is on the way. Passengers aboard a cruise ship found out their ship was on fire, not from the ship's personnel but from cable television showing live coverage shot from a beach two miles away of smoke billowing from the ship. Guests panicked and could have stampeded for the lifeboats, not having proper direction. Public announcements reportedly did not commence until a half hour after the fire was first reported, well after passengers had witnessed the televised coverage and fire-fighting tugboats had arrived on the scene. Guests were then instructed to go to the upper deck at the ship's bow with their lifejackets, as opposed to their designated lifeboat station as all passengers had been told at the mandatory lifeboat drill they attended at departure.

SAMPLE PLANS

PLAN A—ANTICIPATION

How does the maze have to be structured so that it does not fall down on a child?

How can the maze be designed to allow for quick exit?

What needs to happen if an emergency situation, such a fire, occurs?

How can crowd control be maintained so that staff know exactly how many people are in the maze at one time, people can be accounted for and maximum safety numbers will not be exceeded?

What permits, waivers, liabilities, insurance, and fire and public safety regulations need to be in place?

PLAN B—BACKUP

Structural engineer to be hired to design and do structural check

Material flameproofed and certificate obtained

Increase staff—minimum of 30

All staff to be equipped with walkie-talkies—test range and inside/outside maze contact

Key personnel with cell phones—emergency numbers coded into speed dial; test area

Fire extinguishers (tested) and permits as per fire marshal's office

Fire extinguisher instruction for staff

No smoking or open flames allowed on site—signage to be posted

Fire watch towers to be manned at all times—binoculars and megaphones required

Water supply, long hoses (test reach) and buckets to be available for immediate access

Design crowd control system

Ladders in designated areas on outside of maze to assist staff to quickly scale maze and direct people from above to safety

Tall poles (able to be seen by staff and guests inside the maze) with large brightly colored exit sign to be used by designated staff to guide participants to safety in case of emergency

Fire marshal on duty may be required—pending fire regulations

Exit signs may be required—pending fire regulations

On-site medical assistance may be required—pending regulations

Additional exits may be required to be built and clearly marked— pending fire regulations

Loudspeaker—test system

Megaphones—test

PLAN C—CRISIS MANAGEMENT MODE

Designated safety teams go into action, with everyone clear on their responsibility

Team One: Call emergency services, station staff by the main gate to direct them to site

Team Two: Make loudspeaker announcements

Team Two: Responsible for emergency equipment

Team Three: Responsible for staffing exit safety poles

Team Four: Open additional maze exits

Team Five: Scale maze walls and direct guests to safety; use megaphones

Team Six: Head count—stationed at maze entrance and exits

The ABCs of event planning crisis management do not apply only to life-threatening situations. They are event management tools to put to use on anything that could impede or endanger a successful event execution and outcome. They can be major—one facility hosting world leaders for a dinner anticipated what the impact could be if one of the guests fell ill after dinner, especially if only one person became sick. What was served would come under suspicion, as would their kitchen and staff. Their backup plan was to take a small sample from each designated plate, label them noting who had prepared what (some personal chefs were involved, as well as their internal staff) and store them. Should any illness of an unexplained nature occur, food samples of exactly what was served to an individual would be readily available for inspection and food analysis. Nothing untold took place, and crisis management—planned and prepared for—was ready but not required.

At another event involving top world dignitaries, everything was in place, or so the event planners thought. Special meal provisions had been made, anticipated with backup plans in place, but special meeting room needs had not been addressed. Staff had to spring into crisis mode to be able to accommodate the Asian guests' request to have their personal tea makers and rice pot cookers they had brought with them—along with their personal cooks—set up in the meeting room. This was discovered on-site as the meetings were about to commence, not in advance. Extra power and electrical requirements had to be arranged immediately so that the start of the meeting would not be delayed. Staff that had been assigned exclusively to handle the unexpected needs of the VIPs were readily available to spring into action without jeopardizing the event flow by pulling other staff members away from their posts to handle an unexpected situation.

RECAP OF THE ABCs OF EVENT PLANNING CRISIS MANAGEMENT

Plan A—Anticipate

Expect the unexpected. What can go wrong, could go wrong.

Plan B—Backup

Have a backup plan in place. Be prepared.

Plan C—Crisis Management Mode

Establish a chain of command. Discuss expected business behavior and codes of conduct in a take-charge crisis situation. Train a crisis team to be ready to handle all emergencies quickly, quietly and without raising alarm.

> **T I P**
>
> Appoint an official company spokesperson to answer all questions in an emergency. Take note of how governments and major corporations handle the media—one spokesperson in many cases with a lawyer standing by their side, and all other staff instructed to make "no comment" on company or client matters and direct all questions back to the company's point person. What could be said in a moment of crisis could be legally damaging and not representative of the facts.

9
EVENT PLANNING ETHICS, ETIQUETTE AND ESSENTIALS A–Z

A

ACCURACY

Master the art of accuracy. Clients depend on their event planning team to prepare a budget that holds no surprises at the end. Their personal livelihood can depend on the job that you do. Clients depend on their selected event planning team's sense of ethics to guide them safely through the minefield of unexpected costs that can appear at final reconciliation if the event planning company and their suppliers have not been accurate in their cost estimates. If they have contracted with a supplier that has led them down the garden path in the past concerning true cost estimates, they will appreciate honesty and accuracy.

ASSOCIATIONS

Associate and learn from your peers. Take the time to attend meetings and educational seminars, which are a great place to network and exchange ideas. Some of the top industry associations, North American and international, include:

Canadian Special Events Society (CSES) www.cses.ca

Convention Industry Council (CIC) www.conventionindustry.org

Independent Meeting Planners Association of Canada, Inc. (IMPAC) www.impaccanada.com

International Special Events Society (ISES) www.ises.com

Meeting Professionals International (MPI) www.mpiweb.org

Professional Convention Management Association (PCMA) www.pcma.org

Society of Incentive & Travel Executives (SITE) www.site-intl.org

The Association of Bridal Consultants (ABC) www.bridalassn.com

The International Association of Administrative Professionals (IAAP) www.iaap-hq.org

The National Association of Catering Executives (NACE) www.nace.net

The Society of Corporate Meeting Professionals (SCMP) www.scmp.org

B

BALANCE

In the event planning business there are times when it can feel as though you can't catch your breath. There is always a deadline to beat, another proposal to prepare, an event to run and a rapidly changing industry to keep up on. Taking time to put balance into your life can be placed on the back burner, but it is what you require most in order to fully recharge your creativity. When event planners are running on empty or solely on coffee fumes their creativity becomes stagnant. Getting away from the work and focusing on something that brings personal happiness allows you to return with fresh energy and new visions.

BUDDY SYSTEM

During an event, look out for one another and be on the alert for situations that can quickly get out of hand. Buddy up and be prepared to step in where needed.

One night in a bar in Key West a group of men who had been partying heavily after attending a meeting decided to pick up one of their waitresses, and they did—literally. They hoisted her over their heads and passed her along. They were drunk and she was in danger of being dropped, but the more immediate danger to her safety was the overhead ceiling fan they were oblivious to. Staff stepped in and rescued her as she was inches away from the blades.

BUDGETING BACKWARDS

Learn how to quickly project whether or not a destination, venue or event element will fit within your budget parameters. Start with the end in mind and begin to subtract estimated costs. For example, if a client has a budget of $2,500 per person, you would start by deducting the givens, the hard costs that are not optional. These include management fees, on-site staffing charges, communication costs and promotional items (itineraries, document jackets). Then begin to roughly calculate and subtract applicable costs, such as averaged airfares, transfers to and from the airport and on-site parking to see what dollar figure you are left with. From the remainder, deduct accommodation and estimated food and beverage costs based on the number of days, with the balance left to cover any additional items such as decor, entertainment, activities, room rental charges, labor and the like. These estimates do not take into account projected costs for move in, setup, teardown and move out. What budgeting backwards will allow planners to do is provide their client with a quick reality check. If the average airfare is $1,000 and the client wants a seven-night program at a resort where rooms cost over $200 per night, it is immediately obvious that is not a doable option within your $2,500 per person budget. The $2,500 budget will have been eaten up before the cost of a single meal has been factored in, let alone entertainment and other inclusions. A location closer to home may be a solution, or the program may need to be shortened from seven to three or four nights. Guests may need to share rooms or the client must find more money in order to fulfil their event wants. Budgeting backwards can quickly eliminate unnecessary work or filling a client with false expectations of what their budget can provide.

C

CONTRACTS

Have contracts professionally reviewed and prepared by company lawyers. Make sure that clients are fully aware of what they are committing to. For example, in the case of a new venue just opening, clients need to know whether they will receive compensation for cancellation charges from other suppliers if the facility does not open on time, and if they can factor in a penalty contract clause to protect themselves should the facility not open on time. They need to fully understand the ramifications of what they are signing and all possible penalties, liabilities, terms and conditions. If the event planning company is signing the supplier contracts on behalf of the client, it is essential that all relevant clauses from those contracts be included in the event planning company's letter of agreement in the body of the contract or as an attachment.

CONTRIBUTION

If an individual or event planning company can contribute to their industry by giving something back, everyone benefits. It can be done in a variety of ways, some requiring only minutes of your time while others are much larger commitments. One way is being a valued source quoted in industry publications, which contributes to the industry by sharing experiences and knowledge. Other possibilities are sitting on association boards and helping to set industry standards, contributing articles to magazines, teaching seminars at industry educational conferences, being there for a fellow industry member who may require insight or guidance and leading by example—demonstrating a principled approach to the business of special event management.

COST SUMMARY BREAKDOWNS

A cost summary breakdown is the backbone of an event. It is a compilation of all conceivable costs and it is the deciding document on which the client contracts. Event planners have an ethical responsibility to their clients to capture all possible charges, including the ones listed on suppliers' quotes as "not included" and found on their contract terms and conditions and technical and entertainment riders—such as for the top performer who requires first-class airfare for 18 members of their entourage. These are actual costs that the client will be fiscally responsible for and they need to be factored in so that an accurate event projection can be arrived at. Suppliers often list taxes and service charges under "not included" so that costs appear lower than what actual charges will be. Clients need to be presented with an all-inclusive cost summary breakdown that clearly includes applicable dollar amounts for taxes and service charges in their calculations. Don't be flippant when it comes to financial matters. Find out the facts, calculate all possible costs and do the math ethically and honestly. Paint a true picture of anticipated costs. Budget integrity is of utmost importance. Always show fiscal responsibility for your client's and your company's money.

D

DETAIL

The devil is in the details and the details are what set an event apart from others. If the details are not in place, a successful event cannot take place. The details are the foundation that an event is built on. Skip a step or discount a detail and planners are building their event on shaky ground. They'll need to be prepared to handle event emergencies when the cracks in the planning start to reveal themselves.

DOLLARS AND CENTS

Spend your client's dollars and cents wisely. It is better to do one thing with impact than spread the funds out too thinly and have the client disappointed with the outcome. It may be better to stage a chili cook-off at a western event, keep food costs reasonable and be memorable rather than serving another traditional steak and chicken barbecue at a higher cost and having no money left over for entertainment. The client is looking to their planner for expert advice on how to best allocate their spending dollars.

DOLLARS MAKING SENSE

In an effort to save dollars some companies will skimp on the quality of entertainment, but that can make or break your event. Planners are better to hire a great DJ or look for an innovative new show as opposed to booking a mediocre band that plays the equivalent of elevator music. At one event the dance band was so uninspired that within minutes of the dinner presentation all guests left, and the entire ballroom was empty except for the band and one or two company employees. The event was taking place in Las Vegas, the entertainment capital of the world, and the so-so band could not compete and was not going to hold people there. The company would have been better taking their guests as a group to see a spectacular show with top-name entertainment and then letting them run off and play. Event planners can only recommend dollars making sense and can't dictate their client's final decisions. But their suggestions will have been noted and when proven right on the money will give the client a better understanding of where and how dollars would be best spent at the next event.

DRESS CODES IN THE OFFICE AND ON SITE

One event planning co-owner embarrassed her staff at events. She would show up in outfits that would make how Julia Roberts was dressed in the movie *Erin Brockovich* look conservative—high heels, bare legs and tight mini-skirts so short that when she wore her blouse tucked in the shirt tales showed beneath her skirt. Her clients, mainly men in the financial industry, would fondle her openly in front of staff, running their hands up her legs as she sat on their laps. To be at events with the co-owner was embarrassing, and to be associated with her company, which was never viewed as professional, took its toll. Staff who cared about how they were perceived left once they witnessed that kind of behavior firsthand because staying would compromise their personal reputation in the industry.

E

ENERGY

An event must be carefully crafted to have energy and be devoid of dead air. All event elements and inclusions must be mindfully constructed to create anticipation, build to a crescendo and peak on a high, leaving guests animated and full of excitement. Guests should come away knowing that they have attended something very special.

Each event has a pulse and planners must monitor it carefully, bringing emotion and energy into the event planning equation.

ETHICS

Practice ethical personal and business behavior and bring this to all that you do in business and out in the world. Recognize when people start to try to justify their actions, because justification is usually a good ethical compass for gauging when ethics are about to go off track. It is your choice whether to step away or be drawn into something that could have long-lasting personal and professional repercussions and damage your credibility. If you refuse to take part in something that seems unethical and someone is still intent on trying to convince you that what feels wrong to you is essentially right, they are trying to control you and may be looking for a partner in crime or someone to put the blame on. Examples are in the news every day of individuals trusting others instead of themselves, or following orders without questioning whether or not it is the right thing to do. Don't get caught unaware or unprepared.

ETIQUETTE

Practice social and business etiquette skills and become a master of both. They are as important to getting ahead in the event planning industry as learning to play golf or tennis has been for others. They are tools of the trade.

EVENT PLANNING CHECKLIST— FOUR ESSENTIAL STEPS

Event planning consists of four main steps. To ensure a successful special event execution it is essential that none of these steps are skipped. Event planning steps include event design, management, orchestration and coordination.

1. Event Design

Research and Development

Optional Event Enhancement Suggestions

Event Timing and Logistics

Show Flow Outline

2. Event Management

Supplier Quote Review

Preliminary Detailed Cost Summary Breakdown

Event Recommendations

Supplier Re-Costing Based on Final Event Inclusions/Numbers

Cost Summary Breakdown Revision

3. Event Orchestration

Supplier Contract Review and Recommendations to Client

Preparation of Supplier Payment Schedule for Client

Ongoing Supplier Direction

Liaison Between All Event Suppliers and Client

Preparation of Budget Updates

Preparation of Supplier Function Sheets

4. Event Coordination

Pre-Event Meetings With All Suppliers

Event Move In, Installation and Setup

Day of Coordination

Event Teardown and Move Out

Supplier Final Billing Review

Preparation of Reconciliation

Each one of these event planning elements is covered in detail in *Event Planning: The Ultimate Guide to Successful Meetings, Corporate Events, Fundraising Galas, Conferences, Conventions, Incentives and Other Special Events* (John Wiley & Sons, 2000) and *The Business of Event Planning: Behind-the-Scenes Secrets of Successful Special Events* (John Wiley & Sons, 2002).

F

FAIR BUSINESS PRACTICES—RETAINER FOR PROPOSAL RESEARCH AND DEVELOPMENT

One of the largest ethical challenges the event planning industry as a whole faces is how people are being paid for their time and their knowledge, creativity and resources. Companies in the event planning industry are re-evaluating how they do business. The day of reckoning is coming. There are very few professional industries where people do the proper depth of research, development and design and not get paid; however, most event planning proposals are done on spec (speculation) in the hopes of contracting the business, putting their company's very survival at risk. A lawyer may give a client a free half-hour consultation, but without a hefty retainer in hand they are not going to take one step further, and there are no money-back guarantees with their fees should a case not be won or a situation not be resolved. A revolution is in the making, with some event planning companies refusing to provide proposals on spec. The cost of saying yes is too high a cost for their business and staff to pay without some form of compensation. They are choosing to work only with clients who hire their creative services and event planning expertise and pay a nonrefundable advance retainer for proposal development, much as a lawyer would.

Industry experts know that event planning (design) does not stand on its own. In order to present an accurate cost projection to clients, event, management and orchestration (operations) and event coordination must be worked out in advance as well. It is not a matter of simply pulling a pleasing proposal out of the air. Research, timing and logistics must be factored in, otherwise an estimated cost summary breakdown is just a best guess. An unscrupulous planner could appraise an event at $100,000 when in reality it could come in between $150,000 and $200,000 when all the "not included" costs are priced out. Just because something is "not included" does not mean it won't be required and become a very real hard cost. For example, the cost for technical crew meals may not be included in an audiovisual and lighting proposal but they are a condition of the contract. Costs for crew meals must be included for a client to see an accurate reflection of costs. Crew meals—three a day plus breaks—multiplied by the number of staff can add up, and it is better to know the costs up front than be faced with an unpleasant surprise at final reconciliation. And crew meals are just one tiny example. Costs that are left out of a supplier proposal but are a required contract condition can be astronomical. Tenting companies can guess at the costs to cover a swimming pool for guests to dine and dance on and to tent the area, but until they conduct a professional survey (in some cases two or three surveys are required) on a specific pool and deal with the particular intricacies of it and the surrounding area, a true cost cannot be projected. The rate can double or triple depending on what needs to be done, how long it will take to construct, structure engineering to provide a level and sound floor and any special considerations that need to be taken into account, such as professional landscapers to tie mature trees branches up and vacuum the lawn. And until a facility is checked, electrical requirements will not be known. If the facility is found to be underwired, a backup generator or more may be required and that will also affect costs. Entertainment riders have to be reviewed, too. A band may cost perhaps $6,500 for the evening, but the rider may stipulate first-class airfare for the lead singer to be flown from their home city. In some cases, that could equal or exceed the cost of the band's fee to perform.

Planners and their supplies do a tremendous amount of work. Events are designed that range from thousands to millions of dollars. One wrong planning move and an event can fall on its face with all the money spent by clients gone to waste because an objective has not been met. Event planning is a highly skilled profession, but is often treated as a service industry much like the travel industry—where clients can drop in and shop for free information—as opposed to a serious business that is very involved in helping their clients become successful in their business. Events are an integral part of a company's sales, marketing, promotional, communications and branding campaigns. Event planners are often working with and sitting in on meetings with senior executives and top company decision-makers, and are counted on for their expertise. But the same company heads throw event planning companies into a feeding frenzy situation. They create a bidding war where there is only one winner and the rest are not compensated for their expenses. They ask event planning companies to do the job without getting paid—something that they couldn't expect of their own business—but event planning companies and their suppliers are asked to and do so because very few are taking a stand and charging a retainer for research and event development to be credited towards the management fee if the event is a go. If the event does not move forward or they are not awarded the business then at the very least they have been compensated for their time, creativity and communication charges (long distance, couriers, etc.). A few years ago, the airlines banded together to stop paying travel agencies a commission—it started with one and then most followed suit—and travel agencies started charging a fee to issue tickets. It no longer was a service provided to clients for free but for a fee. The consensus is this cannot be allowed to continue in the event planning industry. The event planning industry is taking stock of the value they bring to corporate clients. The events they design can increase a company's marketability and profitability, but they do not share in the rewards. In recent years movie stars had a revelation of the value they bring to the box office and they no longer settle for a salary. The actors that draw people into the theaters also receive a percentage of profits from the back-end, which to them is only fair. Fees for top stars are in the millions because performers know they, not the story line, bring people to the show. They respect what they do and charge accordingly. Event planning companies and their suppliers are penalized, not respected, when they are asked to bid on new business with a multitude of others without being paid for the work they are asked to do. The industry is aware that at times submitted ideas are being taken and used in-house without credit and that companies are being used to comparison shop and keep the client's incumbent on their ethical toes.

Learn from the top lawyers—they receive their fees in advance in the form of retainer—not after the work is done—for their firm's services (the research for the discovery process where each party learns about the opponent's case is not necessarily done by them personally) and charges are billed back to their client based on an established hourly rate. Pick up the telephone to ask a question and there is a charge for their time. Clients learn to limit their requests. Lawyers are on top of their billed minutes and value their time; they will not continue if they are not paid. Before their retainer runs out an invoice for another retainer is sent out. And people pay this without exception—the legal profession has set out an established method of payment for services, as have doctors, dentists, therapists and other professional industries. You cannot take a yoga class or walk out of a store without paying for goods, but event planning companies freely give away over one-hundred-plus hours, in some cases, of their employees' time—which they as a company still have to pay for—in proposal research and development without knowing if they will receive a dime. Some top event planning companies policy charge a minimum flat $15,000 management fee for event design only, and the figure is based on the work they have to do and the hours put in, not on the number of guests. The same charge for design would apply whether it was for an event for two or 2,000. They are minding their own business and working to keep it professional and profitable. If the event is a go the retainer is applied to the management fee.

Business is business. The moment you make an exception to company policy regarding client billing, expect to be burned. Company policy is put in place to protect the employer and employees from being taken in and working for free. It doesn't matter who refers a client to you and how good your relationship is with them. You don't know the referral and they have no loyalty to you or your company. If a retainer is required, do not waiver.

FIRE MARSHALS

Fire marshal rules and regulations must be investigated and adhered to. Events can and have been shut down because proper permits have not be obtained for pyrotechnics, the number of guests exceeds legal limits, sufficient fire extinguishers are not on hand, exit signs are not clearly marked as per fire regulations, special permit liquor licenses have not been executed, fire marshals required to oversee fireworks or indoor pyrotechnic special effects were not hired and the number of washroom facilities is less than required by law based on the number of people attending. Fire inspections can take place without warning—during move in, setup or the actual event, and they have the authority to close everything down immediately. Always make sure that copies of all permits are on hand. Verbal permission from the venue means nothing. Official fire marshal authorization in writing must be received.

FIREPROOFING AN EVENT

There is a serious side to event planning that has to be addressed. Fireproofing an event is often overlooked, although it is a potential pitfall that can jeopardize an event as well as put guests in danger. In December 2002 New York's *Daily News* ran an article about things getting heated up at Travel + Leisure's Rainbow Room benefit for the Children's Advocacy Center of Manhattan. After spending three days preparing miniature Christmas-tree centerpieces, an event planner who was a co-chairwoman was unloading them at Rockefeller Center at 6 a.m. when a fire marshal told her that flammable material couldn't enter the building. The planner protested. She'd worked hard on them and they were for charity. And anyway, they weren't flammable. The fire marshal promptly pulled out a lighter and set one ablaze. Imagine if people attending the event either purchased the centerpieces (as part of the fund-raising efforts) and took them home at the end of the evening and displayed them near open candles, or if at the event a candle, cigarette or cigar had come close to the centerpiece. A tragedy was in the making—both at the event and in people's homes. The event planner should have known to have them flameproofed and obtain written verification. Even items that have been treated with a special fire retardant should be tested. A fire marshal tested one decor item that had been fireproofed and it exploded into flames. Not all companies that offer fireproofing do a job that would pass fire marshal inspection. Use only companies that are experts in their field. Remember, fireproofing alone will not stop a fire from spreading, but it will slow it down.

FUNCTION SHEETS

Function sheets have often been referred to as the event planning bible. They capture all event elements that should be included and lay them out in an exact timeline. The sequence of events is detailed, as are the event inclusions. Function sheets clearly outline event planners' and their clients' event expectations. They are sent to the client and suppliers in advance for review and discussed in detail during the pre-con meetings.

G

GROWTH—PERSONAL AND PROFESSIONAL

Never stop learning—event planning is an industry of constant change. Continue to educate yourself through formal and informal courses and certification. Industry certification includes:

CITE—Certified Incentive Travel Executive (offered by SITE; www.site-intl.org)

CMM—Certification in Meeting Management (offered by MPI; www.mpiweb.org)

CMP—Certified Meeting Professional (offered by CIC;
www.conventionindustry.org)

CSEP—Certified Special Events Professional (offered by ISES;
www.ises.com)

Investigate industry e-mail discussion groups such as MIMlist
Meeting Matters (www.mim.com) where you can participate in
daily conversations with over 2,000 of your peers and get feedback
on issues relevant to your company. Take part in seminars and educational conferences. One successful event planner often volun-
teers his services for setup of major industry educational conferences in order to upgrade his knowledge and pick up tricks of the
trade. The more you know, the better the events you pull off. You
will be ahead of your peers who are content to remain doing the
tired and mundane, and in the process you increase your personal
and professional value to your company and clients.

H

HEALTH

Event planning staff and their suppliers need to make sure that
they stop to take care of their health in the office and on site. This
is not only for their personal well-being but also for the well-being
of the event. Last-minute replacements can be difficult to find and
bring up to speed if someone comes down with an unexpected illness from lack of self-care, or is on the verge of dropping from
exhaustion as the event progresses because insufficient staff have
been scheduled. Event planners should never run an event so tightly that if one on-site staff member becomes ill the success of the
event is placed in jeopardy.

I

INDUSTRY LANGUAGE

Every industry has their own internal language and it is essential to
learn it. A good starting place is *The International Dictionary of
Event Management*, second edition, edited by Goldblatt and Nelson
(John Wiley & Sons, 2001). This is the first and only comprehensive

reference to the growing vocabulary of international event management, with an A to Z coverage of nearly 4,000 terms (more than double the first edition).

INNOVATION

Becoming innovative requires planners to continually grow and learn new job skills. CNN reported that "...a group of proper ladies from Rylstone, England, a hamlet of 40 houses in northern England, made a 2000 calendar of discreet nude photographs of themselves in various housewifely activities. They wanted to remind people that a little erotic fun can be appealing—regardless of age, gender or social class. They sold close to 100,000 calendars and raised more than $750,000 for leukemia research. They also served as an inspiration for others, including a growing number in the United States." Inventive? Yes. Successful? Much more profitable than a rummage sale, and their novelty led the way for firefighters, chefs, gardening clubs and the like to follow suit. Variations of this idea have raised over US$1.5 million for at least 40 causes.

INSURANCE

Find out from each of your suppliers and venues the type of insurance they carry. Make sure that the client has protected themselves and has taken out special event insurance as well. Ensure that the event planning company is covered, too. Should a tragedy occur, all involved could be held liable.

J

JUDGMENT

Learn to use good judgment and not to be quick to judge others. Inexperience and lack of training can create on-site difficulties that could be avoided. Never put people in charge of event elements they have not been fully prepared to handle, because it is not fair to them or to the client. Learning by the "sink or swim method" can be costly all around. Instead, team newbies up with an experienced partner they can learn from.

K

KNOTS

If an event planner is feeling knots in their stomach, their intuition may be kicking in and advising them that there is something critical that has *not* been tied up and requires their immediate attention. Don't discount gut feelings.

KNOWLEDGE

Invest in yourself and seek take-away skills that add to your value. If you put all of your energy into the company you work for and none into yourself, professional success could evade you when or if the time comes to seek a new position. If you limit yourself to just doing your job and not increasing your knowledge you could find yourself less marketable should the company you are working for go under, merge, downsize or choose to look for work elsewhere.

L

LOGISTICS

Event logistics can affect costs. They need to be determined at the planning stage and not left to operations. You can't plan a high-wire act without knowing the structure of the ceiling, rigging points, what type of weights are being used, what type of flooring is required, how the equipment is being transported and whether of not the facility is limited to union labor or not. Leaving logistics to the operations stage created a $100,000 budgeting error for one company because costs had been overlooked in the planning stage. The client was liable for the increased costs and felt the planning company had not been ethical in preparing their initial cost summary breakdown.

M

MANAGE

Manage your time, your life and your event. Each is linked to the other.

N

No

There is a saying: "Never accept a no from someone that was never in a position of authority to give a yes." Valuable time can be wasted trying to get a no changed to a yes or finding a compromise. Too often planners engage in heated debates with a supplier's staff who are not in a position to take the next step and are unwilling to approach their higher-ups with the request. Sometimes the situation can escalate into a power play. Emotion has be removed from the issue. For example, event planners can be passionate about perfection and what they need to achieve a better performance because they are designing and orchestrating a live staged production that allows for no dress rehearsals. Timing and logistics must step in and be presented factually (not emotionally) to the powers that be—those who can change a no to a yes or work with the planners to find a workable solution for both sides. Keeping business etiquette in mind, when moving from a no to a yes the intention is never to do it by stepping on toes, bruising egos (which could still happen but is not done with malice) or by commenting on someone's lack of knowledge or efficiency. It can be done with professional consideration and finesse.

O

One Step More

There is a team building exercise that involves climbing to the top of a telephone pole and jumping off (see www.miravalresort.com). You are securely fastened with ropes and teammates staff the safety ropes. Some people have no trouble scrambling to the top and jumping off. Others cling to the pole part of the way up, afraid to climb higher. In either case, if you make it to the top and jump off or stop halfway up, you are coming down the same way. The point of the exercise is not to get to the top of the pole and jump off, but to take one step more than you are comfortable with. Apply this lesson to the event planning business and in your life. You'll never know what you could miss out on if you don't take one step more. If you settle for less, you get less in life and in your event.

P

PATIENCE

Experienced event planners need to develop patience with staff, suppliers and clients as they move through event planning learning curves. And while patience (calmness, self-control, ability to tolerate delay) is a virtue, planners need to be able to differentiate between someone in a learning curve, someone content to be in a state of inertia, one who may be content to remain in a state of rest unless acted upon by an external force (which may be the planner) and someone who is drowning in deadlines because their company is understaffed and overworked.

PERMITS

The importance of planners receiving copies of all applicable event permits cannot be stressed enough. You can't take someone's word for it when they say all the permits are taken care of. Copies of permits must be in your hand before the event commences. Having obtained necessary permits can lessen legal liabilities and potential criminal charges should anything go wrong. A nightclub and a band ended up under investigation with criminal charges pending when on-stage pyrotechnics caused a fire that resulted in close to 100 deaths, including one of the band members. The band insisted they had been given a verbal OK but the venue said they hadn't been informed that a pyrotechnic display would be taking place. The fire marshal had not issued a permit. The club did not have a sprinkler system in place. The soundproofing installation behind the stage was not fireproofed. No firefighters had been hired by the band or the club to stand by in case of emergency. Other clubs said that the band had surprised them at their venues by including pyrotechnics without permission. Other bands said that the facility in question had allowed them to set off indoor fireworks, and there was documented proof in a magazine that this had occurred. Authorities are checking to see if the club had obtained fire marshal approval and permits for past events. Eventually, past history will be determined. Blame, in the meantime, has been assigned all round. The event organizer was the one stating they had verbal permission but did not make sure they protected themselves by ensuring that all paperwork was in order. Venues, nightclubs and restaurants are often rented out for special occasions, and special effects are often used on stage or as part of an evening finale in private homes and backyards now, as are props and decor. Anyone planning private events needs to know that guest safety, liability and permits are important event elements—its not just food, beverages, decor and entertaining that must be considered. Permits cannot be taken for granted. The repercussions are serious, personally and professionally, and they can be deadly.

PERSPECTIVE

Keep a sense of perspective. What one event planner can easily see may not be as visible to another. Teach what you know to clients, suppliers and other staff members. If others are able to see what you are saying, it may enable them to deal with the issue in a different manner. One experienced car event planner immediately knew that their creative director's vision of having a particular model of car go up the stage stairs was not doable because there was not enough clearance. A trial run was set up before the plan progressed much farther and it was discovered that the event planner was correct. The creative director had no perspective to base this particular event design on, their job experience in this instance was nil, they were unwilling to listen to advice on how best to create their vision and proper research and development had not been done before the creative concept was sold to the client. The planning company was placed in the embarrassing situation of advising the client that the concept they presented and contracted was in fact not possible due to an error on their part.

POLICY

Set personal and office policy in place for appropriate codes of conduct, business ethics and business behavior. Address how issues where you are being asked to cross the line of legal liabilities (e.g., being asked to knowingly serve liquor to underage guests, removing guest from an event, physically restricting anyone) are to be handled. Make the time to review proper procedures.)

PRE-CON MEETINGS

Event planners need to make sure that pre-con meetings take place before the event and that the right people—those who will be overseeing the actual event—will be present. Make sure the meetings are scheduled so that there is enough time to make any changes.

PROTOCOL

Knowledge of proper protocol and cultural sensitivity and aware-
ness are mainstays for event planning at home or abroad. Event
planners must research group demographics and be aware of the
cultural makeup of the guests from the beginning. They must learn
from the client if there are any special needs (due to physical dis-
abilities, health issues and/or cultural requirements) that they need
to be aware of and check with past suppliers to determine the specific needs of the group. Were there any on-site surprises such as
rice pots and tea makers required in the meeting room for a Japanese contingent? Every aspect of the event and the interaction
between guests and staff should be reviewed to make sure that all
cultural observances are in place. Event planners must do their
homework and find out if the group is adventuresome and open to
trying local specialties or if they will offend religious or cultural
beliefs should they offer items such as Taiwanese stir-fried crickets
with raw garlic, chili peppers, scorpions on shrimp toast, waterbugs
stuffed with chicken, Manchurian ants sprinkled on potato strings
or Thai-style fried white sea worms (these items can be found on
the menu of a popular restaurant in California). Event planners
have to check out the menus when doing a private event at a
restaurant or using it for a pit stop on a road rally or team scav-
enger hunt. Even in their own hometown they may be surprised
what is considered nouvelle cuisine. Protocol is a code of correct
conduct and event planning protocol demands that guests not be
subject to event elements that could be deemed offensive, inappropriate or unseemly.

Q

QUESTION EVERYTHING

The event planner's creed is "assume nothing and question everything." Event planners need to keep asking questions until they
fully understand everything and can advise their clients on things
such as costs, liabilities, logistics, timing and insurance requirements. Planners need to know at what time flowers will be at their
peak and fully opened, whether or not cocoa matting or burlap is

the best type of runner to put on a slippery glass slope, and when condensation will occur on an acrylic pool covering that guests will be dining and dancing on so that underwater lighting effects are not ruined and better yet, what can be done to lessen it. They need to be familiar with every event aspect and how it interacts with the others.

R

READ

Read the fine print in contracts, riders and supplier literature such as hotel food and beverage menus. Important stipulations can be missed, for example, a function space charge that will apply should guest numbers drop, or that the venue reserves the right to assign new rooms.

Read industry magazines and keep current. Some respected industry publications include:

Charity Village (non-profit) www.charityvillage.com

Corporate and Incentive Travel magazine
www.corporate-inc-travel.com

Corporate Meetings and Incentives www.corpmeetings.net

Event Solutions magazine www.event-solutions.com

Incentive Magazine www.incentivemag.com

Insurance Conference Planner www.icplanner.com

Marketing Magazine www.marketingmag.ca

Medical Meetings www.medicalmeetings.net

MeetingsNet www.meetingsnet.com

Meeting News www.meetingnews.com

Meeting Professionals International www.mpiweb.org

Meetings & Incentive Travel magazine
www.bizlink.com/meetingscanada.htm

Special Events Magazine www.specialevents.com

Successful Meetings magazine www.successmtgs.com

RECONCILIATION

Devise an internal system that will allow planners to update cost summary breakdowns as the event progresses and changes are made. Staying on top of your client's budget will be invaluable. If they are coming in under budget they may wish to add features, and if the budget shows signs of going over because of client requests and add-ons the time to know is before the event takes place so you can make any necessary adjustments. Maintaining a current budget also serves to make final reconciliation faster and smoother, with less room for surprises.

REPUTATION

Your reputation is what you carry with you through life. In fact it, often it precedes you. People know your name, the work that you do and your business ethics before they actually meet you face-to-face. Companies come and go but your reputation stays with you forever. Take care not to compromise it by working with or for others who do not share the same ethical values as you do.

RESPECT

Respect personal and professional ethical business boundaries, and the codes of conduct of your company and yourself. Respect one another. Never yell, put down others, make unprofessional remarks or display anger in front of staff members or guests. If there is a problem, take it out of the room—out of sight and out of hearing.

S

SITE INSPECTIONS

Never go into an event without having done a site inspection.

STRATEGIC THINKING

Planners who apply strategic thinking to their event design process have discovered a method that successfully works to elevate event planning to a new level. In *The Business of Event Planning*, strategic planning is identified as one of the crucial ingredients in producing outstanding events that meet the expectation of clients and guests.

Employing strategic design for all functions, large or small, is integral to successful special events. Adept event planners know that there is a specific rhythm or flow that must be incorporated into event design and there is a reason behind every choice from food to program elements. Subtle tactical action and strategic event thinking are brought into play, and mastering event design becomes an art form.

A simple cocktail party, consisting of a bar, food and light entertainment, can become a blueprint for much more than a basic cocktail reception. It can be custom tailored so that the cocktail party is not merely a vehicle to provide food and drink to guests but an event planning tool used to meet specific client objectives. Strategic planners look carefully at each element and item to see how they can construct their event to best meet their purpose and stay within the budget, while still being meaningful and memorable. They understand that thought must be given to layout, inclusions and event orchestration. These planners have mastered the art of strategic planning and know that they need to bring something new to the mix. If they don't, the result could be an event that is flawlessly executed but fails to achieve a client's desired results.

Consider a client hosting a cocktail party as the opening event of a weeklong conference. If attendees do not necessarily know one another, one of the client's goals should be to have guests mingling, relaxing and getting acquainted in a comfortable setting.

The first step is placing the bar deep into the room so guests won't huddle near the entrance and around the perimeter. You can provoke discussion by introducing various design, taste, texture and scent elements. There are many ways to accomplish this (depending on the destination, time of year and audience), ranging from an oyster bar, an "ice luge" bar featuring signature martinis sliding not stirred into a guest's glass, and shots of vodka served in ice shooters (a shot glass made out of ice) for a true "icebreaker," to small edible wafer cups with their insides coated with delectable chocolate and filled with shots of Baileys Irish Cream, and herbaceous beverages including thyme, basil, tarragon and rosemary cocktails, such as the Ten Sage cocktail, which is gin with sage, lime sour and orange passion-fruit liqueur.

Events must be strategically designed and planned to achieve specific purposes, and each decision affects your program's balance. You must constantly ask yourself how an event's intrinsic structure will help you to meet your objectives.

Learning how to think strategically will set you apart from the competition. It allows you to maximize the value of bringing people together for your client without incurring additional cost. (The aforementioned ice shooters, for example, cost approximately 50 cents a glass and could easily fit into most budgets, and their value as an "icebreaking" element far exceeds the expenditure. The same applies to the edible chocolate wafer cups.)

In today's economy, the bottom-line dollar amount must make sense, and spending the money by planning strategically can make any event a success.

T

Teach

Each one teach one. Take the time to explain to those new to the business what is being done, why it is being done in a particular manner, what the expected results are and what could be done to make it better. Together we build a better event planning industry. Mentoring can be done in the company, through association educational workshops and in actual schools.

Thank-Yous

Remember to thank others for their help in creating a successful special event.

Timing

Timing is everything in event planning. Every minute counts and all event elements must be factored in. For example, for an awards presentation where guests are coming from the audience, you must calculate in the time it takes winners to make their way to the stage, let the applause die down, accept their award, pose for a picture and leave the stage. If the show flow has only taken the award acceptance time into account, the event will quickly run behind schedule. With televised awards it is the stopping for hugs, kisses and congratulations along the way that slows down the procedure (it is the same at corporate events). Thought must also be given to where the winners will be seated and how difficult it will be for them to make their way to the stage once all the seats are filled with people.

U

UNDERSTANDING

Understand that sometimes things will not go as planned. Everything that could have been done was, but the unexpected occurred and was professionally managed. The outcome may not be as originally desired but only the event planners, their suppliers and the client are the wiser. Guests do not necessarily know exactly what is going to happen or how, and they will probably have a wonderful time and never know that something went wrong.

V

VALUE

Know what your values are and the value they bring. Look to align yourself with others who uphold strong values and value the people they work with.

VISUALIZE

Visualization is a highly skilled art in event planning, and professional planners in the field learn to walk through an event in their minds and clearly see any areas of concern when talking with suppliers and clients. Event planners will have lived the event many times over before it actually takes place. Mastering visualization will also allow a planner to get a physical feel for what will be going on for the guests. For example, a client was looking at doing a lengthy (five-hour) stand-up event, complete with food and beverage. This was not an event where guests could come and go as they please. They were expected to come on time and stay until the end. But it was for older guests and there was very limited seating. Immediately the event planner realized that this picture would not work and felt the guests' unease of juggling plates and glasses with nothing to set them on or for them to set themselves on. Guests would become tired of standing and anxious to slip out and put their feet up.

W

WE

Event planning is never done alone. Wise planners think and talk "we" as opposed to "me."

X

X-RAY VISION

Event planners require X-ray vision to see inside to the heart of an event and sometimes to the heart of a matter. They must be able to see below the surface of what can often not be seen with the naked eye. One client changed the start time of their cocktail reception without telling the event planner and the host and guests began arriving more than an hour early. The bars were set up and ready to go, and the canapés and dry snacks could be quickly readied, but bar staff had been given permission to open the bars only at a specified hour and their food and beverage manager could not be reached to change the start time. The heart of the matter was that the hotel standards required the staff to get approval before doing anything they had not been instructed to do, and their jobs could be at risk if they did not follow company policy. The event planner contacted the hotel general manager, explained the situation and convinced him to instruct the staff to open the bars now, with the client signing off their approval for the additional hour. By realizing what the real impediment was to the solution, the event planner respected the hotel's policy and how their staff upheld the rules but still managed to solve the problem without stepping on too many toes.

Y

YESTERDAY

Event planning is an industry where often everyone—clients, suppliers and event planning companies—want everything done yesterday. It is a fast-paced industry. Event planners need to become skilled at differentiating between a true emergency and a deadline that can be moved to produce a better result. Sales reps need to know how much time it takes to turn around a proposal and what deadlines the office is working on meeting before they go out on a sales call or meeting. This will help them so that they can prepare clients with a realistic timetable.

Z

ZONING LAWS

Event planners must familiarize themselves with event-specific zoning laws and bylaws because they can affect the success of an event. Some areas have noise restriction bylaws and music cannot be played past a certain time. In some areas the time of day doesn't matter and police will be there to investigate should a complaint be called in. Street parking bylaws could hinder a smooth move in, setup, day of coordination, teardown and move out if street parking is limited to one hour, and special permits may need to be obtained for caterers, decor companies and entertainers dropping off equipment or even positioning backup generators. If suppliers receive tickets for parking illegally or are towed away, these charges could be billed back to the client at final reconciliation. Some locales do not allow limousines to gather and park, which would be important should any VIPs be traveling to an event by limo and require the car and drivers to be easily accessible. But the time to find out is in advance of the event so that proper provisions can be made.

10
EVENT PLANNING DOs AND DON'Ts

HOW TO DEVELOP IN-OFFICE AND ON-SITE ETHICS AND BUSINESS ETIQUETTE POLICIES

It is important for every company, and each individual, to establish policies and guidelines on how to avoid displays of unethical behavior and lack of business etiquette. In some cases, individuals may find that they hold themselves to a higher code of conduct than the company they work with. If this is the case, they then need to assess whether or not the company standards are compatible with their beliefs or if they need to look at working for a company that is more in line with their principles. Having an established ethics and business etiquette policy will allow companies to see if codes of conduct are being violated by employees, suppliers, clients and their guests, and determine if the integrity of their business is being compromised by continuing to keep certain individuals in their employ or doing business with suppliers and clients who have demonstrated unethical behavior and business practices. The same applies for suppliers and clients—they need to ask whether or not the event planning companies they are aligning their company with reflect well on their business and their employees. Do their employees exhibit unprofessional behavior? Do they drink on the job? Are they overly familiar with staff and guests? Can you trust them to be discreet and not share confidential information with your competitors? Do they make costly errors? Do the events they produce meet all objectives? These are all questions that need to be asked and answered.

Listed below are sample ethical questions to ask yourself and discuss with peers in the office to use as a basis to start establishing your personal and professional event planning dos and don'ts and acceptable codes of conduct for in the office, on fam trips, site inspections, on site, and from clients and suppliers. Have you or your company ever asked someone to do, been asked to do or done any of the following?

- Used the time and talents of others without fully qualifying the request for proposal from prospective clients?

  Company executives and sales reps sometimes enter into the proposal process without fully understanding, investigating and questioning past history (where have they been, what have they done and what class and style of venues they have used), guest demographics (age, background, location, active or nonactive, adventurous or prefer tried and true, culturally diverse, special interests), client event objectives, budget parameters, proposed event elements, required event inclusions, preferences and other relevant information needed, such as what was and wasn't successful in the past, and if it is a bid situation how many other companies are bidding before proposal research and development can begin. The preparation of a proposal is an investment of time, creative energy and money. A client who supplies only limited information and is not prepared to spend their time answering the questions planners and suppliers need to have answered before they can decide whether or not to enter into proposal preparation is demonstrating a lack of business integrity. The event planning company needs to determine whether or not company policy is such that if pertinent information is not forthcoming, they will not subject themselves, their staff and their suppliers to spending their energy on a project because it may not come to fruition and may just be a client shopping around for creative ideas and sample costs. If an event planning company does decide to proceed and doesn't inform their suppliers that this could be a waste of their time and that the client is not really showing commitment to them or to the event, then the event planning company is not being honest with their suppliers. Suppliers need to know the truth about a proposal's prospects so they can determine whether or not to proceed, take the chance and invest their time and money into preparing a quote.

Determine office criteria for accepting and moving forward with proposal requests.

- Looked to your supplier or event planner to pick up the cost of your personal travel in exchange for being awarded a contract?

  Some clients look for special favors and pricing concessions from event planners when it comes to their personal vacation, and event planning companies have been known to either pick up the cost in exchange for business or approach their suppliers for special rates, upgrades or other amenities. The event planning company may do so without checking to see if they are violating their client's company's code of conduct and in the process placing their company's working relationship with the client at risk. What an individual may put forth as an ultimatum—a signed contract in exchange for personal favors—may not be in keeping with their company policy. If questionable requests are made, question them, don't merely accept them. Have the client put their travel request in writing so that it may be reviewed. Be upfront and advise the client that your company has an established procedure in place to handle personal vacation requests.

  Set guidelines for personal travel booked with or through a supplier. Advise staff and suppliers in writing of your company's policy. Ask to be informed of any requests that breach company policy and that should be reviewed by office management.

- Asked your supplier to provide gifts in kind to you (or your spouse, bosses or clients) for personal use in exchange for "all the good business" brought to them?

  Establish a set office policy about what requests staff are permitted to make of suppliers personally or on behalf of the company's clients. Discuss your company's definition of what would constitute a kickback and a payoff versus an industry perk. Set out clear guidelines on how to handle requests from clients, suppliers and planners and what employee solicitations will not be tolerated by the office. For example, accepting a complimentary room upgrade may be acceptable in the eyes of the company and seen as an industry perk, while accepting a free one-week stay in a hotel may be viewed as a kickback or payoff for business or future considerations.

Establish what is considered a kickback, payoff and perk by the office and how employee and client requests are to be handled. Outline the boundaries and the individual consequences of requesting or accepting a kickback, payoff or perk.

- Asked your supplier to your home or weekend retreat with the intention of requesting them to install sundecks and electrical work at no cost in exchange for awarding a contract?

Some clients and suppliers prefer not to mix business and pleasure. Both have been placed in awkward positions regarding what could be perceived by them as thinly veiled requests to have work done on their client's home or cottage at cost or for free. Are they being hit up for a favor? For work done under the table? Or, is it simply a remark, not a request, being made in casual conversation? To a carpet manufacturer invited to their client's home for dinner, saying, "Don't mind the carpet, we're looking at getting it replaced as soon as we can afford it" could just be a statement of fact, not a request for them to offer to install new carpeting for free or at a favorable rate. Staging companies that hear "This is where we are planning to build the deck when we can afford it. I'd love to be able to do it in time for our daughter's wedding but I don't think I'll be able to afford both. I have the plans right here. How do you think it will look?" may brace themselves for what could come next—"How much would you charge to do the job? Can anything special be worked out, since we do so much business together? I'd hate to give the job to anyone else." Not certain if they are being propositioned or merely asked for their professional advice, clients and suppliers have learned to tread carefully around requests that are questionable and could compromise themselves and their company.

Set company policy regarding interaction between employees, suppliers and clients outside of the office, as well as guidelines for using their company's (client's, supplier's or planner's) services for personal work.

- Made it clear to one of your suppliers that you only drink an expensive alcoholic beverage (or smoke pricey cigars) and that you expect to do so when you are on a site inspection, during meetings and even when visiting at the supplier's office?

Sales reps have been taught in sales seminars and books to pay close attention to clients' personal likes and dislikes. They may actively pursue feedback on favorite food, beverages, passions and pastimes and note preferences in their client files. Mentioning that a certain brand of anything—wine, liquor, cigars, golf clubs, designer clothing—is preferred could be interpreted, rightly or wrongly, by the sales rep as a hint as to what their client would appreciate on their next visit. In some cases they would be right. One employee expected their suppliers to come bearing gifts and was specific about their requests. The arrangement they had worked out was that their supplier would leave the bill in the bag and the employee would then return the item for cash.

Set a price limit on the gift value an employee or office may receive. Ensure that employees are aware that they are to return or politely refuse gifts that exceed the specified amount.

- Accepted fam trips or site inspections to destinations you or your company had no intention of using or recommending and basically used them as personal vacations?

Some event planning companies will permit their staff to travel on fam trips on their vacation time to destinations where having in-depth knowledge about a new product would provide value to the company, as long as it was with a supplier they did business with, and the supplier knew upfront that at this time the company had no clients interested in the area but were looking at it for future consideration. The supplier is then free to decide whether or not it would be appropriate to include this guest or if their company would be better served by inviting someone else who may be able to provide them with immediate business and help them to recoup their financial investment.

Event planning companies and their clients must decide where they stand on fam trips and site inspections. With regard to fam trips, what needs to be addressed is who is eligible to go? What destinations would be considered? Which suppliers would it be acceptable to say yes to and which should be refused? What needs to be determined when it comes to a site inspection is whether or not the client is serious about the destination and will sign a letter of agreement stating they are prepared to finalize the contract upon their return. The planning company and suppliers also need to decide whether or not their company will be charging the client for any expenses from the site inspection should an event not go forward.

- Sent a client to their personal dream destination on a fam trip geared for customers, which is paid for by the venue and not the planner, to a location that the client would never take a group to, as a reward for the client's business?

Suppliers look to their clients to be ethical when it comes to recommending clients to partake in a customer fam trip. Their intention is to sell the destination or facility, not to be used as a thank-you by the planning company in exchange for their client's goodwill. Clients have been sent around the world, hosted by suppliers who only do North American events. Going on a safari, seeing the Orient, South Pacific or the seven wonders of the world may be of personal—not professional—interest.

The planning office and the client's company need to decide what criteria a client must meet in order to be considered for a customer fam trip. Is head office (client) approval required? Planning companies and suppliers need to know they are not violating any of their client's approved company standards by offering or approving a trip for one of their employees.

- Booked directly with suppliers after being introduced to them through hotels and destination management companies while on a hosted fam trip?

This is an unethical business practice. The client, in this case the event planner, would be looking to cut out the third party in the hopes of bringing down the cost of the event by booking direct. How a supplier handles planning companies' requests such as these will determine their future working relationship with the hotel and destination management company, as well as how they are perceived in the industry. Some suppliers will not accept direct bookings if they have been brought in by a third party—they do not want to risk their professional reputation on one booking. Others do but inform the company that brought the planner to them in the first place what is going on. And in some cases, unethical suppliers contact the planner directly after the fam trip and offer to work directly with them and cut out the middleman.

Knowing how to be tactful in sticky situations is important and should be part of office training. Situations and requests should be anticipated in advance and staff directed as to how to respond. They should be told what the company policy is on a planner inquiring as to what the rate would be if they booked directly with your company as opposed to using the services of the host.

- Solicited a client that was introduced to you by an event planning company or supplier?

Clients have been approached by suppliers, after meeting them on the site inspection with their planner, with opportunities to save money if they decide to book with them. One hotel offered a client a substantial savings if they did so. The client declined but questioned their planner's ability to negotiate and wondered why they had been unable to offer the same rates as the hotel. The hotel, in this case, did not know the deal their sales rep was making to the client.

Have procedures been put into place to make staff accountable for their actions? Do employees know company policy with regard to making or receiving offers that would damage business relationships and the company's reputation?

- Neglected to disclose hidden commissions, kickbacks or rebates to clients?

Are kickbacks, hidden commissions and rebates to clients an accepted part of your company's way of doing business? What position, ethically and legally, are you putting yourself in personally and professionally if you are being asked to participate in unethical business practices?

Has company policy regarding kickbacks, hiding extra commission, burying expenses or giving rebates directly to clients been laid out? Do employees have a clear understanding of what is permissible and what is not? What are the legal liabilities they and their office could face by participating in such practices? Do staff know how to handle client requests to be personally compensated or bury costs? Would their company find their actions acceptable if they knew of them?

- Torn down the competition to potential clients?

Many event planning companies and suppliers do not talk negatively about their competition. They simply divert conversation back to the benefits and value their own company brings to the client. If pressed, they still would not respond in a negative light. Rather, they would advise clients that it is their company policy not to discuss the competition.

Establish office codes of conduct for what is acceptable to say if a client requests information on your company's competition.

- Booked meetings just to get bonus points, even if the property may not be the best one for your group?

Clients have been known to do this and so have event planning companies and their staff. Suppliers offer enticing incentives at times. Individuals have taken them and used them personally as opposed to having them applied to the company as a whole.

Are staff permitted to take part in supplier incentives? Can bonus points be used personally or are they pooled to benefit the company? How do employees handle requests from clients to have bonus points made out to them and not their company? Do they know whether on not the individual has the authorization and company approval to make such a request?

- Sent family or friends on client incentive programs and supplier fam trips?

This has often been done in the industry. Suppliers have been openly lied to. Fake business cards have been produced to make it look legit. Suppliers have been known to contact trusted planners in the office to find out exactly how the person being considered for the trip is connected to the office and what role they play.

Is there a clear policy on family and friends receiving industry perks, or taking part in fam trips or client incentive programs? Do staff know the office boundaries? And if the boundaries are overstepped, what should staff do if they become privy to something that is a clear breach of company ethics?

- Extended your stay (or your client's stay) after a meeting and built your personal travel costs into conference costs?

If a client extends their stay, why would a planner care? The planner would care if they are being directed to bury the costs in the event charges. It is not necessarily the company president who makes these requests. Sometimes it is a member of their staff who is only overseeing the event and does not have the authorization to make such a request, and may very well be doing it without the approval of their company. It is not their money or their decision to make. One planner extended their stay after an event to work on reconciliation and invited friends to stay with her and party at the expense of the client. All the expenses were being buried in the client's final billing. Inviting friends to stay was being done without the knowledge or consent of the event planning company. The hotel contacted the company president, concerned about the instructions they received about how to handle the additional charges. The employee was investigated and fired.

Do staff know how to field requests from clients for extended stays that are to be billed back to the company and not paid for personally? Is there a check or safeguard in place so that they do not simply follow the orders of someone from the client's company who may not be in a position to give them and may be doing something underhanded? Discuss ways to broach this with the client tactfully without outright accusation. One option may be having the client sign a form authorizing the expenditure, with a second signature required, such as that of the chief financial officer or the signing officer whose name is on the original contract. In some cases, it has been the event planning company's president that has made such requests to have their personal extended stay built into the client's final bill. Employees in this case, who are being asked to hide costs, could be accessories if the client discovered that they were being charged for expenses they did not incur. Do planning staff know whether it is permissable for them to invite guests to stay with them pre or post event if they are required to be there on business?

- Invited family or friends to stay in your guestroom with you on a program without anyone's knowledge or permission?

This is a lot of risk for little reward, but it has gone on. One event planning company owner went as far as to rent a villa for the duration of her stay and brought her entire family down with them at the client's expense, including babies and toddlers. This was, of course, totally inappropriate, unethical and unprofessional. The children kept running up and demanding attention from their mother in the middle of client meetings and event activities, or calling and waving to the group. Staff were mortified by the lack of business decorum that was displayed by their company head and the client was shocked that family members were on their business trip. They wanted to know exactly who had paid for them to come—was it the event planning company or had they footed the bill? In another case the company president did obtain the permission of their client to bring their family along. The event planning company owner brought his wife and children along, as did his client, and charges for all of them were being absorbed by the client whose company president, who was not at the event, may not necessarily have known about the added expenditure approved by the person he had placed in charge of the event. Guests were upset at seeing the children present because their requests to bring children along to their child-friendly destination had been denied. All the goodwill that the event was to have fostered did not materialize.

Do staff know how to proceed if the client organizing the event decides to bring their family along? Do they have to get authorization that this will be acceptable to the client's top executives? Have office policies and procedures regarding clients or staff inviting guests to stay in their room during an event been discussed?

• Accepted money under the table for services to avoid paying taxes?

For some companies, engaging in this type of unethical behavior could cause them to lose their licenses, and incur other penalties such as going to jail.

Staff need to know how to tactfully turn down such offers. Having a prepared response declining the offer will help your staff avoid potential legal pitfalls, being drawn into further discussion or being accused of making character accusations.

• Marked up supplier invoices to make extra money?

Some planning companies have marked up supplier invoices in addition to their management fee to make extra profit. This can be done in a number of ways because clients do not always see final reconciliation backup billing. One example is the manner of how taxes, service charges and tipping is calculated. For example, if a specialty drink is $10 and the applicable taxes, service charges and gratuities are 15 percent each based on the drink's cost, then the total the client should be charged per drink is $14.50. If the event planning company instead calculates that the percentages are multiplied one on top of each other, the dollar amount changes to $15.20 per drink. The difference is $0.70 a drink in the event planning company's favor. Multiply this by the number of guests and the number of drinks they consume and the additional hidden profit can add up. And this is just one event item.

Some clients would not think to question how taxes, charges and gratuities are calculated. And some planners never ask how their suppliers calculate these expenses as presented to them on their quotes or invoices. One planner, who was having two different ground operators quote on a proposal discovered the difference in how they were tallying the taxes and made sure in the future that they always checked with the local tourist board to make sure they personally knew what percentages should be charged and exactly how they should be calculated.

Instruct staff on how and where to look for possible hidden charges. Set company policy on how to deal with suppliers that have proven to be unethical in their billing. Make sure that staff are aware of preferred suppliers and which suppliers your company does not do business with.

- Obtained a proposal from a supplier on the pretense that the requested service will be outsourced, and then used the ideas in-house without paying them after the supplier has done all the leg-work and saved you time?

Clients have been known to use event planning company proposals as a source of ideas and cost estimates for their in-house staff to work from. Proposals were solicited but it was never the client's intention to contract the business out. Some planning companies, hoping to avoid having this done to them, have start-ed to charge a nonrefundable retainer, which is credited back to the management fee should the proposal go to contract. The retainer may be either a nominal fee or based on an hourly rate that takes into consideration the number of hours that go into researching and developing a proposal. The planning company's intent is not to fully recoup all costs but to weed out clients who are just sourcing ideas. This helps to ensure that their employees spend their time, creativity and energy on clients that are com-mitted to working with them.

Clients need to ensure that their staff practice ethical business prac-tices and set their company ground rules on what these are.

- Overestimated food, beverage and room night potential to get a better rate from a venue?

Some clients feel if they inflate their numbers they will get better rates. Planners need to educate their clients and advise them that specific minimums and guarantees will be outlined in their con-tract and that new rates will kick in should the numbers slide below the threshold.

Planners and sales reps have a responsibility to their suppliers to keep their clients educated about industry rules and regulations. Determine what information your company requires to qualify a proposal request. Past history—final guest count, food and beverage guarantees, budgets and event elements—are examples of some event planning companies' standard prerequisites.

- Assisted a client in their request for "creative accounting" to hide personal expenses?

  One client wanted to write off expenses for a personal party as a charity event, have donations in lieu of gifts, and put the costs through their foundation for payment. Another client wanted to pay for an event for one company through one of their family businesses.

  Staff must be informed how to tactfully handle special requests and know the procedures they must take before acting on their own and agreeing to a client's request. For instance, you may need to advise the client that you are required to check with the company lawyer or accountant to see if what is being proposed is possible, without mentioning that you will also be checking to see if it is ethical by company standards.

- Closed down or had an individual go on vacation without informing clients who may have been counting on being able to reach them and suppliers who have been waiting for payment?

  Personal and professional integrity are what can set you and your company apart from your competition. Treat others as you want to be treated personally and professionally. Be honorable in your dealings with others. Develop business principles that your company and staff can stand behind.

- Acted unprofessionally in dress or demeanor in front of your peers, clients of suppliers, or knowingly wasted others' time by sending jokes, tasteless e-mails or chain letters?

  What are your company's policies and codes of conduct? Where does your company stand on drinking on the job, dress standards and interaction between staff, suppliers, client and guests? What is expected business etiquette in the office and on site?

- Listened in to private conversations, gone through someone's desk without their knowledge, opened someone else's business mail or read another's e-mails?

A discussion with staff needs to take place regarding company security and individual privacy issues. One company's policy was that anything that came into the office was the property of the office, no matter who it was addressed to. It was meaningless if the envelope was marked private and confidential—the receptionist was responsible for opening all the mail and date-stamping it.

Employees need to know the courses of action they should take when they find someone violating company codes of conduct. For instance, what happens when a staff member discovers another staff member going through someone else's in-box? What if it is the company president's mail that is being gone through by unauthorized personnel? One company accountant liked to come in early so that he could go through the president's mail. A staff member saw him and reported him to senior company executives. Would it have made a difference if it wasn't the president's mail he was going through but another colleague's?

Where does your company stand on company security and individual privacy? What rules and company regulations must be adhered to?

- Put your company in financial danger by personal actions?

A client, planner or supplier can place their company in financial danger by accepting a verbal OK as opposed to having changes put in writing and having clients sign off on increased expenses. Should the client deny that they gave verbal approval for an expense, the planner has no backup that the request was approved and the company could be liable for the extra charges. Failing to obtain required permits could result in an event being closed down on the day of the event. If the planner neglected to ensure their supplier had secured proper documentation and fire marshal approval, the event planning company could be held responsible. At one event, a deck built to accommodate the guests collapsed and people were injured. The event planning company and their supplier had not fulfilled one of the contract terms and conditions—a building permit and the services of a structural engineer had been required.

Company policy regarding contract terms and conditions must be laid out and strictly adhered to. Procedures must be put in place that ensure that event elements critical in order for an event to take place or to guarantee guest safety are not overlooked.

- Put yourself or others in a high-risk situation?

One planner placed herself in a high-risk situation when, after a night of heavy partying, a guest followed her back to her hotel room and was insistent on stepping in while she found him a painkiller for his headache. He suggested that she could help him take his mind off his headache in other ways. Instead of opening her hotel room while she was alone on the deserted floor, the planner could have feigned forgetting her key and needing to use the hall telephone to call hotel security to bring her a new set. Once security arrived, she could have requested that security accompany the guest back to his room to make sure that he got there safely and to look after his request for a painkiller, which her company policy and possible legal liabilities prevented her from giving him.

Set out company policy on appropriate interaction, behavior and response from staff when they find themselves placed in potentially compromising and challenging situations.

If you have been in one of these situations, all of which have taken place in the event planning industry, or have been asked to take part in such a scheme, you may want to review your ethical standards and company policies. These questions are to open the door to discussion on unethical business practices in the industry and the ethical policies and procedures you and your company personally and professionally stand behind. Put them in writing, review them and have staff sign off on having been informed on expected company codes of conduct.

- Samples of written policy:

An employee must not intentionally use their position for private gain or the gain of another. Company policy prohibits employees from revealing confidential company and client information.

CONCLUSION

There is a quiet evolution taking place in the event planning industry. Planners are assessing how and with whom they do business. Some event planning companies, taking giant industry leaps forward, have even fired their staff, suppliers and clients for the way they are conducting business. This is something that was unheard of in the past. As well, staff are walking away from companies with questionable business practices, not wanting to have their personal and professional reputations compromised or sullied by association.

Accountability is in the air. People are holding themselves, their companies, clients, suppliers and peers accountable for their actions. Bad behavior is no longer being condoned or overlooked, and neither are bad business ethics. Ethics bars are being raised and business standards have been elevated. No longer will the majority of people in the industry be bought off by a drink or some industry perk, jeopardizing their careers and putting themselves at personal or professional risk. If an ethical or professional boundary has been crossed it will not be ignored. Today, it is viewed as a betrayal of trust to the industry and the individual. Once broken, trust and the credibility of the individual and the industry cannot be easily repaired.

Set high codes of conduct for yourself, office peers, business colleagues, suppliers, clients and their guests, both in and out of the office. Talk about what behavior is expected of the planning staff, as well as what to expect from others during an event. Lapses in judgment reflect not only on the individual but on the company as well. You are judged on the company you keep and the company you choose to be associated with.

Remember that theft is theft, whether it be excessive time stolen from a company for personal chitchat, claiming hours for coming in early but then not working, taking office supplies, padding expenses or making illegal copies of CDs or personal photocopies Theft can be stealing creative ideas, not paying suppliers what they are owed or inflating costs to clients for extra profit.

Two wrongs do not make a right. If the company you work for or do business with is unethical, that does not give anyone else the license to act in the same manner. Hold yourself and the companies you do business with to the highest standards of good business behavior. Walk away from individuals and companies that could put you at personal and professional risk. The cost of closing your eyes to unethical business practices can be high, and can lead to lawsuits, indictment and criminal charges.

Do not allow personal or professional liberties to be taken in or out of the office. Train yourself and others how to be watchful of situations that could compromise reputations and personal safety. Educate each other on what could be encountered during a site inspection, fam trip or an event. Protect one another. Buddy up and be on the alert to rescue each other if needed when alcohol and guests free from everyday restraint become a dangerous mixture.

Social etiquette and business etiquette are not one in the same. Both are equally important to master. Social etiquette includes minding your manners, displaying socially correct behavior in polite society and displaying finely honed dining skills. Business etiquette is making those you do business with feel comfortable, handling business situations appropriately and eliminating barriers that hinder business. Business etiquette is a practiced skill, and it can make or break a career. It is not gender specific.

Remember that the purpose of a business lunch is not just to eat, and that what you choose to order can be as revealing to your dining guests as how you present yourself in business conversation. In event planning, knowledge of worldwide professional conduct, international protocol, business ethics and etiquette is part of the job. You can be undone by an incorrectly fastened button in some countries, and your job is to know which countries these are.

Make every event better with the learning you take from your last event and all those before that. Enhance your and your company's performance by raising standards of acceptable codes of conduct, sharing knowledge, making even an office meeting convey a sense of occasion reflective of what your company does and train each other—planners, suppliers, clients and their staff—as you go along in principled approaches to the business of special event management.

INDEX